100 Brain-Friendly Lessons

For Unforgettable Teaching and Learning (K–8)

100 Brain-Friendly Lessons

For Unforgettable Teaching and Learning (K–8)

Marcia L. Tate

FOR INFORMATION:

Corwin

A SAGE Company

2455 Teller Road

Thousand Oaks, California 91320

(800) 233-9936

www.corwin.com

SAGE Publications Ltd.

1 Oliver's Yard

55 City Road

London EC1Y 1SP

United Kingdom

SAGE Publications India Pvt. Ltd.

B 1/I 1 Mohan Cooperative Industrial Area

Mathura Road, New Delhi 110 044

India

SAGE Publications Asia-Pacific Pte. Ltd.

18 Cross Street #10-10/11/12

China Square Central

Singapore 048423

Senior Acquisitions Editor: Jessica Allan

Content Development Editor: Lucas Schleicher

Senior Editorial Assistant: Mia Rodriguez

Project Editor: Amy Schroller

Copy Editor: Tammy Giesmann

Typesetter: C&M Digitals (P) Ltd.

Proofreader: Sue Irwin

Indexer: Sheila Bodell

Cover Designer: Candice Harman

Marketing Manager: Deena Meyer

Printed in the United States of America

Library of Congress Cataloging-in-Publication Data

Names: Tate, Marcia L., author.

Title: 100 brain-friendly lessons for unforgettable teaching and learning (k-8) / Marcia L. Tate.

Other titles: One hundred brain-friendly lessons for unforgettable teaching and learning (k-8)

Description: Thousand Oaks, California : Corwin, [2020] | Includes bibliographical references and index.

Identifiers: LCCN 2019006747 | ISBN 9781544381572 (pbk. : alk. paper)

Subjects: LCSH: Elementary school teaching—United States. | Middle school teaching—United States. | Lesson planning—United States. | Education, Elementary—Activity programs—United States. | Middle school education—Activity programs—United States. | Learning—United States. | Cognition in children—United States.

Classification: LCC LB1555 .T22 2020 | DDC 371.102—dc23

LC record available at https://lccn.loc.gov/2019006747

This book is printed on acid-free paper.

SUSTAINABLE FORESTRY INITIATIVE

Certified Chain of Custody
Promoting Sustainable Forestry
www.sfiprogram.org
SFI-01268

SFI label applies to text stock

19 20 21 22 23 10 9 8 7 6 5 4 3 2 1

Contents

Acknowledgments   vii

About the Author   ix

About the Contributing Authors   xi

Introduction   1

Chapter 1: A Classroom Climate Conducive to Learning   7

Chapter 2: Instructional Strategies That Work!   13

Chapter 3: A Brain-Compatible Lesson   25

Chapter 4: 25 Sample Language Arts/English Lessons   31
    Grades K–2   32
    Grades 3–5   57
    Grades 6–8   80
    Literary Texts That Teach Story Elements and Skills   98
    Reading Websites   104

Chapter 5: 25 Sample Mathematics Lessons   105
    Grades K–2   106
    Grades 3–5   130
    Grades 6–8   162

Chapter 6: 25 Sample Science Lessons   183
    Grades K–2   184
    Grades 3–5   200
    Grades 6–8   226

Chapter 7: 25 Sample Social Studies Lessons   263
    Grades K–2   264
    Grades 3–5   291
    Grades 6–8   311

Resource: Lesson Plan Template   337

Bibliography   339

Index   341

 Visit the companion website at
http://resources.corwin.com/BrainFriendly-K8
for downloadable resources.

Acknowledgments

There are some people who possess expert knowledge in multiple curricular areas. I don't happen to be one of them. Therefore, I must surround myself with master educators who have more knowledge of specific content than I possess. A deep debt of gratitude goes to the following five content specialists who assisted me with the writing of the 100 brain-compatible lesson plans contained in this book:

Language Arts/English	Simone Willingham, Victoria Hanabury
Mathematics	Lisa Lee
Science	Warren Phillips
Social Studies	Deborah Daniell

These professionals combined their years of experience in effective teaching practices with their knowledge of content to design effective lessons which enable students to master the cross-curricular objectives and standards essential for academic success.

I continue to express my appreciation to the Associates, Pamela Bouie, Jennifer Clowers, Deborah Daniell, Warren Phillips, and Simone Willingham, who work for *Developing Minds Inc.* to spread the word regarding brain-compatible teaching. The Administrative Assistants, Carol Purviance and Harriet Reedy, work to ensure that the entire operation of the company runs with ultimate precision.

The support of my husband, Tyrone, our three exceptional children, and eight incredible grandchildren makes life fulfilling and enables me to do what I do for our company.

Thank you, Jessica Allan, my Corwin editor, not only for your support and recommendations which continue to improve my work but also for your true friendship throughout the years.

About the Author

Marcia L. Tate is the former executive director of professional development for the DeKalb County School System in Decatur, Georgia. During her 30-year career with the district, she has been a classroom teacher, reading specialist, language arts coordinator, and staff development executive director. Marcia was named *Staff Developer of the Year* for the state of Georgia, and her department was selected to receive the *Exemplary Program Award* for the state.

Marcia is currently CEO of the consultant firm she shares with her husband, Tyrone, and has presented her workshops to over 500,000 administrators, teachers, parents, and community leaders from all over the United States and the world, including Australia, Canada, Egypt, Hungary, Oman, New Zealand, Singapore, and Thailand.

She is the author of the best-selling *Worksheets Don't Grow Dendrites* series; *"Sit & Get" Won't Grow Dendrites: 20 Professional Learning Strategies that Engage the Adult Brain; Shouting Won't Grow Dendrites: 20 Techniques to Detour Around the Danger Zones*; and *Preparing Children for Success in School and in Life: 20 Ways to Increase Your Child's Brain Power*. She is also the author of *Formative Assessment in a Brain-compatible Classroom: How Do We Really Know They Are Learning?* which won the 2017 Independent Publishers Book Award. Marcia has written a number of published articles and chapters that have been included in other books. Participants in her workshops call them some of the best ones they have ever experienced since Marcia models the 20 strategies in her books to actively engage her audiences.

Marcia received her bachelor's degree in psychology and elementary education from Spelman College in Atlanta, her master's degree in remedial reading from the University of Michigan in Ann Arbor, and her specialist and doctorate degrees in educational leadership from Georgia State University and Clark Atlanta University, respectively. Spelman College awarded her the *Apple Award* for excellence in the field of education.

Marcia has not only been married to Tyrone for more than 39 years but they are the proud parents of three wonderful children, Jennifer, Jessica, and Christopher. If she had known how wonderful it would be to be a grandmother, Marcia would have had her eight grandchildren, Christian, Aidan, Maxwell, Aaron, Roman, Shiloh, Aya, and Noah, before she had her children. She and her husband own the company, Developing Minds Inc., and can be contacted by calling the company at (770) 918-5039, by e-mailing her at marciata@bellsouth.net, or by visiting either her business website at www.developingmindsinc.com or her personal website at www.drmarciatate.com. Follow Marcia on Twitter and Instagram @drmarciatate.

About the Contributing Authors

Simone Philp Willingham is an Assistant Principal for the DeKalb County School District in Decatur, Georgia. She provides training workshops to teachers, administrators, and parents at both the local and national level. Simone regularly presents to teachers from pre-kindergarten through high school. During her more than twenty-five year career in teaching, she has also been an Instructional Support Specialist, Reading Specialist, classroom teacher, and teacher trainer.

Simone has taught hundreds of students using the 20 brain-compatible strategies with phenomenal success. During her tenure as a Reading Specialist, the standardized reading test scores increased by over 40 percent, and over 80 percent of her EIP students exhibited high growth on all universal screeners and state assessments. She is passionate about teaching and learning and believes that all students can learn, regardless of their background or prior experiences.

Simone holds a bachelor's degree in Sociology and Education from Hunter College, a Master of Science degree as a Reading Specialist from Adelphi University, and an Educational Specialist Degree (Ed.S.) in Administration and Supervision from Lincoln Memorial University. She has also trained with leading innovators in brain-compatible strategies including Marcia Tate, Eric Jensen, and Rich Allen.

Victoria Hanabury is a Technology Design Coach in Austin ISD. She is passionate about designing and facilitating blended learning experiences that drive individual and organizational growth. Before moving to Austin, Victoria taught high school and middle school English in New York City Public Schools and co-developed a web-based program that leveraged push notifications to connect parents with actionable resources for supporting student math achievement. She received her bachelor's degree from the University of Virginia and her master's in teaching from Fordham University.

Lisa Lee is a 32-year veteran educator from Gwinnett County Public Schools (GCPS) in Georgia, one of the nation's top urban school districts. Leading mathematics staff development for the Broad Prize for Urban Education winning district (in 2010 and 2014), Lisa Lee has had extensive opportunities to impact change to the district's 14,800 teachers. Locally, Lisa has served 140 schools with 182,800 students, instructionally developed teachers as the K–12 mathematics coach, worked as the district's K–12 content assessment specialist, led 126 mathematics specialists and coaches in STEM and STEAM initiatives, and has developed district and state lesson studies and assessments.

Mrs. Lee received her bachelor's degree from the University of Georgia and her master's degree from Georgia State University. She has worked alongside with and presented mathematics to the League of Professional Schools, Atlanta Chamber of Commerce, Georgia State University, Piedmont University, National Staff Development Council, and the National Council of Teachers of Mathematics.

Warren G. Phillips is a science workshop presenter who is passionate about brain-based creative teaching using multiple strategies. He has 42 years teaching experience in Southeastern Massachusetts. Warren was NBCT certified in 2000, Time Magazine TOY in 2002, Disney TOY in 2004, USA Today All-USA Teacher Team in 2006, and National Teacher HOF in 2010. He has a bachelor's degree and two master's degrees from Bridgewater State University.

Warren is a co-author of *Science Worksheets Don't Grow Dendrites* with Marcia Tate. He is a contributing author to *Today, I Made A Difference* and *Exemplary Science in Grades 5–8*. He has produced three CDs of science songs called *Sing Along Science*. He has also written a musical for school performances called *The Science Secret*. Warren has been married for 43 years to his wife Karen. They are proud of two wonderful children and two cute grandchildren. He maintains a web page at http://www.singalongscience.com.

An educator for 40 years, Debbie Daniell has taught K–12 and been an administrator in both public and private schools in Georgia. She holds degrees in special education, elementary education, educational leadership, and social studies education. Retiring as K–12 Social Studies Director of Gwinnett County Public Schools in June of 2018, she currently serves as a member of the board of trustees for the Center for Civic Engagement, K–12 GA Social Studies Advisory Board, NSSSA Board of Directors, Georgia Council for Economic Education Program Committee,

and works part-time at the Georgia Center for Assessment at the University of Georgia. In addition, she serves as a school improvement consultant with the Georgia School Boards Association. The founder of DED Educational Resources, Debbie provides training in instructional strategies and school improvement.

Debbie is involved in many professional organizations. Memberships include Georgia Council for the Social Studies, National Council for the Social Studies and Georgia Leadership Association for the Social Studies. A recipient of *Outstanding Social Studies Educator* in 1996 and *2010 Social Studies Supervisor of the Year*, her programs have been awarded Economic Program of Excellence as well as GCSS state program of excellence. As director of K–12 social studies for Gwinnett County Public Schools, she has supervised over 2,000 teachers in writing new curriculum standards, units and lesson plans, benchmarks, and performance assessments. She truly believes that social studies is what we do for the rest of our lives!

Introduction

It is a wonderful time to be in education! We know more about the brain today than we ever have! Teachers instruct brains every day and, therefore, should be experts on how the brain learns. In fact, I believe that the only professionals who should know more about the brain than teachers would be neurosurgeons or neuroscientists. Yet, there are many teachers who have little or no knowledge of how the brain comprehends and retains information.

Therefore, we have students who have little or no love of what happens between the hours of approximately 8:00 a.m. until 3:00 p.m., five days a week, and 10 months out of the year. We even have practices in education that are contradictory to the way brains learn best and wonder why those practices are not successful.

For example, in many instances, we wait too late to teach students a second language. In some school systems, that curriculum does not appear in the scope and sequence until the intermediate or middle school grades. According to the brain research, that is too late! The earlier a second language can be taught, the better. This is the reason that the majority of people in the United States cannot speak a second language as a native speaker.

In a multitude of classrooms in the United States, students are not allowed to talk with their peers during class and, heaven forbid, that a student should want to get out of their seat. Yet, we also know from research on the brain that students should have the opportunity to converse about content and become actively engaged in the learning if we want more of them to remember what is being taught.

SOCIETAL CHANGES

I have been in education for more than 40 years and during the time I have spent plying my trade, society has changed dramatically. Visualize a time when children lived in two-parent families who indulged in home-cooked meals together and, over the dinner table, discussed the goings on of the work and school day. Imagine children getting their vitamin D from playing outside with friends and neighbors and developing those social and motor skills so essential for healthy emotional and physical development. Picture a time when families had only one television and it consisted of only a few channels, yet those channels were the main source of visual entertainment. Parents could determine what was age appropriate and what was off-limits.

We did not even get a color television until I was eight years old. Therefore, when watching *The Wizard of Oz* as a child, I didn't realize that when Dorothy lands in Oz, the movie converts to color! I can recall how the few television channels we had discontinued service after a specified time, the *Star-Spangled Banner* was played and the last question asked for the day was, *Do you know where your children are?*

Now it is over 40 years later and family units have diversified. There are single-parent families, children being raised by other family members such as grandparents, aunts and uncles, siblings, or guardians, and children raising themselves. There are even two-parent families where the parents are so busy working in an attempt to make ends meet financially that they have little time to spend with the children. Many families do not enjoy dinner table talk anymore since life has become so hectic that they do not indulge in this luxury. Home cooking is also at a premium and busy families have replaced nutritious meals with fast food and other less-healthy culinary options. Children now have access to multiple technologies in addition to television right in their bedrooms. These additions include smartphones steeped with social media apps, computers, iPads, iPods, and video games. Therefore, a child's play today often becomes technological and happens indoors, not outside.

BRAIN CHANGES

All human beings are born with approximately 100 billion memory cells called neurons. In utero, the fetus has more than 100 billion neurons but some are pruned way before the baby is born. Each neuron has connections at its ends called dendrites. Every time the brain learns something new, it grows a new dendrite. Therefore, teachers are not only teachers, they are actually *dendrite growers.* Some instructional practices facilitate this growth, while other practices hinder it.

Societal changes appear to come coupled with changes in our brains. Studies have found that young children who watch in excess of more than one hour of television a day had a decrease in the executive function of the brain as well as major delays in language, motor, and cognitive development (Lin, Cherng, Chen, Chen, and Yang, 2015) resulting in less dendritic growth. Speech and language pathologists are relating to me that they are seeing an alarming decline in young children's speech and language development since many parents are using iPads as babysitters rather than the face-to-face communication between parent and child.

Our attention spans appear to have shortened. We want what we want and we want it yesterday! Allow me to share a personal example. I am addicted to popcorn. I recall when growing up how I stood at the stove and popped *Jiffy Pop* popcorn and watched expectantly as the aluminum pan would balloon. I would have to keep the pan in constant motion as it heated and popped or the popcorn would burn. It might take me 20 or more minutes until I was enjoying the delicious rewards of my diligent work. Now, I have difficulty standing at the microwave for only three minutes waiting impatiently while my microwave popcorn completes its cycle. What is the implication, then, for expecting students to sit passively like the students in *Ferris Bueller's Day Off* and listen to a teacher drone on and on about the content? Anyone? Anyone?

Our attention also appears divided. In his book, *How the Brain Learns,* 5th ed. (2017), David Sousa provides a contrasting description of the difference in the newscasts of yesterday and today. He relates that in the past, a viewer of a newscast was solely seeing the face of the reporter. Today, we have become used to multiple people reporting from around the globe while the nonrelated news is scrolling at the bottom of the screen, and stock market averages are changing simultaneously. In the past during a 30-second commercial, only one or two products would be advertised. Now, in 30-seconds, eight or more different products will be showcased.

I even hear students and adults bragging about their ability to multitask. The brain research belies this opinion. Contrary to popular belief and according to Sousa (2017), there is no such thing as multitasking since *the brain cannot carry out two cognitive processes simultaneously* (p.33). If this statement is true, then what can be said for talking on the cell phone while one is driving? One of those tasks is unconscious and that becomes a major problem. The inability to text and drive is an even worse scenario and many states, including my state of Georgia, are legislating hands-free driving.

Allow me to relate a personal true story to illustrate this point. My daughter, Jennifer, was going to get food for dinner when the woman in front of her ran through the red light and up on the sidewalk into three teenagers who were innocently standing on that sidewalk. Jen stopped her car to see if she could be of aid to any of the teenagers who had been hit and was actually holding the hand of a 17-year-old when he passed away. She later found out that this woman was talking on her cell phone while driving and she was having an argument with her husband. While unconsciously driving, her conscious mind was dedicated to the argument leading to the deaths of all three boys since all of them eventually passed away.

INSTRUCTIONAL CHANGES

As society and brains have changed, have schools followed? Many think not! In fact, it has been said that if Rip Van Winkle actually slept for 100 years and then awoke today, the school would be the only entity he would recognize. Lecture has always been and continues to be the primary method of delivering instruction in high schools. According to John Medina's bestseller, *Brain Rules: 12 Principles for Surviving and Thriving at Work, Home, and School*, if keeping someone's interest in a lecture was a business, it would have an 80 percent failure rate (2008, p. 74). Many teachers feel that this method is the fastest way to get a great deal of information over to students in the shortest amount of time. After all, to prepare students for high-stakes testing, content has got to be covered. According to Madeline Hunter, if all teachers are doing is covering content then they would do well to cover that content with dirt, since it will be dead to the memory of students.

While there is so much about the human brain that is still unknown, we know more now than ever and what we believe about the brain is great news for educators! In fact, it is a wonderful time to be a brain-compatible teacher!

For example, it was once believed that the two hemispheres of the brain functioned quite differently. The left hemisphere was thought to house a person's verbal and mathematical abilities as well as the capability to think sequentially and logically. The right hemisphere was believed to govern a person's creative, musical, and artistic abilities. Today we realize that *there is no neuroscientific evidence to support the notion that one hemisphere consistently dominates a person's thinking, learning, or behavior* (Sousa and Pilecki, 2013, p. 9). Therefore, teachers ought to be teaching to both hemispheres of the brain. The 20 instructional strategies delineated in this book and comprising every lesson that follows do just that! For those who prefer left hemisphere, there are lesson plans that include the strategies of storytelling and writing. For the right hemisphere, the list contains drawing and music. Regardless of preferences, the strategies appear to work for all students.

OVERVIEW OF THIS BOOK

Even though the reader will encounter 100 brain-compatible sample lessons in four major content areas, we also believe that there are certain characteristics of a classroom where students' brains can learn at optimal levels. Those include developing a relationship with each student and structuring a classroom where students are optimistic about their ability to do well and look forward to coming to class. Those also include students' abilities to converse with their peers about content and to become physically engaged in the learning. Chapter 1 in this book will delineate some of the characteristics of a brain-compatible classroom, and teachers would do well to implement as many of them as possible.

We also know that even with shortened attention spans and our propensity to attempt to pay conscious attention to more than one thing at a time, there are instructional strategies that take advantage of the way all brains learn best. These strategies have students talking with peers and engaging in multiple ways with content. Chapter 2 will delineate those 20 brain-compatible strategies and provide some definitive research as to why they will work for all students' brains. I do not teach anything to anyone (PreK-12, college, or adult students) without the use of these 20 strategies. And neither should you!

There are five questions that every teacher should ask and answer when planning a brain-compatible lesson. Chapter 3 will be devoted to an in-depth explanation of each of those questions. They are interwoven into a lesson plan which will serve as a template for the 100 cross-curricular lessons provided in this book.

The remainder of the book is a real treat! The content specialists and I pursued national and international standards and objectives in the following four major content areas: *language arts, mathematics, science, and social studies*. Once standards/objectives were identified, at least 25 practical lesson plans were written in each content area using the template provided. The language arts section also includes a list of literary texts that can be used for teaching skills and strategies, as well as suggested websites. The purpose of this book is to help ensure that teachers will have access to effective lessons that, once delivered, accomplish several things:

- Increase academic achievement for every student in any class;
- Decrease behavior problems for every student in any class; and
- Make teaching and learning so much fun!

The plans are meant to be samples of what engaging lessons can resemble and not a plethora of cross-curricular examples. Once teachers get a feel for what brain-compatible lesson plans should include, they can use the template contained in the Resource section of this book to create original lessons regarding those standards and objectives that they must teach.

The plans are also arranged in grade level bands so that teachers have access to plans written both below and above grade level and can be used to differentiate instruction for individual students or meet small, flexible group needs.

When I go into classrooms to model lessons for teachers, I know I have a memorable lesson when students make some of the following comments as the lesson is concluded:

- Is the period over already?
- Class was so good today! Can you come back tomorrow!
- This is the first time Jason hasn't slept through class all school year!

The lessons contained in this book will enable you to garner similar comments and become your students' favorite teacher if you are not already!

1

A Classroom Climate Conducive to Learning

Visualize a classroom where a smiling teacher is standing at the door greeting students by name as they enter. She either asks them about their evening or compliments them on the extra effort expended during yesterday's class. Students love their teacher and their classroom! The walls of the room are painted a pastel blue and the sun gleaming from the bank of windows makes the fluorescent lighting unnecessary. Other visuals on the wall include student work and content related to the objectives being taught. There is calming music playing as students assemble and get settled for the day. Students are permitted to talk with one another but have been taught that if the teacher hears their voices over the music, then they are talking too loudly! A whiff of the essential oil of lavender is in the air since none of the students have allergies. This classroom is a place where students actually want to be!

Students know to look on the board for a sponge activity which will either serve as a review of concepts taught yesterday or an advance organizer on what will be taught today. They get busy! Students are sitting at tables with chairs, rather than desks. This will make student mobility and conversation a great deal easier.

In the pages that follow, you will encounter more than 100 brain-compatible lesson plans in the following four major content areas—English/language arts, mathematics, science, and social studies. While these plans, if implemented, should increase academic achievement for all students, they are not nearly as effective if not implemented in a classroom, similar to the one described above. This teacher takes full advantage of the way all brains learn best. Jensen (2013) describes this concept metaphorically:

> Teachers are the common denominator, and the key factor affecting class climate. They are much more than weather reporters who simply observe or react to class climate; they are the creators of the class climate and, as such, have a huge influence on students' engagement, learning, and overall daily lives. (p.35)

In other words, it is the teacher who makes the difference! The following seven characteristics epitomize a brain-compatible classroom where students are learning at optimal levels and achievement is maximized.

A POSITIVE ENVIRONMENT IS ENCOURAGED

One way to foster a positive environment in class is to develop a relationship with each student. *If your students like you, there is nothing they will not do for you! If your students don't like you, there is nothing they will not do to you!* (Tate, 2014). Students not only work harder for teachers they like but relationships enable them to become more excited about learning, improve behavior, and experience less stress (Jensen, 2013). When a relationship exists, students care what teachers think and feel about them. That relationship can begin with a greeting at the door and continue throughout the lesson as teachers acknowledge students' effort, communicate their high expectations, and encourage students' participation in the lesson.

When the brain is in a positive state, content is more easily remembered. When the brain is under high stress or threat, content that is not related to survival is insignificant. Jokes, riddles, and celebrations not only create a positive learning environment in class but can also facilitate the learning itself (Allen, 2008; Jensen, 2007). Older adolescents are more likely to comprehend the subtleties of humor, satire, or irony than their primary counterparts since their language skills are more highly developed (Feinstein, 2009). Here are a few riddles you can use if appropriate:

- What did the number zero say to the number eight? *Nice belt*
- What did one crow say to another crow that was standing in the road? *Here comes a caw, caw, caw* (car, car, car).
- What did the green grape say to the purple grape? *Breathe! Breathe!*

ROUTINES AND PROCEDURES BECOME HABITUAL

There is no way to have an active, engaging classroom if teachers don't spend a great deal of time teaching those routines and procedures that enable the classroom to function smoothly. This does not happen in a day or even a week. In fact, it takes approximately 21 days or 28 times to make a behavior a habit. Twenty-one days, if practiced once a day and 28 times if practiced more than once a day.

Students have to know when to talk and when to be quiet, when to get up and when to sit down. They have to know how to get into cooperative groups or the behaviors to exhibit when conversing with a partner. When I teach educators, I strike the *G* key of a xylophone with a mallet to get their attention when they are busy. And we stay busy!

This is only one way to get the brain's attention. One teacher told me that when she needs her students' attention she simply says, *Red Robin*. Then the entire class knows to respond *Yum* and immediately get quiet.

Teachers must determine what the routines should be. There are advantages to involving students in that determination. Students will be more likely to comply with a management plan that they helped to develop. Once the rituals are determined, then they should be taught. In fact, effective classroom managers spend more time teaching their rituals during the first few days or weeks of school than teaching their content. Why? So that they can spend the remainder of the year teaching content. Once the rituals are taught, they must be practiced or role played. Actually, have students practice quieting down once a signal is given or talking to a partner at the appropriate voice level.

As students practice, provide feedback as to how students are doing. The feedback may sound something like this. *On a scale of one to ten when quieting down, you earned a six.* Tell students specifically what was right about the behavior but also why it was not a ten. Then give them specific behaviors which will move them in the direction of perfection. More information can be gleaned regarding this characteristic in Chapter 14, "Teach Your Rituals" of my bestseller, *Shouting Won't Grow Dendrites: 20 Techniques to Detour Around the Danger Zones* (2nd ed.).

LEARNING IS PURPOSEFUL AND RELEVANT

How many times has a student asked this question, *Why do we have to learn this?* It is a very legitimate question. When students can't see the connection between what is being taught in class and what happens to them in their world, the question becomes, *Why in the world is it necessary to know this?*

The purpose of the brain was never to score high on a teacher-made or standardized test or to make all *As* on a report card. The purpose of the brain is survival. It is to keep alive the body to which it belongs. Wouldn't it make sense that the content that is closest to what happens in the real world would be the content most remembered? This is why the aforementioned question is asked.

When I teach mathematics and we are setting the objective as to what we will be learning and why we need to know it, I attempt to provide a real-life reason in answer to that question. Once the lesson begins, I rarely, if ever, begin with the word problems in the book. They have no relevance! I make up problems that students might encounter. I even put their names in the problems so that they can visualize themselves solving these real-world problems.

An English teacher related this story. Her students did not comprehend the concept of *propaganda* until she showed them an advertisement of the singer Rihanna wearing a certain brand of lipstick. The ad was filled with positive terms that would encourage anyone to use the lipstick, especially if Rihanna used it. The class discussed the lack of evidence that this lipstick was any better than any other brand. Suddenly *propaganda* made sense.

CONTENT IS TAUGHT IN SEGMENTS OR CHUNKS

My husband and I attended a wedding where the minister did not chunk the vows appropriately. He gave the bride too many of the vows to repeat after him at one time. When he was finished, the bride simply inquired, *Could you repeat that, please?* The congregation chuckled!

The brain can only hold so much at one time. The going rate is seven as the number of isolated bits of information that the brain can hold simultaneously. This is why so many real-world lists come in sevens. Stop reading and see how many lists of seven you can name. Here are some you may have included: astronauts, days of the week, notes on the scale, colors in the rainbow, deadly sins, continents, seas, *Wonders of the Ancient World*, *Habits of Highly Effective People*, and even dwarfs. For additional information to be retained, that information needs to be organized into *chunks* or lesson segments. This is the reason that social security numbers, phone numbers, and credit card numbers are organized into separate sections or chunks—to make it easier for the human brain to remember. Isn't it interesting that with our current dependence on technology, very few people still memorize phone numbers, even if they are chunked?

One of the questions on the lesson plan asks teachers to determine how many chunks or lesson segments of instruction they will need and how much content should be included in each chunk. Additional explanations regarding this characteristic will be included in Chapter 3.

STUDENTS ARE ENGAGED IN CONVERSATION

When I was taught to teach over 40 years ago, I learned that if two students were talking about content, they were accused of cheating! Now we know that if I teach a concept to students and I then ask one student to re-explain or reteach that concept to another student, both brains benefit! In fact, people appear to learn about 70 percent of what they say as they talk and 90 percent of what they say as they do a thing (Ekwall and Shanker, 1988).

A teacher in one of my workshops relayed the following statement: *We spend the first three years of our children's lives teaching them to walk and talk, and the next 15 telling them to sit down and shut up!* Shutting up is not something we want students to do when it comes to talking about content. In fact, according to brain research, the person in the classroom doing the most talking about the content is growing the most brain cells, or dendrites, related to the content (Tate, 2016). In many classrooms, that is the teacher! We have many teachers with major dendritic growth while students sit idly by bored, daydreaming, or devoid of long-term memory. When students talk together about a topic in class, their understanding is improved because they process the information both mentally and verbally (Allen, 2008).

MOVEMENT IS A NATURAL PART OF INSTRUCTION

The purpose of schooling should be to prepare students for success in the world of work. I honestly tried to think of one career in that world that does not involve movement. The only one that came to mind was the guard at Buckingham Palace and even those employees change with one another about every 30 minutes. Therefore, unless we are preparing students to guard the palace, they need to be active. In fact, when our bodies sit for more than 20 minutes, blood pools in our seats and feet. Within one minute after standing, that blood begins to circulate and some of it stands a good chance of ending up in the brain.

One teacher in my class related the following story. Her grandmother knitted her entire life. During her grandmother's last days, she was lying in her hospital bed unconscious and unresponsive. The family had gathered around her to say *Goodbye.* Though unconscious, her grandmother's hands were busy going through the motions of knitting. It was not until her granddaughter came over and told her grandmother that she would finish the piece for her that her grandmother stopped knitting and quietly passed away!

Movement also has an educational benefit! Most content that students acquire while moving ends up stored in a memory system called *procedural* or *muscle memory*. This is one of the strongest memory systems in the brain and is the reason that people rarely forget how to drive a car, ride a bicycle, or play the piano. Gross motor physical activity actually increases the production of totally new brain cells resulting in improved mood, learning, and memory (Jensen and Snider, 2013).

If you have not already, begin to think of content you will be teaching while simultaneously incorporating the brain-compatible strategies of movement or role play. While many teachers use *brain breaks* to infuse movement into the classroom, if the movement becomes a natural part of the learning, those breaks become less essential. Movement will pay big dividends toward student motivation, understanding, and long-term memory!

STUDENTS ARE CHALLENGED BUT REMAIN CONFIDENT

I am a Scrabble player and look forward to playing *Words With Friends* on my cell phone. My sister is my favorite opponent because she is a better player than I am. When she is unavailable, I will play *Solo* (the computer) which makes a move every two minutes. I beat *Solo* at least 90 percent of the time and am often unmotivated to want to play. You see, *Solo* doesn't challenge me! On the other hand, when my sister makes a move, I get excited and am challenged to score higher on my subsequent move than the one she just made. While I do not win many games, my scores are consistently higher than they are when playing *Solo*. When I do win a game against her, there is an indescribable joy!

People find little satisfaction in continually accomplishing tasks that are too easy for them. Let's use the analogy of video gaming. Graphic designers make games that begin at an easy level in order to build up the confidence in the player's brain. Then, when the player is *hooked* and chooses to proceed to the next level, the difficulty level is also increased. Why do students keep playing? Because they have the confidence to believe that they can go to the next level and still be successful. In addition, if the player is doing poorly, no one pops up on a video game, gives the player an *F* and tells them to stop playing! And so the play continues until the performance improves!

Therefore, the appropriate level of content for a student is one where students are confident that they can be successful but there is a low to moderate level of stress. This adrenaline provides a challenge for the brain and keeps students *on their toes!* If the stress level is too low, students lose interest. If it is too high, students may not even attempt the tasks!

2

Instructional Strategies That Work!

*I*f students aren't learning the way we teach them, then we must teach them the way they learn! There is another way to say this. *When you go fishing, do you use bait you like or bait the fish likes?* This is a question I ask educators when I teach my course, *Worksheets Don't Grow Dendrites: 20 Instructional Strategies that Engage the Brain.* While the question always gets a chuckle, the metaphor also makes one think!

Regardless of the learning style or brain research theory, you will find that there are 20 ways to deliver instruction. These ways take advantage of the way all brains learn best. The one thing that all of the following 100 lesson plans will have in common is that they incorporate the 20 strategies delineated in this chapter. Your challenge will be to refrain from planning and teaching another lesson without doing the same—ensuring that you are teaching students in ways that enable them to comprehend and retain.

There are additional multiple reasons why these strategies will work for all students. Those reasons are delineated in the paragraphs that follow.

1. **They increase academic achievement for <u>all</u> students.**

The 20 brain-compatible strategies are powerful and are referenced in the literature whether one is teaching regular education students, special education students, gifted and talented students, or students for whom English is a second language. I recall receiving an email from a Canadian teacher of all autistic students who had spent one day with me learning about the strategies. He was excited to realize that those strategies that he had elected to use with his students following the workshop made a world of difference in what they were able to accomplish academically.

When teaching, I relate the story of my son, Chris, who has characteristics of attention deficit disorder. Chris loved school when he was in kindergarten! In fact, Mrs. Campbell, his kindergarten teacher, will always be his favorite. She even attended one of his baseball games during which he got two hits. I will always believe that those hits were due to the fact that she was present!

By the time Chris got to middle school, Cs became the order of the day, and high school yielded even less favorable results. It dawned on me one day that if he had been taught using the same strategies in the upper grades that were used in kindergarten, Chris might have been more successful throughout his educational career! I tell this story because there are so many parents who have similar academic experiences with their children, particularly boys.

2.   **They address all grade levels and content areas.**

The lesson plans which follow will address four major content areas: English/language arts, mathematics, science, and social studies. Additional content areas could have been included as well since these 20 strategies will work for every single curricular area.

There was a book written by Robert Fulghum titled, *All I Really Need to Know I Learned in Kindergarten*. When you peruse the strategies that follow, you will find that they are used most frequently at the kindergarten level. It is in kindergarten that students draw, move, sing, and simply love being there. As student's progress through the subsequent grades, the strategies decrease from the repertoires of many teachers. Guess what else decreases—academic achievement, student motivation, love of school, confidence in one's ability to be successful, etc., so much so that by the time many students get to middle and high school, the extent of engagement involves listening to the teacher talk and taking the occasional note. Why not use the strategies that work in kindergarten at all grade levels? Therefore, you will find lesson plans in this book at every grade level, and every lesson will be taught using multiple brain-compatible strategies.

By the way, these strategies also increase the likelihood that adults will live to a ripe old age (Mahoney, 2005). Adults who keep their brains and bodies active through exercise or movement, who have a positive outlook toward life through humor and optimism, or who learn to play a musical instrument later in life, tend to live longer than their inactive counterparts.

3.   **They decrease behavior problems.**

Some students disrupt because they are bored. I have had teachers tell me that it is not their job to entertain students! I agree. It is not a teacher's job to entertain! However, it is a teacher's job to engage. If teachers are not finding ways to engage the brains of students, students will find ways to engage their own brains. That engagement just may not be what you want! It could involve talking to the person next to them about things unrelated to content or texting while hiding the cell phone from the view of the teacher.

Other students disrupt because they feel inadequate. They cannot do what the teacher is asking them to do, so they simply cover up that inadequacy with misbehavior. It is much better to be known by your friends as *the class clown*. Very few, if any, students want to be considered *the class dummy*.

When teachers begin to use brain-compatible strategies to deliver instruction, the students who were bored become actively engaged in the lesson and the ones who felt inadequate are successful—and a successful student seldom disrupts the class.

4. **They are consistent with the way adult brains retain information in the world in which we live.**

What came first—school or brains? What a ludicrous question! Everyone knows that human beings had brains long before there was a place called *school*. Therefore, the purpose of the brain was never to make straight *As* in school or score high on a standardized or criterion-referenced test. The purpose of the brain is to assist the body in *surviving* in the world in which it must live. Therefore, the closer a teacher can get the content taught to what actually happens in the world of the student, the more sense that content makes to the brain.

Here are a few examples. Before history was in *writing*, it was passed down through *storytelling*. *Mnemonic devices* abound in the real world! The National Football League is the *NFL* and the Federal Bureau of Investigation is more commonly known as the *FBI*. Thanks to social media, some new abbreviations have been added, i.e., *LOL* or *OMG*. Flight attendants know that passengers need *visuals* to understand the airplane instructions and athletes are constantly *visualizing* their performance before the game or competition even begins. Adults with desk jobs are even cautioned about sitting behind a desk all day and encouraged to *move* or stand while working, and many projects or jobs in the workplace are completed in teams or *cooperative groups*. When teachers are using these strategies in school, they are also preparing students to become college- or career-ready.

5. **With only a few exceptions, the strategies cost very little money.**

In a day and age when school budgets are becoming depleted and money for classroom materials and supplies is at a premium, it is gratifying to know that there are effective ways to deliver instruction that do not require the purchasing of the latest textbook series or expensive educational accouterments. After all, it doesn't cost anything to tell a *story* or a *joke* or to provide students with opportunities to *discuss* content or *reteach* a partner. Students can also get up and *role play* a concept or form a living timeline without expending a dime.

While some of the strategies, like *field trips, manipulatives,* or *technology* require monetary commitments, those expenditures may already be delineated in annual budgets.

6. **They make teaching and learning so much fun!**

I teach model lessons during which I take teachers' classes and teach them for a period of about an hour. Regardless of the content or grade level taught, I always incorporate the strategies. I know I have taught an effective lesson when assessment results indicate that the students not only understand and retain the content but also when the lesson is over and a high school student grabs my skirt as I exit the classroom and tells me that this was the best class she had been in all year!

As I travel the United States working with educators nationwide, I am realizing that the fun has gone out of teaching and learning in many classrooms. Some teachers don't relish delivering content and students don't enjoy coming to school. With all of the emphasis on standardized and criterion-referenced testing, benchmarks, and accountability, many educators are simply not having fun anymore. There are even educators who honestly feel that if students are having fun, they couldn't possibly be learning!

Nothing could be farther from the truth! Rigor and fun are not mutually exclusive. According to Cooper and Garner (2012), it is possible for learning to be both enjoyable and rigorous! Just visualize going to your challenging workplace daily where you don't enjoy what you have chosen as your profession. What an unhappy life you would live! In fact, the saying is, *If you love your job, you will never work a day in your life! It will not be work. It will be play!* By the way, people who play actually live longer than people who simply work! (Mahoney, 2005).

BRAIN-COMPATIBLE STRATEGIES

These miraculous but practical strategies are as follows:

Brainstorming and Discussion

In one workshop that I facilitate, I show an excerpt from the movie *Ferris Bueller's Day Off.* If you have seen this movie, then you can visualize the scene where the teacher, Ben Stein, is doing 100 percent of the talking. He then pauses and asks for a student response with the words, *Anyone? Anyone?* while almost simultaneously answering his own questions. All of the students appear in a comatose state. One has even fallen asleep and is drooling on his desk. While the scene was designed to be comical, it was indicative of what many classrooms still resemble today—a teacher doing all the talking while students sit passively like sponges supposedly absorbing as much content as possible.

Researchers are relating that when students actually talk with one another and share ideas about content, they are more likely to process and recall what they are learning (Sousa and Pilecki, 2013). Therefore, allowing students to brainstorm ideas or participate in a lively discussion regarding a higher-order, open-ended question is a very effective teaching tool for fostering creative thought.

Drawing and Artwork

John Dewey had the right idea many years ago when he stated that thinking in art precedes thinking in other curricular areas (Dewey, 1934). Over 80 years later, very little has changed. The arts are being integrated into science, technology, engineering, and math programs. Thus, *STEM* Programs are becoming *STEAM* Programs. Why? Because research is telling us that the arts can be very beneficial to the brain. They increase attention and cognitive skills and upgrade brains by teaching sequencing and processing skills (Jensen and Snider, 2013).

Many students, including my son Chris, are such great artists! Use that talent to your advantage. Peruse your curriculum and determine which curricular objectives can be drawn or integrated into art projects. The time will be well worth it!

Field Trips

Visualize yourself as a student in elementary, middle, or high school. Recall a time when you and your classmates got on a school bus and journeyed to a distant location to accomplish a curricular objective. While you may have long forgotten the objective, you probably still remember the things you saw while on the field trip. The purpose of the brain is survival in the actual world in which we live. Spatial memories acquired during the authentic, experiential experiences of a field trip stay embedded in the brain and, therefore, need no rehearsal (Fogarty, 2009). Is it any wonder that those things perceived in the real world are long remembered while other things taught within the confines of a classroom can be easily forgotten!

Virtual field trips can also be included in this strategy as well as the strategy of technology. These types of field trips broaden the horizons of students since they enable students to *travel* to places that would be inaccessible or cost prohibitive.

Games

When students hear the words, *Let's play a game!* the stress level in their brains decreases while the retention rate increases. The use of games, including technology-based gaming, appears to be increasing exponentially and is highly effective for raising academic achievement and increasing student engagement (Hattie, 2012). David Sousa (2017) suggests that students create original quiz games, even in secondary schools, to test other students' knowledge of a concept previously taught.

Just always be certain that the purpose of any game created or played in class is to introduce, teach, or review content. There is little time for anything else! By the way, playing games is one of the things that keep older people living. The saying is, *You don't stop playing games because you grow older. You grow older because you stop playing games!*

Graphic Organizers, Semantic Maps, and Word Webs

Graphic organizers—also referred to as concept, mind, semantic, or thinking maps—involve taking content from the curriculum and visually plotting it to show and identify the relationships among the ideas. This strategy is particularly effective with English language learners (Konrad, Joseph, and Itoi, 2011) or students with learning disabilities (Sheriff and Boon, 2014) but is actually beneficial for all students.

When lecturing, accompany your lecture with a mind map. Do not give students the mind map in advance. As you draw the organizer on the board, have them draw it along with you. The fact that you are providing a visual to accompany the content as well as having students draw what you are drawing can facilitate understanding and long-term retention.

Humor

Comedian John Cleese made this statement, *He who laughs most, learns best!* Nothing could be truer when it comes to teaching and learning. Since I.Q. is not fixed, brains that are susceptible to adverse environments are equally influenced by positive, enriching environments (Jensen, 2013). Therefore, classrooms, where humor is the order of the day and students look forward to coming to class, can make all the difference in academic achievement. Laughing together is one of the best ways for people to strengthen their immune systems, build relationships, lift their spirits, and relax (Silver, Berckemeyer, and Baenen, 2015).

Humor has both the physiological benefits of increasing oxygen, creating a surge of endorphins, and decreasing blood pressure and stress as well as the psychological benefits of gaining students' attention, creating a positive climate, and increasing retention and recall (Sousa, 2017). In most middle and high schools, there is a class clown. This is the student who loves to make others laugh, often at inappropriate times. Put that talent to use! Jim Carrey's teacher made a deal with him that if he completed his in-class work and homework daily, then the last two minutes of class would belong to him for joke-telling. What a win-win for both teacher and student!

Never confuse humor with sarcasm. They are on opposite ends of the continuum. Any comment meant to tease or demean a student can, at the very least, interfere with higher-level thinking (Jensen, 1995) and destroy the positive classroom environment so conducive to optimal learning.

Manipulatives, Experiments, Labs, and Models

Manipulatives, whether physical or virtual, work since they help students build links between the symbol or object and the mathematical ideas represented (National Research Council, 2009). However, they can be used both during surface learning and deeper understanding. Using manipulatives to move from *physical representations through visual representations to symbolic representations* appears to result in significant gains in mathematics achievement, especially for those who are struggling (Gersten et al., 2009).

Therefore, Unifix cubes or geoboards in mathematics, experiments or labs in science, and building models across the curriculum are all examples of the use of manipulatives. Some teachers think that only young students need manipulatives, but there is such a strong correlation between the hands and the brain that manipulatives can accelerate the mathematical abilities of high school students as well (Curtain-Philips, 2018).

Metaphors, Analogies, and Similes

The strategy of metaphors, analogies, and similes is one of the most powerful ones on the list of 20. Students are capable of comprehending new and difficult concepts when those concepts are compared to dissimilar ones that students already understand. Metaphors can apply to both skill and context learnings, are rich in imagery, and useful for bridging the gap between what the learner already knows and other new learnings (Sousa, 2017).

Creating metaphors and analogies are two of four strategies that help move students from concrete to abstract, from existing to new knowledge, and from separate to connected ideas (Dean, Hubbell, Pitler, and Stone, 2012). However, teacher guidance or modeling is a must if students are to apply this strategy appropriately.

Mnemonic Devices

Mnemonic devices, while developed by the ancient Greeks to help them remember the dialogue in plays, can be used by students to greatly increase their memory (Sousa, 2017). These devices include acronyms and acrostics and can be found in every content area. Acronyms are letters in a word that stand for the content to be remembered. For example, to recall the *Great Lakes,* we simply remember *HOMES* or *H*uron, *O*ntario, *M*ichigan, *E*rie, *S*uperior. Acrostics are sentences where the first letter in each word stands for the content to be recalled. For example, *Please Excuse My Dear Aunt Sally* can assist students in remembering the order of operations in mathematics – *P*arenthesis, *E*xponents, *M*ultiply, *D*ivide, *A*dd, *S*ubtract.

If students are old enough, have them create their own mnemonic devices. According to Feinstein (2009), adolescents find acronyms and acrostics more memorable when they personally create them.

Movement

Of all the strategies on the list, this one is my favorite—not only because it correlates strongly with long-term memory but also because it is so much fun! It is actually a teacher's best friend! When students move while learning, content stands a better chance of ending up in long-term or procedural memory. This strategy is the reason that people seldom forget how to drive a car, ride a bike, type, or play the piano. It has been said that *Sitting is the new smoking!* Lack of movement appears to have just as detrimental an effect on the body as does smoking cigarettes.

This strategy does not have to be time consuming. If the sample lesson plans do not include movement as a strategy, you can still include it in your lesson. Simply having students stand up and mentally process content every few minutes increases blood flow and could temporarily reduce the stress of sitting (Jensen and Snider, 2013). Having students stand if they agree with the answer of another student and remain seated if they disagree is a simple technique that requires no preparation. Begin thinking about those objectives you teach that could easily use some movement. You and your students will be better for it!

Music, Rhythm, Rhyme, and Rap

Students who teachers believe are incapable of remembering content are often walking down the hall singing the lyrics to every song, rhyme, or rap that they hear. Even many Alzheimer's patients who may not respond to anything else verbally, often respond to the lilting sounds of a familiar song. Newer evidence is showing that music may assist in building and strengthening connections between cells in the cortex of the brain and is being used when rehabilitating stroke patients (Sousa, 2017).

Provide songs to assist students in retaining content. Jeff Green's *The Green Book of Songs by Subject* (2005) is a valuable resource for selecting appropriate songs to teach content. If students are old enough, have them create their own songs, rhymes, and raps. Adults are even learning more about the life of Alexander Hamilton in a few hours of song and dance while attending Lin-Manuel Miranda's Tony Award-winning Broadway show *Hamilton* than they may have learned in all of their history classes.

Project-Based and Problem-Based Learning

The purpose of the brain is to solve problems in the world in which its body lives. Therefore, when students are asked to become involved in real-life projects or solve problems that can occur in the actual world, content simply makes more sense. I think that students instinctively know that! In fact, an Indiana University survey asked 81,000 high school students to name some of their preferred learning strategies when at school. Sixty percent of them stated that they wanted to participate in group projects (Jensen and Nickelsen, 2014) especially those that involved technology. Since students also said in the survey that they wanted to use their creativity in school, problem-based learning also fulfills that need. According to Fogarty (2009), "the more complex the problem, the more complex the brain activity" (p. 167). Many of the plans which follow will include projects and problems which will creatively engage the brains of your students.

Reciprocal Teaching and Cooperative Learning

There are many advantages to having students work with partners or in small groups when experiencing content. First of all, an increased number of students can be engaged simultaneously. Second, when students have opportunities to talk about or teach one another what they are learning, they are able to use the cognitive strategies of questioning, summarizing, clarifying, and predicting (Rosenshine and Meister, 1994).

According to Hattie, Fisher, and Frey (2017), when learning mathematics, students need whole-class and small-group opportunities to talk about their questions, thinking, and arguments. The good news is that this research also seems to apply when students are learning anything. In fact, according to Hattie's research, reciprocal teaching is one of the top ten most effective teaching strategies with an effect size of 0.74.

Role Plays, Drama, Pantomimes, and Charades

When you have students act out the definition of a vocabulary word, dramatize a scene from history, or depict the steps in a math word problem, you are using the strategy of role play. Role play results in both increased student engagement as well as a deeper understanding of academic content (Bender, 2017).

In one lesson I taught, we played Charades where students would take turns selecting a vocabulary word and acting it out. Other students had to guess which word was being depicted. The word was *exhausted*. One third grader selected the word, looked at the card on which the word was written, and then fell out on the floor. While I inquired as to whether or not she was hurt, she reminded me that she was simply doing as she was told—acting out her word. No student would soon forget the meaning of *exhausted*!

Storytelling

If you have doubts about the impact of storytelling on the brain, just experience a lecture or speech where the speaker begins to tell a story. Even those who were not previously paying attention begin to do so! If the story is funny or emotional, its attention and retention value is increased.

Brains retain content better when that content is connected together. Stories have beginnings, middles, and ends and student's brains can follow the content of a story. According to Stibich (2014), telling good stories is like weightlifting for the brain since stories force listeners to make connections between their feelings, ideas, and the world at large.

While storytelling is an integral part of any language arts classroom, it is actually cross-curricular. Teachers can tell the story of the algebraic equation in math or the phases of mitosis in science. And after all, what is history if not a story?

Technology

According to the *Secretary's Commission on Achieving Necessary Skills (SCANS)* Report (1991), a person's ability to select, apply, maintain, and troubleshoot equipment including computers and other technology is a workplace competency required of high school students to be successful following graduation. Therefore, any use of this strategy should pay large dividends to students in their chosen profession.

While the use of technology is very important, there are 19 other strategies which deserve consideration. Too much reliance on this strategy solely may limit a student's ability to accomplish another workplace competency on the *SCANS* Report—interpersonal skills. These skills are defined as a person's ability to participate as part of a team of people from diverse backgrounds. Encourage students to strive for balance. This will prepare them for workplace success.

Visualization and Guided Imagery

While visuals are things students can see, visualization involves seeing in the mind's eye and is an effective way to retain content. Imagery, or the visualization of objects, arrays, and events related to new learning is a major way the brain has of storing information (Sousa, 2017). In fact, according to David Sousa (2017), when the brain creates images, the same parts of the visual cortex are activated as when the eyes actually process input from the real world.

Therefore, having students image the meaning of a vocabulary word, a specific period of history, or the steps in a math word problem or science experiment is a very worthwhile endeavor. Having them imagine what life will be like 50 years from today or what would have happened if they had been born 100 years before they were is also meaningful for long-term memory.

Visuals

With an abundance of cell phones, computers, laptops, television, etc., we are bombarded with information that is taken in visually. According to neurologist Judy Willis (2006), at least 50 percent of students in any classroom are likely to be visual learners. Since "the brain processes visuals up to 60,000 times faster than words" (Gregory and Chapman, 2013, p.23), PowerPoint, visuals on the document camera or Smartboard, or posters on the wall in support of the learning are essential if the content is to be processed and remembered.

There is even physical evidence to support that the visual cortex in the brains of students today is actually physically thicker than it was in my brain when I was their age. (Tate, 2016). Since students begin so early encountering visuals, they have had many years to perfect this modality.

Work Study and Apprenticeships

One of the concerns with secondary schools is their tendency to cover a tremendous amount of content without giving students an opportunity to apply that content in the context of authentic situations (Wiggins and McTighe, 2008). In fact, Aristotle had the right idea thousands of years before when he said, *One learns to do by doing!* In other words, the best way to teach anyone anything is to immerse them in the actual tasks required to master the knowledge or skill.

This is the reason that internships, externships, and apprenticeships are vital, particularly for high school and college students. It is one thing to sit in a classroom and read about the skills and abilities required to do a job. It is another thing to actually work with someone who is currently doing the job and who is willing to equip you with on-the-job training.

Writing and Journals

What is more memorable for students' brains—to write in longhand or to type on a computer? The answer may surprise you! Scientists from Princeton University and the University of California tell us that writing notes by hand is much better for long-term memory of ideas and conceptual information than typing on a laptop, tablet, or computer.

So while it is certainly necessary that we provide opportunities for students to interact with the technology, there will be times when it is simply more productive for them to write. However, since the brain can only pay conscious attention to one thing at a time when lecturing, have students listen to the lecture and then write or write first and then listen to the lecture. To attempt to do both simultaneously will not be nearly as productive.

These are the 20 brain-compatible strategies that will be a part of every lesson which follows. To teach the human brain without the use of instructional strategies that take advantage of the way it learns best should be considered malpractice!

3

A Brain-Compatible Lesson

There are five questions that every teacher should be asking and answering when planning a memorable lesson. These five questions are reflected in the lesson plans which follow and are outlined below. Is it necessary that teachers write down the answers to the questions when planning? No! Teachers might have a required lesson plan format that is different from the template contained in this book. Is it necessary that teachers ask the five questions? Absolutely!

SECTION 1: LESSON OBJECTIVE

What Do You Want Your Students To Know and Be Able To Do?

I have been taught Stephen Covey's *7 Habits of Highly Effective People*. I learned that Habit Two of the seven is *Begin with the End in Mind*. In other words, before you begin a task, visualize a successful outcome to that task. Then plan just how you will ensure that the successful outcome becomes a reality. Planning a lesson is no different!

Teachers are given approximately the same amount of instructional time annually but asked to teach more and more content and to do it all well! They are then assessed by how well their students have mastered the content delivered; therefore, teachers will be tempted to just cover content.

However, if all teachers are doing is delivering content, then they should do what Madeline Hunter suggests and cover the content with dirt because it is dead to memory. To leave out the activity is to leave out the memory!

Before you begin to plan a lesson, visualize what you want your students to know, understand, and be able to do once that lesson is completed. Then, and only then, will you be ready to actually plan the lesson. Learning begins with the teacher, and hopefully the student as well, knowing what the desired results are and then working backward to where the student starts the lesson (Hattie, 2012). Here is an analogy that Covey uses. A pilot of an airplane cannot possibly plan the flight route until the destination has been determined.

In their book, *Understanding by Design* (2005), Wiggins and McTighe refer to this concept as *backward lesson design.* The starting point should then be determined by the student's prior knowledge and where the student falls in the learning process. Wiggins and McTighe relate that teachers must *shift their thinking* regarding the student learning they are seeking and the evidence that the learning has taken place before even considering what activities will be used to deliver the learning (2005).

The 100 lesson plans contained in this book begin with the end in mind and state what students should know and be able to do at the beginning of each plan itself.

SECTION 2: ASSESSMENT

How Will You Know That Students Have Mastered Essential Learning?

Note that this is the second question in the lesson plan template and not the last question. There is another way to ask it. *How will you know when students know?* What will you do both during (formatively) and after (summatively) the lesson to determine whether students have learned what you need them to learn?

When my sisters and I were in school, it was always important to us and our parents that we make good grades. My father had the highest of expectations for our success. I can still hear him saying, *On the report card, a grade of C means Fair. My children are not fair. They are exceptional!* We lived up to those high expectations!

I always wanted to score well on any test to be administered; therefore, I spent a great deal of time in my room studying. However, I usually had to guess what was going to be assessed. If I guessed correctly, I made an *A.* If I guessed incorrectly, I was upset because my studying time had not been productive. Today's lesson planning involves not only telling students what you expect them to know, understand, and be able to do but also how those expectations will be assessed.

These assessments can, and probably should be a combination of more traditional selected types of assessments (such as multiple choice, matching, or short-answer items) and constructed types of assessments (such as products and performances). Selected types help to ensure that students are familiar with the formats encountered when taking teacher-made, benchmark, or summative assessments. Constructed types are more aligned with the way many students learn and are more indicative of what will be expected of them in the actual world of work.

Each of the following lesson plans will indicate the specific assessments that will be used to determine what students should know, understand, and be able to do and how we will know when they can do it. Those assessments should be a combination of both authentic and traditional forms of assessment if we really want to know if all students are learning.

SECTION 3: WAYS TO GAIN/MAINTAIN ATTENTION

How Will You Gain and Maintain Students' Attention?

Whether we like it or not, when we are teaching, we are vying for the attention of our students. If our lesson is not worthy of that attention, then it is going elsewhere. Years ago, that attention could be directed toward talking to a peer about things totally unrelated to the learning or writing and passing a note which was often intercepted by the teacher. Today, a lack of attention could still result in talking with a peer or texting while the teacher is oblivious to what is happening. Students can even be quiet and maintain eye contact with the teacher while simultaneously not paying a bit of attention to what is being taught.

There are four major ways to gain and keep the attention of students. They are *need, novelty, meaning,* or *emotion.* Note the word "or" which means that a teacher does not need to employ all four ways to get the student's attention. One of the four is sufficient.

Consider *Need, Novelty, Meaning,* or *Emotion*

Need

The brain tends to pay attention to and remember things it perceives the need to remember. For example, when I was working on my master's degree in remedial reading at the University of Michigan, my grade in one course was dependent on the ability to increase the reading level of a high school student whom I tutored for one semester. My student was a ninth grader who was reading at approximately a third- to fourth-grade level and impatiently waiting to drop out of school due to his inability to read his textbooks. After I had tried a variety of instructional techniques, it dawned on me that Ricardo's immediate need was to secure his driver's license and ultimately become more mobile. I went to the motor vehicle's bureau and secured a driver's manual from which I taught Ricardo sight words, the use of context clues, and other essential language arts skills and strategies. Was I able to get his reading to grade level? No, I regret that I simply did not have enough time. Did his performance improve? Absolutely! When the semester ended, Ricardo had the confidence to believe that he could take and pass his written driver's test and I became one of his favorite teachers!

Students acquire knowledge so much easier when they perceive the need for the information. Some of the following lesson plans use *need* to gain the attention of students.

Novelty

Our brains pay attention to those things in the environment that look or sound new or different. For example, before we bought a house in the subdivision where we raised our three children, I was apprehensive due to the fact that a railroad track ran right beside it and I thought the passing trains would be disturbing. I asked some of the neighbors if that was the case and they assured me that it would not be. We bought the house and moved into it. For the first week, I could set the clock by the noise of the passing trains which were right on schedule. I was upset since I figured the neighbors had not been truthful with me. The recognition of that noise lasted only a few weeks and then I, too, failed to notice. They say that people who live near airports experience the same thing.

If teachers want students to stop paying attention to their lessons, then they will want to teach the same way every day with little or no novelty in the lesson. Simply changing the teacher's location in the classroom as the lesson is being taught adds some novelty, but the 20 brain-compatible strategies on which the lessons in this book are based will help to ensure that instruction continues to be taught in new and different ways.

There is no magic number of strategies which should be included in each lesson. The lesson objective should guide the determination of which one's fit the best. However, to use the same strategy too often is not a good thing! Many school systems today are thinking that every lesson should reflect the strategy of technology. While that strategy is certainly important, it becomes mundane and as boring as a worksheet if every lesson revolves solely on that one strategy.

Meaning

If teachers want to make lessons meaningful, they should think of ways to connect the content of those lessons to the lives of their students. This concept was delineated as one of the characteristics of a brain-compatible classroom in Chapter 1 and goes a long way in answering the question, *Why do we have to learn this?*

The strategy of *metaphor, analogy,* and *simile* enables teachers to take a concept that they must teach and make it more meaningful by connecting it to another real-world concept that students already understand. For example, telling students that a main idea and details are like a table and legs, or the layers of the earth are formed like the dirty clothes in a laundry basket with the most recent layers of clothes on top makes difficult concepts much easier to comprehend. Helping them to understand that the Richter scale for measuring the intensity of earthquakes is an example of a logarithmic scale would be another example of making content meaningful.

Emotion

Of the four ways to gain the brain's attention, *emotion* is the most powerful! The brain does not remember *days*! It remembers moments! Therefore, anything that happened in the world that had an emotional impact on the public will be long remembered. For example, visualize where you were on January 28, 1986, when the *Challenger* exploded. If you were old enough, you will probably recall that we lost seven astronauts that day including Christa McAuliffe, an extraordinary American teacher from New Hampshire who was specially selected to join the other six astronauts on the space shuttle.

However, I do not want to use a negative definition of emotion when talking about teaching and learning. If you were ever in the classroom of a teacher you disliked, you will never forget being in that teacher's room, but you are unlikely to recall much of the content taught. This is probably due to the fact that your brain was in survival mode while sitting in that class.

Teachers should want students to recall their content. Therefore, they must teach with passion and enthusiasm. According to Eric Jensen (2013), teachers can positively affect the state of students' minds simply by being in a positive state themselves. Passion and emotion are contagious! I have even told my husband, Tyrone, that the day I facilitate professional learning or teach students with no passion or enthusiasm, that day will be the last day I work as an educational consultant!

SECTION 4: CONTENT CHUNKS

How Will You Divide And Teach The Content To Engage Students' Brains?

As stated in Chapter 1, most human brains can hold approximately seven isolated bits of information simultaneously. This is the reason that so many real-world lists come in sets of seven. If I want my students to hold more, then I should chunk or connect the content. It is in this section of the plan that the teacher determines how much students' brains can hold at one time. That amount determines the size of a chunk or lesson segment. The amount of content contained in one chunk may be different for a special education student than for a gifted, regular education, or ESL student.

Students with poor working memory can be supported if taught in fewer and smaller chunks of content (Jensen, 2013). A chunk, then, is one segment of a lesson objective. Many lessons will have only one chunk since the entire objective can be addressed. However, multiple activities may be used in teaching that one chunk.

Let's use this analogy to explain the concept of chunking. Visualize this scenario. You are listening to a speaker and the speaker tells you that he will be addressing three points or concepts in the speech. Now, your brain is positioned to listen for those three points and you are disappointed if those points are not made. Each point would then include a strategy for getting the point across to the audience, such as visuals, storytelling, or the use of an analogy.

A teacher must determine which brain-compatible activities will be incorporated into each chunk. Due to the large amount of content to be taught, some teachers are tempted to leave out the student activity and simply tell students what they need to know in a boring lecture. What they don't know is that for most students, to leave out the activity is to leave out the memory!

Activities in each chunk should include those that indicate a gradual release of responsibility on the part of the teacher and an increase in responsibility on the part of the student. The motto, *I do, we do, you do* depicts this relationship perfectly and will be reflected in the lesson plans which follow.

SECTION 5: BRAIN-COMPATIBLE STRATEGIES

Which Will You Use To Deliver Content?

As teachers are integrating the activities into the designated chunks, the 20 brain-compatible strategies should be reflected. A place is provided on the template for teachers to check off which strategies have been included. I am mindful of including at least one strategy for my visual learners (i.e., graphic organizers, visuals, visualization), at least one strategy for my auditory learners (i.e., brainstorming and discussion, reciprocal teaching and cooperative learning, or storytelling), at least one strategy for my tactile learners (i.e., drawing and artwork, manipulatives, or writing) and at least one strategy for my kinesthetic learners (i.e., movement, role play, or project-based learning) in every lesson. If a lesson is planned, and not one strategy is used to deliver instruction, then the lesson is not brain-compatible and should be planned again.

The lessons which follow are written in an attempt to enable teachers to begin teaching in brain-compatible ways. They represent a small sample of plans regarding standards and objectives which many teachers must deliver. Once you get the hang of planning and teaching this way, the creation of subsequent plans becomes much easier. So, hop on board and enjoy the ride into brain-compatible teaching!

4

25 Sample Language Arts/English Lessons

LANGUAGE ARTS GRADES K–2 LESSON 1

High-Frequency Words

Lesson Objective(s): *What do you want students to know and be able to do?*

Read common high-frequency words by sight (e.g., the, of, to, you, she, my, is, are, do, does).

Assessment (Traditional/Authentic): *How will you know students have mastered essential learning?*

Have students create a story using at least three to five sight words.

Ways to Gain/Maintain Attention (Primacy): *How will you gain and maintain students' attention? Consider need, novelty, meaning, or emotion.*

Students will sing sight words and use colorful fly-swatters to "swat" sight words they see around the room.

Content Chunks: *How will you divide and teach the content to engage students' brains?*

Lesson Segment 1: Identify Commonly Used Sight Words in Context (Dolch Word List)

- **Activity 1: Singing/Body Spelling**

On chart paper, write the following song for an anchor chart. When introducing the chart, sing to the tune of "Are You Sleeping."

All Am Are At

Ate Be Black Brown

But Came Did

But Came Did

Do Eat For Get Good Have

Do Eat For Get Good Have

He Into

He Into

After singing the song twice, have students body spell the words as a group. To body spell, have students stand up and emulate the actions you make. For example, to spell the word, "all," extend your arms out for the letter *a* and stretch your arms up twice for the two letters *l*. If a letter extends below the line, like a *p*, have students bend over from the waist and touch their toes. Challenge the students by having them spell the words and do the motions faster and faster.

• Activity 2: Inside Out Spelling

Distribute index cards with the sight words written on each card, to students. Play upbeat music such as *Do the Twist* by Chubby Checker. Have the students form inside out circles to do *air spelling*. Ten students will stand in the inner circle facing out and 10 students will stand on the outer circle facing in. The outside circle will go first. The students will say the word and spell it in the air with their hands for the students on the inside. Then, the students on the inside circle will share their words. When the music plays, students will rotate clockwise and repeat the same routine until all students have air spelled their words.

When students are done, place the words on the word wall using the color green (vocabulary words may be written in purple).

• Activity 3: Fly Swatter Activity

As a review, have students use fly swatters as they read around the room. As they travel around to the word wall and anchor charts, students will *swat* and recite the words they recognize.

Next, when rotating to literacy centers, create a station called *Word Work*. Activities in the word work center can include:

- Using magnetic letters, have the students build the sight words introduced during that week. Have words that were previously introduced reinforced by seeing the word with fidelity on sight.
- Using shaving cream or grits inside a container, students practice spelling their sight words. It even smells or feels good too.

• Activity 4: Splashes of Sight Words

Create *Splashes of Sight Words* paint cans with the students. Use the "Splashes of Color" handout from the book, *Engage the Brain: Graphic Organizers and Other Visual Strategies, Grade 2*, page 86. Ahead of time, draw or glue a picture of the paint can. Preview old magazines to ensure pictures are appropriate for primary aged students. Have students cut out as many sight words as they can find and glue them on the paint can. The cans can be displayed or kept in their Readers Workshop folders.

Lesson Segment 2: Use Commonly Used Sight Words in a Story

• Activity 1: Story Writing and Illustrating

After reviewing the sight words introduced for the week, distribute primary story paper to the students (the kind with a square box at the top for illustrations and lines at the bottom for writing). Have the students write and illustrate a story with at least five sight words in them. Allow the students to take turns sharing their stories with the class.

Brain-Compatible Strategies: *Which will you use to deliver content?*

__X__	Brainstorming/Discussion	__X__	Music/Rhythm/Rhyme/Rap
__X__	Drawing/Artwork	_____	Project/Problem-Based Learning
_____	Field Trips	_____	Reciprocal Teaching/Cooperative Learning
_____	Games		
_____	Graphic Organizers/Semantic Maps/Word Webs	_____	Role Plays/Drama/Pantomimes/Charades
__X__	Humor	_____	Storytelling
_____	Manipulatives/Experiments/Labs/Models	_____	Technology
		_____	Visualization/Guided Imagery
_____	Metaphors/Analogies/Similes	__X__	Visuals
_____	Mnemonic Devices	_____	Work Study/Apprenticeships
__X__	Movement	__X__	Writing/Journals

Name _____ Date _____

Splashes of Color

Directions: Look through a magazine and cut out samples of a color you like. Try finding many different shades of that color. Glue your samples onto the paint can. Now glue the sight words cut from the magazines onto the colored paint cans.

LANGUAGE ARTS GRADES K–2 LESSON 2

Rhyming Words

Lesson Objective(s): *What do you want students to know and be able to do?*

Recognize and produce rhyming words.

Assessment (Traditional/Authentic): *How will you know students have mastered essential learning?*

Have students create their own rhyming word flipbooks with a partner or individually.

Ways to Gain/Maintain Attention (Primacy): *How will you gain and maintain students' attention? Consider <u>need</u>, novelty, meaning, or <u>emotion</u>.*

Begin the lesson by using voice intonation to read or sing the first two pages from Dr. Seuss's *Hop on Pop* to pique students' curiosity. In addition, pin words to your clothing and have objects available that represent the words pinned to you.

Content Chunks: *How will you divide and teach the content to engage students' brains?*

Lesson Segment 1: Recognize Rhyming Words

- **Activity 1: Match My Rhyme**

As students gather on the carpet for the lesson, read or sing words from the first five pages of Dr. Seuss's book, *Hop on Pop*. Ask students why they think you are reading or singing these random words and sentences. Then, introduce the concept of rhyming words to the students. Ahead of time, prepare an anchor chart entitled, *Rhyming Words*. Explain that rhyming words are words that have the same ending sounds like the ones you just said to them. Provide an example such as "hop" and "pop" and write them on the chart. Now, reread the first five pages from the story. Then, ask the students, *Did you hear any other words that rhyme?* Elicit responses from the students and chart rhyming words using different colors as a visual.

Prior to the lesson, prepare enough sets of rhyming words and illustrations on index cards for at least 10 to 12 pairs of students. In addition, fold 10 to 12 sheets of 11×14 construction paper in half. Mix up the cards and distribute them to pairs of students along with one sheet of construction paper. Have the students find matches and place them on the left and right sides of the construction paper. When students have finished, they can go around the room to view other classmates' rhyming pairs.

- **Activity 2: Green Egg Rhymes**

Ahead of time, glue and write pictures of rhyming words on jumbo craft sticks and on cutout pictures of green eggs. The words should come from the story *Green Eggs and Ham* by Dr. Seuss.

Place them in plastic bags for the students to use after the mini-lesson. Begin the lesson by reading the story to the students. During the first reading, allow students to just listen for enjoyment. The second time, ask them to listen for the rhyming words they hear. You may choose to just read half of the book to adjust for students' attention spans.

Afterward, divide students into pairs. Distribute bags with craft sticks and green egg cutouts. Instruct students to match the pictures on the green eggs to the corresponding rhyming word found on the craft stick. They can use tacky clay or glue sticks to attach the egg on the craft sticks. Once pairs are done, play upbeat music and students can conduct a *rhyming walk* to see the matches their classmates found in other groups.

Lesson Segment 2: Produce and Create Rhyming Words

- **Activity 1: Rhyming Word Book**

Ahead of time, collect appropriate magazines filled with rich rhyming word pictures. To save time, you may cut out several before the lesson or students may find their own. Review rhyming words by allowing students time to walk around the room to discuss rhyming words they have learned during this unit. Afterward, distribute magazines or pictures to the students. In addition, give each student an 8×11 sheet of construction paper folded vertically. Cut the top layer of each to create five flaps (you may do this or draw dashed lines for students to do it by themselves to strengthen cutting skills.). Next, tell students to glue each picture on each of the five outer flaps. Then, on the inside, have them draw a picture of a word that rhymes with the picture on the outer flap. Have students label each picture with the matching word.

Brain-Compatible Strategies: *Which will you use to deliver content?*

__X__	Brainstorming/Discussion	__X__	Music/Rhythm/Rhyme/Rap
__X__	Drawing/Artwork	_____	Project/Problem-Based Learning
_____	Field Trips	__X__	Reciprocal Teaching/Cooperative Learning
__X__	Games		
_____	Graphic Organizers/Semantic Maps/Word Webs	_____	Role Plays/Drama/Pantomimes/Charades
_____	Humor	__X__	Storytelling
__X__	Manipulatives/Experiments/Labs/Models	_____	Technology
		_____	Visualization/Guided Imagery
_____	Metaphors/Analogies/Similes	__X__	Visuals
_____	Mnemonic Devices	_____	Work Study/Apprenticeships
__X__	Movement	__X__	Writing/Journals

LANGUAGE ARTS GRADES K–2 LESSON 3

Phonemes

Lesson Objective(s): *What do you want students to know and be able to do?*

Produce the initial, medial vowel, and final sounds in three-phoneme words. Make new words by adding or substituting individual phonemes in one-syllable words.

Assessment (Traditional/Authentic): *How will you know students have mastered essential learning?*

Have students create a *Short Vowel Book* to be used during the Readers Workshop period.

Ways to Gain/Maintain Attention (Primacy): *How will you gain and maintain students' attention? Consider need, novelty, meaning, or emotion.*

Instruct students to slap their thighs, clap their hands, or snap their fingers to help reinforce beginning, medial, and ending sounds in a word.

Content Chunks: *How will you divide and teach the content to engage students' brains?*

Lesson Segment 1: Make New Words by Adding or Substituting Phonemes

- **Activity 1: Slap, Clap, Snap**

On an anchor chart, write all the three phoneme words in the –at family. Bring in as many of those objects as possible so students can see its relevance to the real world. Tell students that they will be looking at several words and objects today. Instruct them to give the sounds of the word after you say the word and will slap, clap, and snap at the same time. For example, if the students sound out the word "cat," when they say, "c," they will slap their thighs. When they recite the sound, "a," they will clap once and when they say, "t," the students will snap their fingers. Repeat this same pattern for several words.

To evaluate what students have learned, call out the same words using different directions. Have the students slap, clap, or snap when you ask for the beginning or ending sound. For example, say the word "cat." Allow the students to repeat after you. Then, ask for the beginning sound and its motion. Students should pronounce the *c* sound and slap their thighs at the same time. If you ask for the ending sound, they should pronounce the *t* sound and snap their fingers.

For additional practice, have the students log onto IXL.com and practice beginning, medial, and ending sounds.

- **Activity 2: Let Me Be Your Substitute**

In advance, write the letter *a* on five different clothespins, and do the same for the remaining vowels. Write the beginning, middle, and ending consonant, vowel, consonant word on chart paper (example—dog). Discuss the beginning, middle, and ending sound found in the word. Afterward, take a sticky note and cover the vowel. Place all clothespins in a paper bag. Have the students pull a pin from the bag. The student will orally pronounce the letter found on the pin, and determine if it would be a good substitute for the letter *o* found in the word "dog." Continue to pull different vowels until there are no more possible sounds for that word.

Distribute a sheet of 8x10 construction paper folded in fours. Ask students to select four of their favorite words learned today. Instruct them to write each word in a square and illustrate it.

• Activity 3: Cut It Out!

Ahead of time, laminate the *Word Building* handout for students to use throughout the year. Distribute the handout (found on page three from this lesson plan), a Ziploc bag, and four pictures from a magazine. Have students cut out the letters individually and place them near their plastic bag (to be housed in their Readers Workshop folders afterward). Next, spread out the four pictures. Using letter tiles, arrange the letters to create the words that match the picture.

Afterward, allow students to create a short vowel book (select a vowel you have been working on). Staple five half sheets of white copy paper in between two sheets of construction paper and staple the edges. Have students use resources around the room including the words from the activity along with the Word Wall to write, for example, long o words in the book. Next, allow the students to illustrate each word. Instruct students to keep the books in their Readers Workshop folders.

Brain-Compatible Strategies: *Which will you use to deliver content?*

__X__	Brainstorming/Discussion	_____	Music/Rhythm/Rhyme/Rap
__X__	Drawing/Artwork	_____	Project/Problem-Based Learning
_____	Field Trips	_____	Reciprocal Teaching/Cooperative Learning
_____	Games		
_____	Graphic Organizers/Semantic Maps/Word Webs	_____	Role Plays/Drama/Pantomimes/Charades
_____	Humor	_____	Storytelling
__X__	Manipulatives/Experiments/Labs/Models	_____	Technology
		_____	Visualization/Guided Imagery
_____	Metaphors/Analogies/Similes	__X__	Visuals
_____	Mnemonic Devices	_____	Work Study/Apprenticeships
__X__	Movement	__X__	Writing/Journals

Word Building

a	a	a	a	b	b	b
c	c	c	d	d	e	e
e	f	f	g	g	g	g
h	h	i	i	i	i	i
j	j	k	k	l	l	l
m	m	m	n	n	o	o
o	o	o	p	p	q	q
r	r	s	s	s	t	t
t	u	u	u	v	v	w
w	x	x	y	y	z	z

Adapted by: Simone Willingham

LANGUAGE ARTS GRADES K–2 LESSON 4

Word Analysis Skills

Lesson Objective(s): *What do you want students to know and be able to do?*

Know and apply phonics and word analysis skills in decoding words.

Assessment (Traditional/Authentic): *How will you know students have mastered essential learning?*

Students will create an original poster and draw or find as many words they can in a magazine that correspond to the designated rime. Once students draw a picture or glue a picture to the poster, they will be challenged to write the word that matches the picture.

Ways to Gain/Maintain Attention (Primacy): *How will you gain and maintain students' attention? Consider* <u>need</u>*, novelty,* <u>meaning</u>*, or* <u>emotion</u>*.*

Divide students into three to four teams. Have various pictures taped around the room (at least 10). Then, call out a blend (for example, pronounce "bl"). Play upbeat music like the instrumental version of the song *Beat It* by Michael Jackson. When students hear the music, instruct teams to travel to the picture beginning with that blend so they can become familiar with decoding and blending. Repeat this process for several words.

Content Chunks: *How will you divide and teach the content to engage students' brains?*

Lesson Segment 1: Know and Apply Phonics and Word Analysis Skills While Decoding Words

- **Activity 1: Shaving Cream Words**

Assign groups of students index cards of words with common rimes (ug, ot, it). Spray shaving cream on students' desks. Students can use a craft stick to make a smooth layer on their desks or on a plastic tray. Then, instruct students to select a card and recite the onset (initial letter) then the rime (the group of letters following the onset). As the students recite the onset and rime, they will write the letters with their fingers as they recite (they can also use the craft stick). Then, when they have written the entire word, the students will pronounce what they wrote in the shaving cream. Repeat the process for all the words.

- **Activity 2: Word Drawings**

After introducing a new rime or word pattern, distribute a sheet of construction paper, folded in fours, to each student. Ask students to write four words from the pattern in each square on the paper. Instruct students to visualize what that word means to them and how they can use it in their everyday lives. Next, students will draw a picture about what that word means to them, including the word itself. For example, if the student has the word "book," they may draw eyelashes and pupils inside the two letters between the "b" and "k." They can also draw a picture of some glasses around those letters including a visual of a book.

• Activity 3: Blending Hustle

Instruct students to sit in a circle on the floor. Place rimes on index cards in different places around the room. Next, distribute index cards and pencils to the students. Assign students to work in teams of two. When a student's team is called, and they hear the song *The Hustle* by Van McCoy, they will *two-step hustle* to a rime or blend. As a team, students will have to create a word with that rime and write it on their card. The challenge is that teams must *two-step* to each card or they will lose their turn. The team that creates as many words as they can in one minute wins lunch with the teacher.

• Activity 4: Poster Sounds

Ahead of time, collect age-appropriate magazines with rich pictures for the students. Distribute construction paper, scissors, magazines, and glue sticks to students. Assign each student a rime or word family to focus on. Instruct students to write the rime in the middle of the paper using a bold marker. Then, allow students to cut pictures from magazines or draw pictures that include that rime. For example, if a student is assigned the "ing" rime, they may find a picture of someone singing, which they will use as the word "sing." The students will cut and glue the picture to the paper or draw the picture on the paper. Then, challenge students to sound out and write the word that corresponds to the picture.

Brain-Compatible Strategies: *Which will you use to deliver content?*

__X__	Brainstorming/Discussion	__X__	Music/Rhythm/Rhyme/Rap
__X__	Drawing/Artwork	_____	Project/Problem-Based Learning
_____	Field Trips	__X__	Reciprocal Teaching/Cooperative Learning
__X__	Games		
_____	Graphic Organizers/Semantic Maps/Word Webs	_____	Role Plays/Drama/Pantomimes/Charades
_____	Humor	_____	Storytelling
__X__	Manipulatives/Experiments/Labs/Models	_____	Technology
		__X__	Visualization/Guided Imagery
_____	Metaphors/Analogies/Similes	__X__	Visuals
_____	Mnemonic Devices	_____	Work Study/Apprenticeships
__X__	Movement	__X__	Writing/Journals

LANGUAGE ARTS GRADES K–2 LESSON 5

Main Topic and Details

Lesson Objective(s): *What do you want students to know and be able to do?*

Identify the main topic and retell key details in a text.

Assessment (Traditional/Authentic): *How will you know students have mastered essential learning?*

Engage students in a project to create an ice cream cone that represents the main idea and supporting details in a text.

Ways to Gain/Maintain Attention (Primacy): *How will you gain and maintain students' attention? Consider need, novelty, meaning, or emotion.*

Tell students that the main idea is like an ice cream cone. Demonstrate with an ice cream cone, ice cream, and scoop during the explanation.

Content Chunks: *How will you divide and teach the content to engage students' brains?*

Lesson Segment 1: Identify the Main Topic in a Text

- **Activity 1: Main Idea Video**

Play the short clip from the site Brainpopjr.com entitled *Main Idea and Key Details*. Afterward, complete the activities and short quiz using the ActivBoard. Have students take turns answering the questions on the board.

- **Activity 2: Text Message Metaphor**

Review the concept of the main idea/main topic with students. Compare the main idea to a text message. When we send a text, we send the most important or main message. Show the students an example of an appropriate text message from your phone while you demonstrate.

Next, read the first three pages from the literary text *Thomas' Snowsuit* by Robert Munsch (or another appropriate book) to the students. Afterward, play upbeat music, such as *Happy*, by Pharrell Williams, to have the students visit with a clock appointment. Tell them to take turns discussing what they feel is the main idea. Give students at least three to five minutes to discuss. When they are finished, elicit responses from the students. Using the graphic organizer as an anchor chart, write the main idea in the rectangle on the chart. Discuss why they were able to distinguish their answer along with supporting evidence from the text.

- **Activity 3: Cell Phone Silhouette**

Review the main idea from *Thomas' Snowsuit*. To emphasize the analogy to the cell phone, bring in at least five different pictures and silhouettes of cell phones. Have the students trace their favorite cell phone silhouette on construction paper and decorate. Once students are done, allow them to place the silhouettes in the Readers Workshop folders or reading book bags to use with key details later on. Laminate for extended use throughout the school year.

Lesson Segment 2: Identify the Key Details in a Text

- **Activity 1: Detail Phone Call Metaphor**

Review the main idea from the text, *Thomas' Snowsuit*. Ask the students to refer back to the cell phone and ask them to take out their paper phones. Ask, *We now know that when you send a text message like the main topic, you are sending the most important idea. But sometimes, we want to provide the person with more information. When we want to give specific details about the topic, how would we use the phone?* Students' responses should include *calling people on the phone for more details.* Tell them that today, we will be calling our friends to provide them with supporting details about a topic.

Read pages 1-5 from *Thomas' Snowsuit* to the students. During the first reading, ask students to listen for enjoyment and the main idea. During the second reading, ask students to pay attention to the details that support the main idea. Then assign students to work in pairs. Distribute the *It's All In the Details* handout and a sliver of paper to the students. Instruct the students to attach the sliver of paper on the cell phone using Velcro on the back. Write the main idea on the paper attached to the phone. This represents the text message. As a team, have them create at least three details that support the main idea and write them on the handout. When students are finished and hear the instrumental version of the song *Call Me* by Blondie, they will put their cell phones to their ears and call their partner to discuss the details. This emphasizes the point that you *text* the main idea but you *call* to discuss the details.

- **Activity 2: Main Idea and Details**

To bring it all together, assign or ask students to select a book from the classroom or their reading book bag. As they read, remind them to use the analogy of the cell phone to help them reinforce the concepts.

Next, students will create their own paper ice cream cone and three scoops of ice cream. Provide models and silhouettes for the students. Glue the paper ice cream cone and detail scoops on construction paper to build their own main topic ice cream cones. The main idea is the cone itself and the supporting details are represented by each scoop on top.

As a special treat, once students have displayed their ice cream cones, they can enjoy the actual ice cream and cone treats brought in for the demonstration on the first day of this plan.

Brain-Compatible Strategies: *Which will you use to deliver content?*

__X__ Brainstorming/Discussion	__X__ Music/Rhythm/Rhyme/Rap
__X__ Drawing/Artwork	_____ Project/Problem-Based Learning
_____ Field Trips	__X__ Reciprocal Teaching/Cooperative Learning
_____ Games	
__X__ Graphic Organizers/Semantic Maps/Word Webs	_____ Role Plays/Drama/Pantomimes/ Charades
_____ Humor	__X__ Storytelling
_____ Manipulatives/Experiments/Labs/ Models	__X__ Technology
	_____ Visualization/Guided Imagery
__X__ Metaphors/Analogies/Similes	__X__ Visuals
_____ Mnemonic Devices	_____ Work Study/Apprenticeships
_____ Movement	__X__ Writing/Journals

It's All in the Details

Detail 1:

_____

_____

_____

_____

_____

Detail 2:

_____

_____

_____

_____

_____

Detail 3:

_____

_____

_____

_____

_____

LANGUAGE ARTS GRADES K–2 LESSON 6

Story Details

Lesson Objective(s): *What do you want students to know and be able to do?*

Use key details to describe characters, settings, and major events in a story.

Assessment (Traditional/Authentic): *How will you know students have mastered essential learning?*

Students will create a story based on a picture found in a magazine or from a group of pictures selected in advance from the internet. The students will write a possible setting, names for characters, and how events correspond with the picture.

Ways to Gain/Maintain Attention (Primacy): *How will you gain and maintain students' attention? Consider need, novelty, meaning, or emotion.*

Come in dressed like Grandma from the story *Little Red Riding Hood.* Ahead of time, on chart paper, write the words, **Title** _____, **Character** _____, **Setting** _____, **Event 1** _____, and **Event 2** _____. Ask students to figure out who you are and from which story. Once students figure out who you are, fill in the lines next to **Title** and **Character**.

Next, ask students questions about the character, setting, and events. Fill in the remainder of the chart as you elicit responses from the students.

Content Chunks: *How will you divide and teach the content to engage students' brains?*

Lesson Segment 1: Use Key Details to Describe the Characters in a Story

- **Activity 1: Hare and Bear Traits**

Read the story *Tops and Bottoms* by Janet Stevens to the students. During the first reading, ask students to listen to it for enjoyment. During the second reading, stop and ask clarifying questions that focus on the main characters, and how their actions influence the outcome of the story.

Assign students to work in pairs. Distribute a sheet of construction paper, folded in half, to each pair. Next, instruct them to draw a picture of the bear on the left and the hare on the right. Instruct students to write at least three to five words to describe each character in each column. In addition, allow them to provide supporting evidence for each trait. Share with the class.

- **Activity 2: Blooming Characters**

Ahead of time, encourage students to use a familiar book they have read in class or one found in their Readers Workshop book bags. Distribute a sheet of construction paper along with a flower cut out. Students can use the flower cut out for their writing or may use it as a model to create their own picture on the paper provided. Have the students write the main character's name in the middle of the flower. Then, have them write character trait words to describe the character on the petals. Next, draw an arrow next to each petal and provide supporting evidence from the story.

Lesson Segment 2: Use Key Details to Describe the Setting in a Story

• Activity 1: Setting Mobile

Explain to students that the setting of a story involves where and when the story takes place. Ask students to think about places in their house. Ask them to name the different parts of their homes or apartments. Tell them that they just described various settings where many stories can take place.

Next, divide students into groups of three and appoint a facilitator. Distribute an 8×10 sheet of construction paper with four holes punched at the bottom, four strings of yarn, and four index cards (with holes punched at the top) to each team. As a group, instruct students to refer to movies and books they've read. On the construction paper, have them write the word, *SETTINGS*, with a marker in the middle. Then, on each index card, have students write and illustrate possible places where a story can take place. Attach the index cards to the "SETTINGS" paper to create a mobile. Allow students time to share their mobiles before displaying them around the room.

• Activity 2: Setting It Together

Read a story to the class with multiple settings, such as *Charlotte's Web*. Divide students into five different groups and assign a facilitator. Distribute chart paper and markers to each group. Assign each group a specific setting from the story. Instruct the students to draw detailed pictures of their group's setting.

Next, display the posters in the front of the room. Distribute five sticky notes with the numbers 1-5 written on them to each group. Play upbeat music, such as *The Electric Slide* by Marcia Griffiths. When the music plays, instruct students to label the settings in the order they appeared in the story. Afterward, discuss selections and place the posters in the correct order to remain on display.

Lesson Segment 3: Use Key Details to Describe Major Events in a Story

• Activity 1: Beginning, Middle, and End

Place students in four cooperative groups of four to six. Appoint a *facilitator* for each group. Provide the 5W's, a sheet of chart paper, markers, and multiple copies of a selected piece of literature, such as *A Chair for My Mother* by Vera Williams. Have students work together to complete the following tasks:

- Group 1—Draw a picture that creates a retelling of the beginning of the story. The facilitator will ensure that each student gets a chance to draw or contribute to the poster.
- Group 2—Draw a picture that creates a retelling of the middle of the story. The facilitator will ensure that each student gets a chance to draw or contribute to the poster.
- Group 3—Draw a picture that creates a retelling of the end of the story. The facilitator will ensure that each student gets a chance to draw or contribute to the poster.
- Group 4—Draw a picture that creates an additional ending to the story. What do the students think happened after the end of the story? The facilitator will ensure that each student gets a chance to draw or contribute to the poster.

- **Activity 2: Role Play It**

After reading a story to the class, divide students into three groups. In each group, assign one student to act out the events that happened in the beginning of the story, another to role-play events from the middle, and another, the end. Assign the remaining students the role of creating an illustration for the background or setting. Provide time for students to practice and present to the rest of the class.

Lesson Segment 4: Use Key Details to Describe Characters, Setting, and Major Events in a Story

- **Activity 1: Picture It**

Students will create their own original story based on pictures from the internet or magazines. Distribute pictures from magazines or appropriate pictures from the internet along with a sheet of construction paper to the students. Have students create a title for their picture based on what they can evaluate from the illustration. Next, have the students assign a name to their main character. Based on the picture, the students assign a setting and two events and details about their picture. When they have finished, allow students time to present their original stories to the class.

Brain-Compatible Strategies: *Which will you use to deliver content?*

__X__	Brainstorming/Discussion	__X__	Music/Rhythm/Rhyme/Rap
__X__	Drawing/Artwork	_____	Project/Problem-Based Learning
_____	Field Trips	__X__	Reciprocal Teaching/Cooperative Learning
_____	Games		
_____	Graphic Organizers/Semantic Maps/Word Webs	__X__	Role Plays/Drama/Pantomimes/Charades
_____	Humor	__X__	Storytelling
__X__	Manipulatives/Experiments/Labs/Models	_____	Technology
		_____	Visualization/Guided Imagery
_____	Metaphors/Analogies/Similes	__X__	Visuals
_____	Mnemonic Devices	_____	Work Study/Apprenticeships
__X__	Movement	__X__	Writing/Journals

LANGUAGE ARTS GRADES K–2 LESSON 7

Questioning

Lesson Objective(s): *What do you want students to know and be able to do?*

Ask and answer *Who, What, Where, When, Why,* and *How* questions to demonstrate understanding of important details in a text.

Assessment (Traditional/Authentic): *How will you know students have mastered essential learning?*

Select a short biography of a historical figure to read to the students. Then ask them *Who, What, Where, When, Why*, and *How* questions related to the article or text. Have the students complete questions about the biography using a body silhouette template.

Ways to Gain/Maintain Attention (Primacy): *How will you gain and maintain students' attention? Consider* <u>need</u>, <u>novelty</u>, *meaning, or emotion)*

Have the students view the video clip below about answering questions. After reading the text, pass the plastic cow around the circle to represent Ferdinand in the story. Next, read *The Story of Ferdinand* and have students use a plastic cow (to represent Ferdinand) to answer questions about the text.

Content Chunks: *How will you divide and teach the content to engage students' brains?*

Lesson Segment 1: Ask and Answer *Who, What, Where, When, Why,* **and** *How* **Questions**

- **Activity 1: How Do I Answer?**

Place the words *Who, What, Where, When, Why*, and *How* on the ActivBoard. Tell students that they will learn how to answer these types of questions. Play the "Answering Questions" video clip using the following link: https://www.youtube.com/watch?v=C2fWZHaNugc. After viewing the video, have students identify a 12:00 appointment. Play the music from the game show, *Jeopardy!* When the music begins, have students meet with a clock appointment and discuss what they have learned about answering the 5Ws. Discuss and share responses as a class.

- **Activity 2: Ferdinand Who?**

Review the words *Who, What, Where, When, Why*, and *How* on the Smartboard. Select a book of interest from the book list such as *The Story of Ferdinand* by Munro Leaf. Then ask students to sit in a circle. Give a child a plastic cow or bull. This animal will be named after "Ferdinand" as a manipulative from the story. Ask him or her one of the sample questions below. As they answer, have the student pass Ferdinand to the next classmate. After several students have answered the questions, distribute construction paper, crayons, and pipe cleaners to the students. Have them draw a picture of their favorite part of the story and explain why they like that part best (they can use pipe cleaners to enhance their illustrations). Have students dictate as you write and allow more advanced students to begin formulating their own sentences. When students are done, display their writing around the room.

Sample questions—*"Who is the main character in the story? What did Ferdinand want to do more than anything? How did the story end?"*

• Activity 3: Apple Tree Details

Read an article or nonfiction text to the students. Then, place students in cooperative groups of four to six. Appoint a facilitator for each group. Provide a tree sketched on brown 11x16 construction paper. Then, give each student in the group a cutout of an apple with one of the 5W's written on each apple. Have students answer their question on the back of the apple. Once the students are finished, have them share their question and answer with the group. Finally, allow the facilitator to glue the stem of each apple to the group's tree. Once the groups are done, the facilitator will share the group's tree with the rest of the class.

• Activity 4: Body Details

Read an article or nonfiction text to the students. Older and more advanced students may choose their own biography based on their individual Lexile level. Then, provide pairs of students with an outline of a body.

In the head, instruct students to write the name of the text along with their name. In the left arm, write two sentences about who they are. In the right arm, write two sentences about what they accomplished. In the middle of the body, include the date when they were born, the year they did something important, and the year they died. In the left leg, write why they invented an item or did something important. In the right leg, draw a picture of the person. Add decorative details as needed.

Brain-Compatible Strategies: *Which will you use to deliver content?*

__X__	Brainstorming/Discussion	_____	Music/Rhythm/Rhyme/Rap
__X__	Drawing/Artwork	_____	Project/Problem-Based Learning
_____	Field Trips	__X__	Reciprocal Teaching/Cooperative Learning
_____	Games		
__X__	Graphic Organizers/Semantic Maps/Word Webs	_____	Role Plays/Drama/Pantomimes/Charades
_____	Humor	__X__	Storytelling
__X__	Manipulatives/Experiments/Labs/Models	__X__	Technology
		_____	Visualization/Guided Imagery
_____	Metaphors/Analogies/Similes	__X__	Visuals
_____	Mnemonic Devices	_____	Work Study/Apprenticeships
__X__	Movement	__X__	Writing/Journals

LANGUAGE ARTS GRADES K–2 LESSON 8

Opinion With Facts

Lesson Objective(s): *What do you want students to know and be able to do?*

Write opinion pieces in which a topic is introduced, an opinion stated with reasons provided for supporting that opinion, and a conclusion is conveyed.

Assessment (Traditional/Authentic): *How will you know students have mastered essential learning?*

Engage students in writing a piece that states an opinion and uses examples to show why that opinion is held.

Ways to Gain/Maintain Attention (Primacy): *How will you gain and maintain students' attention? Consider need, novelty, meaning, or emotion.*

Show students a bowl of fresh carrots cut into bite-sized pieces. Tell the students, "Carrots are nutritious and they are the best vegetable ever." Next, distribute carrots for students to eat (obtain parents' permission ahead of time). Observe the students' faces and ask them what they think. Say, "Do you agree with me? Is there a problem?" Guide students to recognize that what you just said may not be a fact. Instruct students that when they hear upbeat music and if they like the carrots, stand on the right side of the room, if they don't, stand on the left side.

Content Chunks: *How will you divide and teach the content to engage students' brains?*

Lesson Segment 1: Recognize Opinion Statements

- **Activity 1: Commercials**

Have students view an age-appropriate commercial. Tell them that the people making the commercials want you to buy that product so they make it sound as appealing as possible. They tend to make some opinions sound like facts. Distribute *F* and *O* sets of letters attached to craft sticks to each student. Read facts and opinions about the commercial. When the students hear a fact, they hold up the *F* stick, when they hear an opinion, they hold up the *O*.

- **Activity 2: Disney Is the Best**

Show students commercials, brochures, posters, and books about Disney World. Then place students in heterogeneous groups of four. Give each group a sheet of poster board and markers. Write the following statements on the board, *Disney World is the best place to visit, Disney World has many attractions for families to see.* Assign two groups to work on statement one and two groups to work on statement two. Groups assigned to the first statement will design a poster in favor of this point of view and two supporting reasons for their opinion. Groups assigned to statement two will design a poster displaying at least four attractions Disney has to offer. Afterward, have groups share their posters with the class. Guide students to see that although the posters from both assignments are similar, the first statement was based on opinions and the second was based on facts.

Ahead of time, design a T-chart with the word *Facts* on the left and *Opinions* on the right. Elicit responses from students that distinguish the facts and opinions found in their Disney World posters. Write their responses on the appropriate side of the T-chart. Discuss.

Lesson Segment 2: Write an Opinion Piece With Reasons and Conclusion

• Activity 1: *Hey Little Ant*

Read the book *Hey Little Ant* by Phillip and Hannah Hoose to the students twice. The first time, ask students to listen to the book for enjoyment. During the second reading, ask students to listen for the boy's opinion and the ant's opinion along with the arguments each character presents. In addition, ask them to listen closely to the conclusion at the end.

Next, assign students to work in pairs. Appoint one student to write the ant's opinion about being stepped on and two reasons supporting his opinion, and the other students will write the boy's opinion and two reasons supporting his point of view. Have both sides write a conclusion. Afterward, allow students to take turns role-playing their statements.

• Activity 2: What's My Opinion?

On an anchor chart, create a graphic organizer similar to the one on page 52 from the book *Reading and Language Arts Worksheets Don't Grow Dendrites* (2nd Edition) by Marcia Tate. Model by writing the following opinion statement on the chart *Our Class Should Have a Goldfish as a Pet* in the middle circle. Modify the organizer by drawing only one square on each side of the circle. Elicit two supporting statements for the squares (examples—fish are easy to take care of; they are inexpensive; they will teach us responsibility). Next to each square, draw an arrow and write supporting details for each statement. For the conclusion, instruct students to restate their opinion with a concluding statement. Transfer the sentences from the organizer to written format on another sheet of chart paper for students to view as a model.

Afterward, have students work in pairs to create an opinion piece using the model above. Sample arguments may include:

The best color is blue.

PE is the best class at school.

Dogs are the best animals.

Pizza is the best dinner to eat on a Friday night.

The worst habit is biting your nails.

Brain-Compatible Strategies: *Which will you use to deliver content?*

__X__	Brainstorming/Discussion	_____	Music/Rhythm/Rhyme/Rap
__X__	Drawing/Artwork	_____	Project/Problem-Based Learning
_____	Field Trips	__X__	Reciprocal Teaching/Cooperative Learning
_____	Games		
__X__	Graphic Organizers/Semantic Maps/Word Webs	__X__	Role Plays/Drama/Pantomimes/Charades
_____	Humor	__X__	Storytelling
__X__	Manipulatives/Experiments/Labs/Models	_____	Technology
		_____	Visualization/Guided Imagery
_____	Metaphors/Analogies/Similes	__X__	Visuals
_____	Mnemonic Devices	_____	Work Study/Apprenticeships
__X__	Movement	__X__	Writing/Journals

LANGUAGE ARTS GRADES K–2 LESSON 9

Compare and Contrast

Lesson Objective(s): *What do you want students to know and be able to do?*

Compare and contrast two or more versions of the same story by different authors or from different cultures.

Assessment (Traditional/Authentic): *How will you know students have mastered essential learning?*

Using a graphic organizer, the students will be able to evaluate similarities and differences between two stories from different cultures.

Ways to Gain/Maintain Attention (Primacy): *How will you gain and maintain students' attention? Consider need, novelty, meaning, or emotion.*

Show off your rhythmic skills by hula hooping for your students. While you hula hoop for a minute, ask the students to observe characteristics of your skills by paying attention to how long the hoop stayed around your waist, how many times it dropped to the ground and the motions you used with your hips. Afterward, invite another teacher or student to hula hoop. Next, ask students to look for similarities and differences between you and your opponent. Discuss the results.

Content Chunks: *How will you divide and teach the content to engage students' brains?*

Lesson Segment 1: Compare and Contrast Two Characters in a Text

- **Activity 1: Hula Hoop It**

Distribute two hula hoops and 15 index cards to pairs of students. Each student in the pair will have their own hula hoop. Student A will observe Student B hula hooping for one minute. During this time, have Student A observe how long Student B was able to hoop along with how many times the hoop dropped to the floor and the motion they used. After one minute, the students will switch places and Student B will observe Student A.

Once they are done, have the students lay their hula hoops on the floor to resemble a Venn diagram. Label the top of each hoop with their name. Then, have students write three to five things they observed about the way they each hula hooped that are different and at least three things they shared in common. Place the differences in each other's respective circles and the commonalities in the middle.

- **Activity 2: Compare It**

Read the story *Little Red Riding Hood* to the students. Afterward, assign students to work in pairs. Have the students write the title of the story at the top of the paper. Next, instruct students to draw a Venn diagram using two different colors for each circle. Then, label the left side *Little Red Riding Hood* and the right side *The Wolf*. Guide students to include details about each character under their respective circles and similarities in the middle. After completing the diagram, allow students to draw pictures on each side to match the statements written in the circles. Share with the class.

Lesson Segment 2: Compare and Contrast Two or More Similar Stories

• Activity 1: What's The Difference?

Tell students that they will be building on the skill comparing and contrasting. Tell them that today they will be comparing and contrasting the traditional story of *Little Red Riding Hood* with the Chinese version, *Lon Po Po*, by Ed Young. First, review the story *Little Red Riding Hood* with the class. Refer to previous anchor charts. Then, read *Lon Po Po* to the students. Ask the students to listen to the story for enjoyment during the first reading. Before the second reading, ask students to listen for the differences between the two literary pieces.

Assign students to work in pairs. Next, distribute a sheet of 11×14 construction paper, glue, and two copies of a basket picture, which will serve as a graphic organizer. Have them write the title and author at the top of each of the baskets. Then, instruct students to write elements from each story inside the baskets. When they are finished, cut out the baskets and glue them to the far sides of the construction paper while leaving room in the middle. Write similarities from both stories in the central section between the baskets. Draw a picture of a character on both sides to match each story. Then, have pairs present one set of comparison/contrast from their organizers. Afterward, have students tell which story is their favorite and explain why.

Brain-Compatible Strategies: *Which will you use to deliver content?*

__X__	Brainstorming/Discussion	_____	Music/Rhythm/Rhyme/Rap
__X__	Drawing/Artwork	_____	Project/Problem-Based Learning
_____	Field Trips	__X__	Reciprocal Teaching/Cooperative Learning
_____	Games		
__X__	Graphic Organizers/Semantic Maps/Word Webs	_____	Role Plays/Drama/Pantomimes/Charades
_____	Humor	__X__	Storytelling
_____	Manipulatives/Experiments/Labs/Models	_____	Technology
		_____	Visualization/Guided Imagery
__X__	Metaphors/Analogies/Similes	__X__	Visuals
_____	Mnemonic Devices	_____	Work Study/Apprenticeships
__X__	Movement	__X__	Writing/Journals

LANGUAGE ARTS GRADES 3–5 LESSON 1

Decoding Multisyllabic Words

Lesson Objective(s): *What do you want students to know and be able to do?*

Decode multisyllabic words using common affixes and roots and determine how these change a word's meaning.

Assessment (Traditional/Authentic): *How will you know students have mastered essential learning?*

Students will create new words using commonly used affixes and prefixes by adding them to a variety of root words. In addition, the students will create a flipbook to increase vocabulary understanding by applying prefix and suffix knowledge.

Ways to Gain/Maintain Attention (Primacy): *How will you gain and maintain students' attention? Consider need, novelty, _meaning_, or emotion.*

Bring in an actual live plant as a metaphor and visual to connect students to the idea of root words and suffixes. The students will see the roots of the plant (root word) and the leaves or flowers (suffix or prefix) and how prefixes and suffixes add meaning to a word.

Content Chunks: *How will you divide and teach the content to engage students' brains?*

Lesson Segment 1: Comprehend the Purpose of Prefixes

- **Activity 1: Identifying Roots and Affixes Through Metaphor**

First, show a picture of a plant and discuss the importance of the root and the leaves. The base word is like the root (it supports the word) and the leaves are like the prefix (adds beauty to the plant just like the prefixes add meaning to the root word). Next, write the word "refill" on the board. Ask them to analyze the word and identify the root and prefix. Tell students that "fill" is the simplest form and "re" changes the meaning.

Next, read the touchtone text *Pre- and Re-, Mis- and Dis-, What Is a Prefix* by Brian Cleary aloud to the students. As you read the text, have students listen to the story for enjoyment. Then, read the book a second time. Ask students to listen and specifically make note of the prefixes applied in context during the story. These prefixes are highlighted in color for students as a visual. As a second option, instead of reading the book, visit Brainpop.com and use the video entitled *Prefixes and Suffixes*. After the video, students can divide into two teams and complete the quiz as a game.

- **Activity 2: Recognizing Prefixes**

Close the book and ask students to list as many prefixes as they can possibly remember from the story. Give students two minutes to complete this task. After two minutes, have students share their lists with one another. Have students identify an energizing partner or appointment from another table. Play the instrumental version of Pharrell Williams' song, *Happy*. When the song begins, have students travel to their partner and take turns sharing their prefixes.

Lesson Segment 2: Comprehend the Purpose of Suffixes

• Activity 1: Prefix/Suffix Card Game

Read the touchtone text *Full- and Less-, Er- and Ness-, What Is a Suffix* by Brian Cleary aloud to the students. Have students play the Prefix/Suffix Card Game. To play, the teacher will distribute the "Commonly Used Prefixes/Suffixes" sheet along with a set of index cards to groups of four students (the teacher will already have these words prewritten on each colored card).

Red Index Cards		White Index Cards	Blue Index Cards	
Prefix	*Meaning*	**Base Words**	**Suffix**	*Meaning*
re-	again	able	**-ful**	full of
dis-	not, opposite of	learn	**-less**	without
un-	not	happy	**-ly**	characteristic of
pre-	before	like	**-y**	like
im-	not, opposite of	agree		
non-	not	kind		
mis-	wrong, bad	read		
		paint		
		lead		

• Activity 2: Building New Words

Next, have students take turns building new words using either a red and white index card or a white and blue index card. When students create the new word, they will write the new word on a sheet of construction paper.

Lesson Segment 3: Integrate Both Prefixes and Suffixes

• Activity 1: Creating a Flipbook

Have students create a flipbook. Using the words from their construction paper, students will select four words from one prefix or suffix family (example—four words beginning with dis- or four words ending with –ly). Ahead of time, fold a sheet of 11×14 copy paper in half. Use scissors to create four flaps. On the front of each flap, students will write, define, and illustrate each word. Under each flap, students will write the base word along with its definition and illustration. Students can share these books with each other and use them as a resource during the Writers Workshop block.

Brain-Compatible Strategies: *Which will you use to deliver content?*

_____	Brainstorming/Discussion	__X__	Music/Rhythm/Rhyme/Rap
__X__	Drawing/Artwork	_____	Project/Problem-Based Learning
_____	Field Trips	__X__	Reciprocal Teaching/Cooperative Learning
__X__	Games		
_____	Graphic Organizers/Semantic Maps/Word Webs	_____	Role Plays/Drama/Pantomimes/Charades
_____	Humor	__X__	Storytelling
_____	Manipulatives/Experiments/Labs/Models	__X__	Technology
		_____	Visualization/Guided Imagery
__X__	Metaphors/Analogies/Similes	__X__	Visuals
_____	Mnemonic Devices	_____	Work Study/Apprenticeships
__X__	Movement	__X__	Writing/Journals

LANGUAGE ARTS GRADES 3–5 LESSON 2

Writing

Lesson Objective(s): *What do you want students to know and be able to do?*

Write explanatory informational texts that examine a topic and convey ideas and details clearly.

Assessment (Traditional/Authentic): *How will you know students have mastered essential learning?*

Students will create an informational brochure detailing why people should move to a specific city or town.

Ways to Gain/Maintain Attention (Primacy): *How will you gain and maintain students' attention? Consider need, novelty, _meaning_, or emotion.*

Bring in a plethora of brochures from Six Flags, other amusement parks, doctor's offices, and hotels for students to use as visuals. You may visit your local Chamber of Commerce and travel agencies for additional copies.

Content Chunks: *How will you divide and teach the content to engage students' brains?*

Lesson Segment 1: Distinguish Elements and Formula for Informational Writing

- **Activity 1: *INFO* Anchor Chart**

Ahead of time, develop an anchor chart with the formula for informational texts (see below).

Discuss the importance of the *INFO* outlined on the chart. Have students write the formula in their Writers Workshop Notebook or another note-taking guide.

Informational Writing

I Introduction

N Name 3 facts

F Facts require supporting details

O Offer a conclusion

- **Activity 2: Identifying Informational Text**

Distribute several brochures to student groups of four or less, a stack of sticky notes, and four colored pencils or markers (red, purple, green, pink). Allow students opportunities for flexible seating options—work in the corner, in the hallway, etc. Have students select four brochures from which to work. As they read through each, have students write the introduction (blue marker), three facts (purple marker), one supporting detail for each fact (green marker) and a conclusion (pink marker) on sticky notes. When the groups are finished, have them place the sticky notes on the brochure. Repeat the directions for the remaining brochures.

- **Activity 3: Viewing Student Work**

When the students have completed the brochures in their groups, have them rotate through each group to view one another's work. Play Buster Poindexter's song, *Hot, Hot, Hot*, as a prompt for the student to travel to each group. Give students about two minutes at each table.

Lesson Segment 2: Create a Brochure Incorporating Informational Writing

- **Activity 1: Applying the *INFO* Formula**

Have students view a short informational video from YouTube about a particular city of interest. The video clip of Atlanta, Georgia, is included as an example (Atlanta-CityvideoGuide-YouTube). Next, have students select a city of interest. They can check out books from the Media Center, visit Britannica.com, collect brochures from travel agencies, and view informational videos from YouTube .com. Have them use the Informational Writing Formula (pictured) to summarize their findings.

- **Activity 2: Creating an Original Brochure**

Provide a sheet of 8×10 construction paper folded into thirds. Once students have selected a city of interest, have them use the information from the graphic organizer to create a brochure. Provide colored markers and pencils for students to create vivid illustrations. The brochure should be created according to the following guidelines:

Outer Flap—Title, Illustration, and Student's Name

Inner Left Flap—Introduction to the brochure

Middle—Fact, three supporting details, illustration

Right—Fact, three supporting details, illustration

Back Right—Fact, supporting details, illustration

Back Middle—References

Back Right—Illustration of the outline of the city

Brain-Compatible Strategies: *Which will you use to deliver content?*

__X__	Brainstorming/Discussion	__X__	Music/Rhythm/Rhyme/Rap
__X__	Drawing/Artwork	__X__	Project/Problem-Based Learning
_____	Field Trips	__X__	Reciprocal Teaching/Cooperative Learning
_____	Games		
__X__	Graphic Organizers/Semantic Maps/Word Webs	_____	Role Plays/Drama/Pantomimes/Charades
_____	Humor	_____	Storytelling
_____	Manipulatives/Experiments/Labs/Models	__X__	Technology
		_____	Visualization/Guided Imagery
_____	Metaphors/Analogies/Similes	__X__	Visuals
__X__	Mnemonic Devices	_____	Work Study/Apprenticeships
__X__	Movement	__X__	Writing/Journals

LANGUAGE ARTS GRADES 3–5 LESSON 3

Plot Structure

Lesson Objective(s): *What do you want students to know and be able to do?*

Read grade-level texts with purpose and understanding to support comprehension (plot).

Assessment (Traditional/Authentic): *How will you know students have mastered essential learning?*

Students will complete a *Plot House* individually using a piece of literature.

Ways to Gain/Maintain Attention (Primacy): *How will you gain and maintain students' attention? Consider need, novelty, meaning, or emotion.*

Have students work with a partner to complete *Plot Mountains* on large sheets of chart paper paired with a literary text. Have them then compare the plot structure of a text to the parts of a house and evaluate the elements of the plot to create a *Plot House*.

Content Chunks: *How will you divide and teach the content to engage students' brains?*

Lesson Segment 1: Recognize Elements of Plot

- **Activity 1: Drawing a *Plot Mountain***

On a sheet of chart paper, draw a *Plot Mountain*. Label the mountain with parts of the plot: bottom left (**conflict**), left outside middle (**rising action**), top (**climax**), bottom right (**outcome**). Discuss each component and its importance to the overall plot of a text.

- **Activity 2: Singing the "Plot Song"**

Display the words from the "Plot Song" below and have students sing and move to the lyrics.

- **Activity 3: *Head First***

Read the first four pages from the story *Head First* by Mike Dion. Complete the conflict and the rising action sections of the mountain during the mini-lesson.

- **Activity 4: *Plot Mountain* Continued**

Distribute sheets of chart paper to pairs of students along with copies of the text. If copies of the text aren't available, the teacher can record himself or herself reading the story ahead of time. Then, students can watch the teacher read the remainder of the story on iPads with their partner. Students will complete the remainder of the plot mountain from the first activity.

- **Activity 5: Plot Structure**

Distribute the *Plot House* graphic organizer on construction paper from the resource *Engage the Brain: Graphic Organizers and Other Visual Strategies, Grade 5*, page 87. Allow students to select a piece of literature with a plot structure (see the Literary Texts list found on pages 98–103). Students can provide illustrations for each area in the house.

Brain-Compatible Strategies: *Which will you use to deliver content?*

__X__	Brainstorming/Discussion	__X__	Music/Rhythm/Rhyme/Rap
__X__	Drawing/Artwork	_____	Project/Problem-Based Learning
_____	Field Trips	__X__	Reciprocal Teaching/Cooperative Learning
_____	Games		
__X__	Graphic Organizers/Semantic Maps/Word Webs	_____	Role Plays/Drama/Pantomimes/Charades
_____	Humor	__X__	Storytelling
_____	Manipulatives/Experiments/Labs/Models	__X__	Technology
		_____	Visualization/Guided Imagery
__X__	Metaphors/Analogies/Similes	__X__	Visuals
_____	Mnemonic Devices	_____	Work Study/Apprenticeships
_____	Movement	__X__	Writing/Journals

Plot Song

By: Simone Philp Willingham

To the tune of *Crank That*

The conflict is the beginning
Of the story
It identifies the problem
Yeah there's a problem

Rising action
How they solve it
Rising action
How they solve it
Rising action
Take the steps
How to solve the character's problem

The climax shows suspense
In the story
It's so exciting
That it has us biting our nails

Then go down
The solution
Then go down
Solve the problem
Then go down
To the outcome
Then go down
How it all turns out!

LANGUAGE ARTS GRADES 3–5 LESSON 4

Descriptive Details

Lesson Objective(s): *What do you want students to know and be able to do?*

Write narratives to develop real or imaginary events or experiences using appropriate techniques, descriptive details, and a clear sequence of events.

Assessment (Traditional/Authentic): *How will you know students have mastered essential learning?*

Students will use descriptive details to write their own personal narratives.

Ways to Gain/Maintain Attention (Primacy): *How will you gain and maintain students' attention? Consider need, novelty, meaning, or emotion.*

Take individual pictures of the students role-playing an event that has happened to them either at home, during a vacation, or during school. Students will use these pictures to write a personal narrative about the picture.

Content Chunks: *How will you divide and teach the content to engage students' brains?*

Lesson Segment 1: Recognize Elements of a Personal Narrative

- **Activity 1: Personal Narrative Chart**

Write the *Personal Narrative* chart below and post it on the wall. Explain to students that writers often write about their own personal experiences. Tell students that today they will write a personal narrative. Review the elements of the personal narrative from the chart below. Have students take notes in their writing journals.

- **Activity 2: Personal Pictures**

Take pictures of students engaged in different actions. Distribute printed pictures to individual students. Have students brainstorm and discuss possible events that their pictures evokes. Using the graphic organizer on page 57 from *Reading and Language Arts Worksheets Don't Grow Dendrites* (2nd Edition), have them begin brainstorming ideas about their pictures.

Lesson Segment 2: Identify Personal Narratives in Literature

- **Activity 1: Author Engagement**

Read the first two pages from the story *Love You Forever* by Robert Munsch or *When I Was Young in the Mountains* by Cynthia Rylant to the students. Discuss how the author engaged the reader during the introduction. Then, have students use ideas from the literary text to add ideas to their graphic organizers. Afterward, have them share their introductions with the class for feedback.

- **Activity 2: Details and Descriptive Words**

Finish reading one of the texts from Activity 1. Have students listen for enjoyment for the first time. The second time, ask them to listen for details and descriptive words. After listening, have the students take notes in their journals and add descriptive words to their notes. Use the graphic organizer to help complete their drafts and a revision checklist to help guide their writing. Next, use the tools from WritingA-Z.com to complete their pieces.

- **Activity 3: Movie Stars**

When students have completed their writing, record them reading their finished pieces using an iPad or another device. Show the movie to other classes or to parents on Curriculum Nights, etc. Students can refer to their live movies throughout the year as they develop into prolific writers.

Brain-Compatible Strategies: *Which will you use to deliver content?*

X	Brainstorming/Discussion	____	Music/Rhythm/Rhyme/Rap
____	Drawing/Artwork	____	Project/Problem-Based Learning
____	Field Trips	____	Reciprocal Teaching/Cooperative Learning
____	Games		
X	Graphic Organizers/Semantic Maps/Word Webs	**X**	Role Plays/Drama/Pantomimes/Charades
____	Humor	**X**	Storytelling
____	Manipulatives/Experiments/Labs/Models	**X**	Technology
		____	Visualization/Guided Imagery
____	Metaphors/Analogies/Similes	**X**	Visuals
____	Mnemonic Devices	____	Work Study/Apprenticeships
X	Movement	**X**	Writing/Journals

Personal Narrative

Introduction:

Attention grabber: statement, question, dialogue

Identify: Who? Who did what, where, when?

Opinion: State the importance of the event or give a clue about it.

| **Beginning** (of event) | **Middle** (of event) | **Beginning** (of event) |

supporting detail | supporting detail | supporting detail
supporting detail | supporting detail | supporting detail
supporting detail | supporting detail | supporting detail

Conclusion:

– restate opinion in your own words (explain importance)

– personal comment on event

LANGUAGE ARTS GRADES 3–5 LESSON 5

Opinion/Point of View

Lesson Objective(s): *What do you want students to know and be able to do?*

Write opinion pieces on topics supporting a point of view with reasons and information.

Assessment (Traditional/Authentic): *How will you know students have mastered essential learning?*

Students will participate in a group project to create commercials with reasons to support their opinion statements.

Ways to Gain/Maintain Attention (Primacy): *How will you gain and maintain students' attention? Consider need, novelty, meaning, or emotion.*

Define the word "opinion" as a view or judgment formed about something, not necessarily based on fact. Read the first five pages from the text *I Wanna Iguana* by Karen Kaufman. Ask students the following: *Based on the first few pages, do you think Alex will convince his mom to allow him to get an iguana?* Discuss.

Content Chunks: *How will you divide and teach the content to engage students' brains?*

Lesson Segment 1: Recognize Opinions and Facts in Literature

- **Activity 1: Fact/Opinion Strips**

In advance, write facts and opinions from *I Wanna Iguana* on sentence strips. Read the remainder of the story to the students. Post a *Facts From the Text* and an *Opinions From the Text* chart on two opposite walls in the room. Divide students into teams. Distribute sentence strips to the teams. Play upbeat music. Instruct teams to place the strips on the chart that represents either a fact or an opinion.

Lesson Segment 2: Recognize Opinions and Reasons in Commercials

- **Activity 1: Opinions and Reasons**

Remind students that in the story *I Wanna Iguana*, Alex was able to give his opinion with supporting reasons in detail. Provide students with the graphic organizer from *Reading & Language Arts Worksheets Don't Grow Dendrites*, page 57, to complete as a whole class. Give the students the topic, *All Classes Should Have Recess for 20 Minutes Every Day*.

   Have students form their opinions on the topic. In groups of four, have students brainstorm at least four ideas supporting their reasons for recess or not. Have them share with the class.

- **Activity 2: Point of View and Reasons**

Place students in heterogeneous groups of four. Give each group one copy of the graphic organizer along with a topic. Samples are provided below or use a topic that you feel is relevant for your class. Have each group form their point of view and four supporting reasons for their opinion.

- **Activity 3: Commercial Creation**

Remind students that advertisers use commercials to persuade their viewers to purchase a particular product or convince them to think about a particular position. Using the opinion and four supporting reasons they developed in the previous activity, assign each student in the group with a role to create a commercial. They can create props and illustrations to enhance their presentations. Using iPads, students will role-play and record their commercials to convince their audience of their position.

Sample Topics

Dogs Make Better Pets Than Cats

Spinach Is the Best Vegetable

Six Flags Is the Best Amusement Park

Football Is the Most Fun Sport to Play

Brain-Compatible Strategies: *Which will you use to deliver content?*

X	Brainstorming/Discussion	**X**	Music/Rhythm/Rhyme/Rap
X	Drawing/Artwork		Project/Problem-Based Learning
	Field Trips	**X**	Reciprocal Teaching/Cooperative Learning
	Games		
X	Graphic Organizers/Semantic Maps/Word Webs	**X**	Role Plays/Drama/Pantomimes/Charades
	Humor	**X**	Storytelling
X	Manipulatives/Experiments/Labs/Models	**X**	Technology
			Visualization/Guided Imagery
	Metaphors/Analogies/Similes	**X**	Visuals
	Mnemonic Devices		Work Study/Apprenticeships
X	Movement	**X**	Writing/Journals

LANGUAGE ARTS GRADES 3–5 LESSON 6

Character Traits

Lesson Objective(s): *What do you want students to know and be able to do?*

Provide an in-depth description of a character while drawing on specific details in a text.

Assessment (Traditional/Authentic): *How will you know students have mastered essential learning?*

Students will create a character trait suitcase based on the events from a literary text.

Ways to Gain/Maintain Attention (Primacy): *How will you gain and maintain students' attention? Consider need, novelty, meaning, or emotion.*

Create a life-size silhouette of a body that represents the class. Using colored pencils, have students take turns writing a character trait word inside the body that best describes them. Instruct students to write their name next to their word. Define the word "character" and discuss what supporting evidence should look like.

Content Chunks: *How will you divide and teach the content to engage students' brains?*

Lesson Segment 1: Recognize Traits of a Character in Literature

- **Activity 1: Character Traits in Literature**

Read the story *Alexander and the Terrible, Horrible, No Good, Very Bad Day* to the class. The first time, have the students listen for enjoyment. The second time, read the first seven pages and ask students to listen for the character trait words to describe Alexander. On chart paper, write the character trait word on the left side. Then, ask students to think of two examples or evidence for each trait from the text. Write the examples on the right. The students should distinguish at least two traits from the text.

- **Activity 2: Character Portrait**

Distribute copies of the story *Alexander and the Terrible, Horrible, No Good, Very Bad Day* to pairs of students to create a *Character Portrait*. In the middle of the construction paper, draw a figure to represent Alexander. Label three parts of the portrait with an additional character trait word that describes him. Under each word, write two examples or evidence to support each trait.

- **Activity 3: Gallery Walk**

Once pairs have completed the character sketch, display their masterpieces on the walls around the room. Play upbeat music. Each time you play the music, have pairs rotate to each picture to see what their classmates created. Discuss differences in traits and the types of evidence used from the text.

- **Activity 4: Character Traits in Literary Texts**

Assign pairs of students a text that emphasizes a character and several traits. You may select a text from the *Literary Texts That Teach Story Elements* list. Students will take turns reading. Next, have students use the graphic organizer to distinguish at least four character traits from the story along with supporting evidence from the text.

- **Activity 5: Character Suitcase**

Use the graphic organizer to create a *Character Suitcase.* Distribute file folders, brown construction paper, and colored pencils to pairs of students. Have each pair draw a picture of a book character on the outside of the file folder. Using the colored pencils, have them write four words around the character. Inside, have them write each character trait word on the left side and the supporting evidence on the right. Finally, have students use the brown construction paper to create a handle to complete their suitcases.

As an extension, based on the character's personality, students can draw and cut out at least two items that the character would possibly take with them on a vacation. Place the items in their suitcase. Set time aside for students to share their suitcases and why they selected the items placed in the suitcases.

Brain-Compatible Strategies: *Which will you use to deliver content?*

X	Brainstorming/Discussion	**X**	Music/Rhythm/Rhyme/Rap
X	Drawing/Artwork	____	Project/Problem-Based Learning
____	Field Trips	**X**	Reciprocal Teaching/Cooperative Learning
____	Games		
X	Graphic Organizers/Semantic Maps/Word Webs	____	Role Plays/Drama/Pantomimes/Charades
____	Humor	**X**	Storytelling
X	Manipulatives/Experiments/Labs/Models	____	Technology
		____	Visualization/Guided Imagery
____	Metaphors/Analogies/Similes	**X**	Visuals
____	Mnemonic Devices	____	Work Study/Apprenticeships
X	Movement	**X**	Writing/Journals

Character Traits

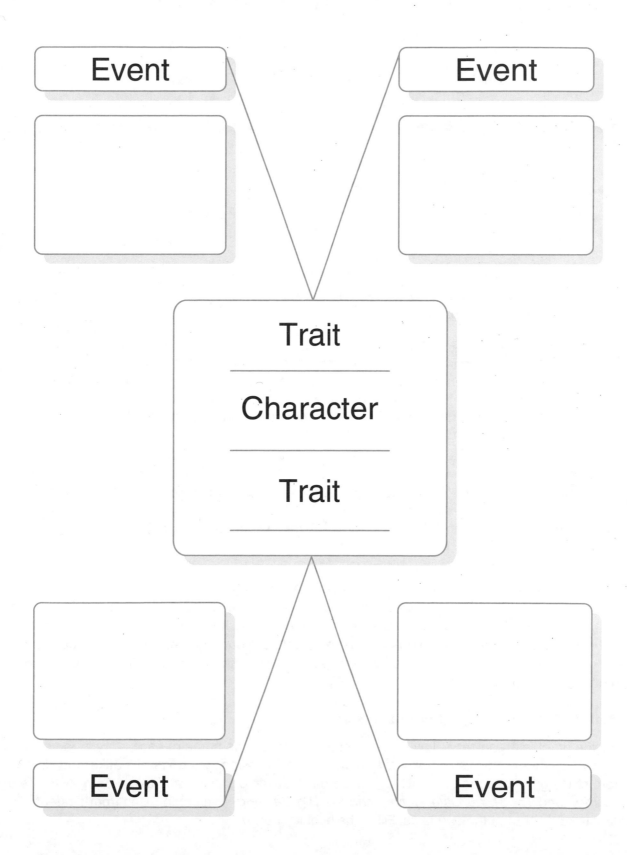

LANGUAGE ARTS GRADES 3–5 LESSON 7

Compare and Contrast

Lesson Objective(s): *What do you want students to know and be able to do?*

Compare and contrast the overall structure of events, ideas, concepts, or information in two or more texts.

Assessment (Traditional/Authentic): *How will you know students have mastered essential learning?*

Students will engage in opportunities to practice comparing and contrasting people in the class.

Students will evaluate comparisons and contrasts in two literary texts.

Ways to Gain/Maintain Attention (Primacy): *How will you gain and maintain students' attention? Consider need, novelty, meaning, or emotion.*

Hold up an analog clock and digital watch (or a watch from a phone or device). Ask students to compare the two. Explain that when we say that both are used to tell time, we are *comparing* them (using words like *and, both, too, like, similarly*)—showing how they are alike. When we say the analog clock can be displayed on the wall and a phone clock goes in your pocket, we are *contrasting* the two (using words like *but, unlike, different*)—telling how they are different. Place these examples on an anchor chart as a visual.

Content Chunks: *How will you divide and teach the content to engage students' brains?*

Lesson Segment 1: Compare and Contrast Two or More Characters in a Text

- **Activity 1: Like Me?**

Distribute hula hoops and 15 index cards to pairs of students. Each student in the pair will have their own hula hoop. Lay them flat on the ground so they overlap to resemble a Venn diagram. Next, have the student label the top of each hoop with their name. Then, have students write five things they have in common and five things that are different from one another on the index cards. Have them place the similarities in the middle overlapping circle of the hoops and the differences in the two outer circles of the hoops.

- **Activity 2: Compare and Contrast Texts**

Draw the graphic organizer below on chart paper and write the name of each story in the squares below. Ask students to listen for ways in which the following two texts are alike and different before reading them to the group. Then, read the first seven pages from *The True Story of the Three Little Pigs* and *The Three Little Wolves and the Big Bad Pig*. Elicit responses from students that compare and contrast the two texts. Fill in the bubbles below.

- **Activity 3: Flip Books**

Have pairs of students read two tales (refer to the *Literary Texts That Teach Reading Skills* list for suggested books.) Have each partner create a four-layer book with two sheets of different colored cardstock paper according to the following directions. Stack two sheets one on top of the other, leaving an inch and a half from the bottom. Fold the top over and staple the top edges. There should be four flaps. On the top flap, title the activity, Compare/Contrast Flipbook. Next, write the story titles on the next two flaps. On the last flap, write both titles (to show how they are alike). Start with the last flap to write two ways in which the two texts are alike with supporting details. Under the other flaps, write how the texts are different. Illustrate each flap to exhibit the tale's unique features.

Brain-Compatible Strategies: *Which will you use to deliver content?*

X	Brainstorming/Discussion	____	Music/Rhythm/Rhyme/Rap
X	Drawing/Artwork	____	Project/Problem-Based Learning
____	Field Trips	**X**	Reciprocal Teaching/Cooperative Learning
____	Games		
X	Graphic Organizers/Semantic Maps/Word Webs	____	Role Plays/Drama/Pantomimes/Charades
____	Humor	**X**	Storytelling
____	Manipulatives/Experiments/Labs/Models	____	Technology
		____	Visualization/Guided Imagery
X	Metaphors/Analogies/Similes	**X**	Visuals
____	Mnemonic Devices	____	Work Study/Apprenticeships
X	Movement	**X**	Writing/Journals

Compare and Contrast Texts

Differences

Similarities

Differences

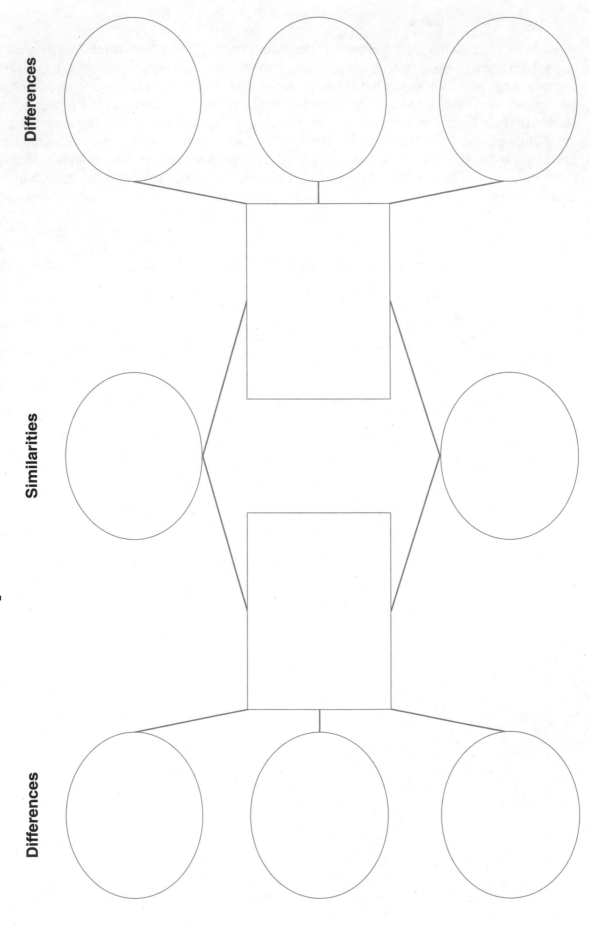

LANGUAGE ARTS GRADES 3–5 LESSON 8

Drawing Inferences

Lesson Objective(s): *What do you want students to know and be able to do?*

Refer to specific details in a text when drawing inferences implicitly from the text.

Assessment (Traditional/Authentic): *How will you know students have mastered essential learning?*

Students will evaluate inferences with a variety of literary texts.

Ways to Gain/Maintain Attention (Primacy): *How will you gain and maintain students' attention? Consider need, novelty, meaning, or emotion.*

Define the word "inference" on chart paper with examples. Students will sing the "Inference Song" to reinforce the concept.

Content Chunks: *How will you divide and teach the content to engage students' brains?*

Lesson Segment 1: Draw Inferences From Pictures

- **Activity 1: Inferences From Pictures**

In advance, cut out several pictures from magazines. Have students select a picture and write a two to three sentence inference about the picture on an index card. Next, tape or glue the picture and index card to both sides of a craft stick. Students will count off in turn from 1 to 6. All the students that called the same number can go to one section of the room. Repeat the procedure until all number groups have been assigned a section of the room to meet. Play upbeat music, such as *Let's Groove Tonight*, while the groups are assembling. Have students share pictures and inferences with the group.

- **Activity 2: Matching Inferences**

Introduce the steps in making an inference after singing the "Inference Song" (see below). In advance, write or glue statements on two different colored index cards (statements in the left column—blue; inference statements in the right column—white). Assign pairs of students to match the event with its corresponding inference. Afterward, students will select their favorite event/inference, glue both cards on a sheet of construction paper, and illustrate the events.

There are dark clouds in the sky.	It will rain.
I didn't hear the alarm go off this morning.	I was late for school.
I tripped as I gave a speech in front of the class.	I felt embarrassed.
I was up doing homework until 11:00 last night.	I am exhausted.
I invited 20 friends to my birthday party.	I am elated.

Lesson Segment 2: Draw Inferences From Literature

● **Activity 1: Inferences From Texts**

Remind students that an inference is information that is not stated directly by the author in a text. In advance, write the heading "Inferences We Concluded" on chart paper. Assign a selection from a text and a sticky note to individual students (refer to the Literary Skills Text List). Instruct each student to write an inference on his or her sticky note. Afterward, have students place their sticky note on the chart. As a group, discuss the inferences placed on the chart. During the discussion, have students support their inference by providing evidence from the text.

Brain-Compatible Strategies: *Which will you use to deliver content?*

__X__	Brainstorming/Discussion	__X__	Music/Rhythm/Rhyme/Rap
_____	Drawing/Artwork	_____	Project/Problem-Based Learning
_____	Field Trips	__X__	Reciprocal Teaching/Cooperative Learning
_____	Games		
_____	Graphic Organizers/Semantic Maps/Word Webs	_____	Role Plays/Drama/Pantomimes/Charades
_____	Humor	_____	Storytelling
_____	Manipulatives/Experiments/Labs/Models	_____	Technology
		_____	Visualization/Guided Imagery
_____	Metaphors/Analogies/Similes	__X__	Visuals
_____	Mnemonic Devices	_____	Work Study/Apprenticeships
__X__	Movement	__X__	Writing/Journals

Inference Song

By Simone Willingham

To the tune of *Are You Sleeping*

Read the question

Read the passage

To see what it's about!

What can it be about?

Find the facts and opinions

They help you answer the questions

Think about the clues

Bring in your own knowledge

What does your evidence say

What does your knowledge suggest

Think about it slow

What do I really know?

Then draw and inference right away

With process of elimination

What can you conclude?

What can you infer?

ENGLISH GRADES 6–8 LESSON 1

Socratic Seminar

Lesson Objective(s): *What do you want students to know and be able to do?*

Prepare for and participate in a Socratic Seminar, building on others' ideas and expressing their own using textual support.

Assessment (Traditional/Authentic): *How will you know students have mastered essential learning?*

Students' preparedness should be assessed by collecting seminar annotations and partner pre-work. Track student discussion contributions in real time and via a digital backchannel. Call on students to reflect orally on the overall quality of the discussion.

Ways to Gain/Maintain Attention (Primacy): *How will you gain and maintain students' attention? Consider need, novelty, meaning, or emotion.*

Create a digital anticipation guide using Google forms. Have students fill out the form on computers as a warm-up. Include the following thematically linked questions:

1. There is never a good enough excuse for stealing.

2. Everyone deserves a second chance.

3. If someone does something that hurts you, you should still treat them with kindness and respect.

4. We can learn a lot by listening to people who are older than us.

Project aggregate google survey response data to demonstrate divergent thinking and help students collectively anticipate and engage with ideas that will arise during reading and discussion.

Next, invite students to stand up, find a partner, and discuss their response to the first survey statement for one to two minutes. Encourage them to provide clear reasoning to back up their stated opinions. After a minute or two, have students move again to find a new partner, and continue this process to generate discussion around each survey statement.

Content Chunks: *How will you divide and teach the content to engage students' brains?*

Lesson Segment 1: Prepare for and Participate in Socratic Seminar

- **Activity 1: Annotation Protocol**

Distribute the short story *Thank You Ma'am* by Langston Hughes. Briefly share background information about the author. Facilitate a *popcorn* read aloud of the story in which one student reads aloud for a paragraph or two and then "popcorns" the reading responsibility to another student.

Build in stopping points for students to turn and talk, annotate, and process. Remind them that you will collect their annotations as evidence of seminar preparation.

Suggested annotation protocol:

- Vocabulary: Circle important/unfamiliar vocabulary you come across while reading. Define the words in the margin.
- Reading Observations: Jot a few-word summary of what is happening, including key facts and details. This is especially helpful if the text is wordy or confusing.
- Key Quotes: Underline quotes that seem important and that you would like to come back to. Jot down thoughts in the margin.
- Ahas!: Put an exclamation point and a quick note next to sections of text that make you feel something intense or connect in some way.
- Questions: Jot down questions (with a question mark) in areas that make you wonder or feel confused.

- **Activity 2: Partner Pre-Work**

Partner students and give them time to work together on preparing *evidence-based* answers to the seminar analysis questions. They should be ready to refer to specific quotes and page numbers.

1. Discuss the characters and setting in the story using evidence from the text. What traits do the characters demonstrate? What details of the setting seem important?

2. What is the big conflict in the story? What causes this conflict?

3. Look up the word "integrity." Is Luella Jones a person of integrity? Is Roger? Defend your answer using evidence from the text.

4. What is the theme of this story? What pieces of evidence support your claim?

5. Create an original question to pose to the group. Use your annotations!

- **Activity 3: Discussion**

Arrange your classroom such that students are seated in two concentric circles. The inner circle will speak first while the outer circle takes notes digitally in a shared Google doc. Groups will then switch places and repeat the protocol.

Set norms for whole-class discussion and use a timer to keep the inner circle on track. Provide 15 minutes for the first group to discuss the first couple of analysis questions at their own pace and pose their additional questions to the group. Track student participation.

During the inner circle discussion, ask students in the outer circle to listen carefully and record their thinking/feedback in a shared Google doc. This will serve as a running record of the conversation and help students stay engaged. Try dividing the document into a graphic organizer with four quadrants to help them capture different types of thinking:

Quadrant 1: I AGREE with _____ because....

Quadrant 2: I DISAGREE with _____ because....

Quadrant 3: When I heard____ I started to THINK DIFFERENTLY because....

Quadrant 4: This conversation is making me WONDER....

Ask the groups to switch places and repeat the protocol.

• **Activity 4: Seminar Reflection**

Lead a discussion to reflect on the successes and challenges of the seminar.

If possible, provide students with time to write out reflective responses before they share aloud. This will give them time to process their thoughts more fully.

In an effort to maintain a safe and inclusive discussion space, encourage students to avoid mentioning names unless they are sharing specific, positive feedback.

- What did the group do well?
- How might the group improve for next time?
- How did your thinking shift or change as a result of hearing ideas from others?
- What questions does this story leave you asking?

Brain-Compatible Strategies: *Which will you use to deliver content?*

__X__	Brainstorming/Discussion		_____	Music/Rhythm/Rhyme/Rap
_____	Drawing/Artwork		_____	Project/Problem-Based Learning
_____	Field Trips		__X__	Reciprocal Teaching/Cooperative Learning
_____	Games			
__X__	Graphic Organizers/Semantic Maps/Word Webs		_____	Role Plays/Drama/Pantomimes/Charades
_____	Humor		__X__	Storytelling
_____	Manipulatives/Experiments/Labs/Models		__X__	Technology
			_____	Visualization/Guided Imagery
_____	Metaphors/Analogies/Similes		_____	Visuals
_____	Mnemonic Devices		_____	Work Study/Apprenticeships
__X__	Movement		__X__	Writing/Journals

ENGLISH GRADES 6–8 LESSON 2

Irony

Lesson Objective(s): *What do you want students to know and be able to do?*

Identify and interpret irony in context and analyze its role in the text.

Assessment (Traditional/Authentic): *How will you know students have mastered essential learning?*

As an exit slip, students will write a literary response paragraph in which they cite and explain one example of irony in *The Gift of the Magi* and describe how O. Henry uses the literary device to impact readers.

Ways to Gain/Maintain Attention (Primacy): *How will you gain and maintain students' attention? Consider need, novelty, meaning, or emotion.*

Project or print out some examples of ironic signage and see if your students can find the humor. You can find many examples online. Give students time to pair-share and discuss each sign. This will undoubtedly make them laugh and warm them up for identifying irony in the context of a short story.

Content Chunks: *How will you divide and teach the content to engage students' brains?*

Lesson Segment 1: Understand Irony

- **Activity 1: Video Notes**

Ask students to watch the 7-minute Khan Academy video on irony (free online) and take notes on situational, verbal, and dramatic irony. Consider making this a flipped assignment. Students can watch the video on their phones or computers at home and then come into class ready to practice.

- **Activity 2: Whole Group Discussion**

Discuss the signs as a class and give students time to ask questions about the Khan Academy video. Ask them if they can think of other examples of irony in literature, music, or life. They are likely more familiar with irony than they think.

- **Activity 3: Shared Reading**

Distribute copies of *The Gift of the Magi* by O. Henry. You may want to define some of the challenging/unfamiliar words for students in advance of the read aloud to aid with comprehension. Instruct students to listen and follow along with a dramatic reading of the story (several versions are available for use on YouTube). They should place a star next to anything they think might be an example of irony. Stop the recording periodically to give students think time and ask check-in questions.

- ### Activity 4: Group Work

Distribute a graphic organizer so students can record examples of irony in the text in one column, identify whether the example is situational, dramatic, or verbal in a second column, and interpret the meaning in a third column. Complete a sample entry together, using the first example of irony from the story. Give students time to work in partners or small groups to complete the organizer.

- ### Activity 5: Debrief

Invite students to come up to the board and record examples of irony or share them in a digital space like Padlet. You can organize sections of the board by page or line number to ensure that groups share different examples.

Discuss student-generated examples and ask the class to consider why O. Henry makes use of irony in this short story. How does this literary device help him craft an effective tale?

Brain-Compatible Strategies: *Which will you use to deliver content?*

X	Brainstorming/Discussion	**X**	Music/Rhythm/Rhyme/Rap
___	Drawing/Artwork	___	Project/Problem-Based Learning
___	Field Trips	**X**	Reciprocal Teaching/Cooperative Learning
___	Games		
X	Graphic Organizers/Semantic Maps/Word Webs	___	Role Plays/Drama/Pantomimes/Charades
X	Humor	**X**	Storytelling
___	Manipulatives/Experiments/Labs/Models	**X**	Technology
___	Metaphors/Analogies/Similes	___	Visualization/Guided Imagery
___	Mnemonic Devices	**X**	Visuals
X	Movement	___	Work Study/Apprenticeships
		X	Writing/Journals

ENGLISH GRADES 6–8 LESSON 3

Research Topics

Lesson Objective(s): *What do you want students to know and be able to do?*

Brainstorm and consult with others to develop a viable small group research topic.

Assessment (Traditional/Authentic): *How will you know students have mastered essential learning?*

Evaluate the quality of the student research topic reflections and conference with groups as needed.

Ways to Gain/Maintain Attention (Primacy): *How will you gain and maintain students' attention? Consider* <u>need</u>, <u>novelty</u>, *meaning, or emotion.*

Connect to the real world and share a couple of examples of how professional teams brainstorm collaboratively, develop solutions, and iterate together before launching a final product, campaign, etc. Tell students that they are going to work together to identify a problem facing their school community, research the problem, and develop a tangible solution collaboratively. The first step in this process is a collaborative brainstorming session.

Content Chunks: *How will you divide and teach the content to engage students' brains?*

Lesson Segment 1: Brainstorm to Develop a Research Topic

- **Activity 1: Independent Braindump**

Have students sit together in their designated research groups. Direct them to independently jot down as many community problems as they can think of on scrap paper, post-its, or in a blank digital document. Encourage them to go as wide as possible and not discount any of their ideas in this initial ideation phase.

- **Activity 2: Small Group Brainstorm and Consultation**

If students can access the internet through computers or their mobile phones, encourage them to use dotstorming.com for this part of the lesson. Using this resource, each group member can add their proposed ideas to a digital "board" where they can collaborate. (If your students do not have access to technology, they can use sticky notes, chart paper, and pens/pencils instead.)

Ask students to take turns sharing each of their identified community problems with the group. They should add a new card to their group's online Dotstorming board each time they share. If two people have the same idea, they do not need to add another card. At this point, encourage students to reserve judgment and ask only clarifying questions as needed.

Next, give each group member a few minutes to silently and independently identify the two problems they believe are most pressing/interesting from the combined list of ideas. They should "upvote" these ideas on the Dotstorming board and write a short comment explaining their rationale for upvoting.

Activity 3: Debrief and Topic Selection

Provide students with a few questions to evaluate the viability of the most upvoted school community problem, which will potentially serve as their research topic. If there is more than one top contender, these questions will help students determine which topic to consider. If the most upvoted solution does not seem viable based on their initial discussion, students can go back to the Dotstorming board and evaluate another proposed idea.

Suggested evaluative questions:

- How might we begin researching this problem? What resources (technology, people, etc.) might help us learn more about how the problem is impacting our school community?
- Does this problem impact people that we know personally? Could they help us in our investigation? How?
- Do we know of groups or individuals who are currently trying to address this problem? What are they doing? How might we find out more information?
- Do we have initial ideas about how we might help solve or address this problem? What are they?

After students have unpacked research viability, provide a digital or physical space for them to share their selected topic with you and the rest of the class. It might be helpful to provide them with a sentence frame such as:

Our group has decided to research _____ because _____. The first thing we plan to do to learn more about this problem is_____.

If students can thoughtfully complete this reflection they are likely prepared to dive into a supported small group research process.

Brain-Compatible Strategies: *Which will you use to deliver content?*

__X__	Brainstorming/Discussion	_____	Music/Rhythm/Rhyme/Rap
_____	Drawing/Artwork	__X__	Project/Problem-Based Learning
_____	Field Trips	__X__	Reciprocal Teaching/Cooperative Learning
_____	Games		
__X__	Graphic Organizers/Semantic Maps/Word Webs	_____	Role Plays/Drama/Pantomimes/Charades
_____	Humor	_____	Storytelling
_____	Manipulatives/Experiments/Labs/Models	__X__	Technology
		_____	Visualization/Guided Imagery
_____	Metaphors/Analogies/Similes	__X__	Visuals
_____	Mnemonic Devices	_____	Work Study/Apprenticeships
_____	Movement	__X__	Writing/Journals

ENGLISH GRADES 6–8 LESSON 4

Text Analysis

Lesson Objective(s): *What do you want students to know and be able to do?*

Cite strong and thorough evidence to support your analysis of the text.

Assessment (Traditional/Authentic): *How will you know students have mastered essential learning?*

Assess Flipgrid responses informally or using a simple rubric. Flipgrid allows you to create a simple rubric from within the platform.

Ways to Gain/Maintain Attention (Primacy): *How will you gain and maintain students' attention? Consider need, novelty, meaning, or emotion.*

Students will be more inclined to read and enjoy informational texts if we provide them with engaging opportunities to share their insights with one another.

Start this lesson by engaging students in a discussion about why reading news is valuable. What are some of the challenges associated with consuming news? How can we address these challenges? How do students typically get their news (TV, internet, magazines, etc.)? Which news outlets do they enjoy? Chart out the group's thinking.

Content Chunks: *How will you divide and teach the content to engage students' brains?*

Lesson Segment 1: Cite Strong and Thorough Evidence to Support Your Analysis of the Text

- **Activity 1: Model and Directions**

Project the text of an accessible news article that you've read recently. If possible, annotate the text in advance using a digital annotation tool like Kami (www.kamihq.com). Point out how you identified the author's claim or claims and noted supporting evidence. Next, show students a model Flipgrid video (like the one you expect them to create) to establish benchmarks for the assignment and clarify instructions.

- **Activity 2: Identify Claim and Evidence**

Give students time to select a news article that interests them. You might suggest sites like Newsela, Science News for Students, and the New York Times Learning Network if students aren't sure where to begin, encourage them to draw from the list you created together at the beginning of class as well. Students should annotate the text using a digital tool like Kami.

- **Activity 3: Pair-Share**

After reading, ask students to stand and pair-share about the following:

- Share the title and source of your selected article.
- Why did you select this article?
- What is the author's big claim or purpose for writing?
- What evidence does the author share to support his or her claim(s)?
- What are your personal reactions to this text? Agreements? Disagreements? Connections?

Talking through the prompts with a partner will help students prepare to create their short video responses. If possible, familiarize them with the scoring rubric in advance of the pair-share so that they can provide one another with thoughtful constructive feedback.

- **Activity 4: Flipgrid Videos**

Give students time to complete and post their video responses. They should answer the same guiding questions they used in the pair-share.

After students have posted their own video, they can view other student responses. Ideally, hearing from their peers will inspire students to check out additional informational texts that sound compelling.

Brain-Compatible Strategies: *Which will you use to deliver content?*

__X__	Brainstorming/Discussion	_____	Music/Rhythm/Rhyme/Rap
_____	Drawing/Artwork	_____	Project/Problem-Based Learning
_____	Field Trips	__X__	Reciprocal Teaching/Cooperative Learning
_____	Games		
_____	Graphic Organizers/Semantic Maps/Word Webs	_____	Role Plays/Drama/Pantomimes/Charades
_____	Humor	__X__	Storytelling
_____	Manipulatives/Experiments/Labs/Models	__X__	Technology
		_____	Visualization/Guided Imagery
_____	Metaphors/Analogies/Similes	__X__	Visuals
_____	Mnemonic Devices	_____	Work Study/Apprenticeships
__X__	Movement	__X__	Writing/Journals

ENGLISH GRADES 6–8 LESSON 5

Character Development

Lesson Objective(s): *What do you want students to know and be able to do?*

Analyze how complex characters develop over the course of a text.

Assessment (Traditional/Authentic): *How will you know students have mastered essential learning?*

Circulate and informally assess FLATS organizers to gauge student success as the lesson unfolds. Assess and provide feedback on individual student work products (videos, journal entries/letters, and visual representations) as desired. This lesson will also help students engage in valuable pre-thinking, and you might decide to conclude with a formal, scored class discussion of the short story.

Ways to Gain/Maintain Attention (Primacy): *How will you gain and maintain students' attention? Consider need, novelty, meaning, or emotion.*

Ask students to think about whether or not their facial expressions, statements, and actions actually reflect how they are feeling on an average day. Encourage them to stand and think-pair-share about this topic and then discuss briefly as a group. Students will likely note that emotions are complex, and there is often a mismatch between how we perceive people and what they are actually experiencing internally.

Tell students that skillful authors create characters who are just as complex as we are. They don't always *say and do* exactly what they are feeling and thinking. As skillful readers, we must carefully examine the evidence authors provide about their characters, and then make thoughtful inferences about a character's motivations, internal experience, and overall function in the story.

Tell students that they will read a short story called *Blue* by Francesca Lia Block (available at commonlit.org). This story contains complex characters who impact one another in a variety of ways to shape the overall story. Explain that students will have an opportunity to select and analyze one character they find particularly intriguing. Let them know that they will choose from a menu of options to express their thinking creatively later in the lesson.

Content Chunks: *How will you divide and teach the content to engage students' brains?*

Lesson Segment 1: Analyze Complex Characters

- **Activity 1: Author Background + Initial Reading**

Share brief background information about the author to provide students with context before reading. Distribute copies of *Blue* and lead the class in a shared *popcorn read* of the story, where one student stands and reads one page or paragraph aloud, and then "popcorns" the next page or paragraph to a classmate. Alternatively, ask students to read the story in its entirety independently.

During this initial reading, students should simply take in the story and get a sense of the characters. Encourage them to annotate as desired. Their reading goal is to determine which character they find most intriguing.

At the end of the initial reading, give students time to determine which character they find most intriguing and then turn and talk with a nearby thought partner. They can use the following questions to guide their conversation:

- Which character did you find most intriguing?
- Why did this character stand out to you? Did you find them relatable? Did you find them off-putting? Explain.
- How does this character seem to impact/relate to other characters in the story?

- **Activity 2: FLATS Graphic Organizer + Second Reading**

Tell students that it is helpful to organize the evidence authors *directly provide* about characters and examine it as a whole before making inferences or drawing conclusions about them. Share the mnemonic device "FLATS", which students will use to organize evidence from the text about their selected character.

You can pre-create a graphic organizer for students or have them make their own chart to record evidence of their selected character's **F**eelings, **L**ooks, **A**ctions, **T**houghts, and **S**tatements.

Direct students back to the text and give them time to complete a second reading and fill out the FLATS organizer for their selected character.

- **Activity 3: Character Analysis Using Creative Options**

Now that students have collected and examined all of the direct evidence related to their chosen character, ask them to combine their findings with inferential thinking to create a character representation. Give them a menu of creative options:

- Write a letter or journal entry from the perspective of your selected character, combining what you know from the text itself and your own inferences to shape your language.
- Create a visual representation connected to your selected character and an accompanying descriptive paragraph, combining what you know from the text itself and your own inferences to shape your visual creation and descriptive language.
- Make a YouTube "confessional" video in which you speak from the character's perspective, combining what you know from the text itself and your own inferences to shape your talking points.

- **Activity 4: Gallery Walk**

Give students the opportunity to share their work with one another. Each student can display their creative piece at their desk or somewhere around the room. Provide time for students to circulate with sticky notes and leave comments for one another. Make sure to establish norms for this feedback process. For example, you might instruct students to leave only *warm* feedback if you will not be providing time for them to iterate further on these particular work pieces.

Brain-Compatible Strategies: *Which will you use to deliver content?*

__X__	Brainstorming/Discussion	_____	Music/Rhythm/Rhyme/Rap
__X__	Drawing/Artwork	__X__	Project/Problem-Based Learning
_____	Field Trips	__X__	Reciprocal Teaching/Cooperative Learning
_____	Games		
__X__	Graphic Organizers/Semantic Maps/Word Webs	_____	Role Plays/Drama/Pantomimes/Charades
_____	Humor	__X__	Storytelling
_____	Manipulatives/Experiments/Labs/Models	__X__	Technology
		_____	Visualization/Guided Imagery
_____	Metaphors/Analogies/Similes	__X__	Visuals
__X__	Mnemonic Devices	_____	Work Study/Apprenticeships
__X__	Movement	__X__	Writing/Journals

ENGLISH GRADES 6–8 LESSON 6

Central Ideas and Supporting Details

Lesson Objective(s): *What do you want students to know and be able to do?*

Determine central ideas or themes of a text and analyze their development.

Summarize the key supporting details and ideas.

Assessment (Traditional/Authentic): *How will you know students have mastered essential learning?*

Assess each group's central idea/theme statements and evidence on the shared Padlet before they begin writing independently. Provide guidance as needed. Collect student writing samples and assess individually or ask students to switch papers and provide peer feedback using a rubric.

Ways to Gain/Maintain Attention (Primacy): *How will you gain and maintain students' attention? Consider need, novelty, meaning, or emotion.*

Invite students to watch a music video that will inspire discussion, such as *Hall of Fame* by The Script (available on YouTube). Distribute or project the song lyrics for students to consider alongside the video.

Ask students to reflect on and discuss the following questions with a partner:

1. What is the central idea or theme (MAIN MESSAGE) of this song?

2. Which specific images or moments from the music video or song lyrics help develop this message? How so?

Lead the class in a shared discussion of the song's meaning and how the video/lyrics help develop the artist's overall message. Create and record a shared central idea/theme statement to use as a model.

Tell students that, as musicians and filmmakers, writers use specific words and images to share key messages with readers. Now they will be tasked with applying this same thought process to a shared text.

Content Chunks: *How will you divide and teach the content to engage students' brains?*

Lesson Segment 1: Determine Central Ideas or Themes and Analyze Their Development

- **Activity 1: Independent Reading**

Distribute "Everyday Use" by Alice Walker or another short story that maps to your curriculum. Instruct students to read the story carefully and place a star next to any parts of the text they think illuminate the central idea/theme/main message Walker is trying to convey.

- **Activity 2: Group Work**

Ask students to work in small groups to develop a shared central idea/theme statement and find at least three pieces of text evidence that help develop this message over the course of the text. Refer students back to the model you created at the start of class as needed.

Invite students to share their central idea/theme statement and related evidence/analysis digitally via Padlet. You can set up a collaborative board for your class at https://padlet.com.

Give students the opportunity to move around the room, review the submissions from other groups, and provide digital feedback if there is time. (*Do you agree or disagree with the proposed central idea/theme statement? Does the evidence the group selected effectively support the proposed central idea/theme statement?*)

- **Activity 3: Independent Writing**

Ask students to independently compose a powerful paragraph in which they state the central idea/theme in "Everyday Use" by Alice Walker and analyze its development over the course of the text using at least two to three pieces of properly cited text evidence. Remind students that it is important to analyze *how* the evidence they selected helps the author develop her overall message.

Encourage students to use a central idea/theme statement from another group's Padlet entry if they feel it is stronger than their group's, *or* to create their own new statement.

Note: If there are students in your class who require strong writing models, consider writing a model powerful paragraph based on the music video, providing sentence starters, and/or posting an example of proper quote citation.

Brain-Compatible Strategies: *Which will you use to deliver content?*

__X__	Brainstorming/Discussion		__X__	Music/Rhythm/Rhyme/Rap
_____	Drawing/Artwork		_____	Project/Problem-Based Learning
_____	Field Trips		__X__	Reciprocal Teaching/Cooperative Learning
_____	Games			
_____	Graphic Organizers/Semantic Maps/Word Webs		_____	Role Plays/Drama/Pantomimes/Charades
_____	Humor		__X__	Storytelling
_____	Manipulatives/Experiments/Labs/Models		__X__	Technology
			_____	Visualization/Guided Imagery
_____	Metaphors/Analogies/Similes		__X__	Visuals
_____	Mnemonic Devices		_____	Work Study/Apprenticeships
__X__	Movement		__X__	Writing/Journals

ENGLISH GRADES 6–8 LESSON 7

Analyzing Texts

Lesson Objective(s): *What do you want students to know and be able to do?*

Analyze texts of historical and literary significance, including how they address related themes and concepts.

Assessment (Traditional/Authentic): *How will you know students have mastered essential learning?*

Informally assess expert presentations. Grade exit slips to determine students' ability to explain connections between thematically linked texts using clearly explained evidence.

Ways to Gain/Maintain Attention (Primacy): *How will you gain and maintain students' attention? Consider need, novelty, meaning, or emotion.*

Play a song about immigration such as *Now* by Miguel. Ask students to listen carefully and consider:

- What is the tone of the song?
- What is the theme of the song?
- How do specific lyrics help Miguel develop his overall message?

Tell students they will be working collaboratively to analyze multiple texts that are thematically related to the song they just heard using the jigsaw method. This strategy requires student groups to become experts on their assigned text, and then share their learning with the rest of the class.

Content Chunks: *How will you divide and teach the content to engage students' brains?*

Lesson Segment 1: Analyze Documents

- **Activity 1: Group Work**

Divide students into groups and distribute a graphic organizer. Students can work inside a collaborative Google doc to complete the organizer or take their own notes on a printed handout. Have them consider multiple aspects of the text, such as:

- Who is the author/speaker in this piece?
- What is the historical context?
- Who is the intended audience?
- What is the overall tone? Which lines of text contribute to the overall tone?
- What is the theme of the text? Which lines of text help develop the theme? Explain.

Consider grouping students around the following texts, which are all available digitally via Common Lit (www.commonlit.org):

> Group 1: *Puerto Rican Obituary* by Pedro Pietri
>
> Group 2: *America and I* by Anzia Yezierska
>
> Group 3: *The New Colossus* by Emma Lazarus
>
> Group 4: *Fish Cheeks* by Amy Tan

- **Activity 2: Expert Presentations**

Invite student groups to present to the class on their assigned text. They can use the structure of the graphic organizer to divide up talking points. The rest of the class should take notes during expert presentations. Encourage each group to field questions from the class for a few minutes after they have finished their initial presentation.

- **Activity 3: Exit Slip**

Give students access to all of the assigned readings. Ask them to select one text in addition to the one they analyzed in their expert group, and respond to the following prompt:

Explain how the two texts you selected address related themes or concepts, using evidence from both texts to support your thinking.

Encourage students to use the notes from the expert presentations to help develop and organize their responses.

Brain-Compatible Strategies: *Which will you use to deliver content?*

__X__	Brainstorming/Discussion	__X__	Music/Rhythm/Rhyme/Rap
_____	Drawing/Artwork	_____	Project/Problem-Based Learning
_____	Field Trips	__X__	Reciprocal Teaching/Cooperative Learning
_____	Games		
__X__	Graphic Organizers/Semantic Maps/Word Webs	_____	Role Plays/Drama/Pantomimes/Charades
_____	Humor	_____	Storytelling
_____	Manipulatives/Experiments/Labs/Models	__X__	Technology
_____	Metaphors/Analogies/Similes	_____	Visualization/Guided Imagery
_____	Mnemonic Devices	_____	Visuals
_____		_____	Work Study/Apprenticeships
__X__	Movement	__X__	Writing/Journals

ENGLISH GRADES 6–8 LESSON 8

Listening Responsively

Lesson Objective(s): *What do you want students to know and be able to do?*

Listen responsively to a speaker by framing inquiries that reflect an understanding of the content and describing the speaker's position using reference to evidence.

Assessment (Traditional/Authentic): *How will you know students have mastered essential learning?*

Keep track of student input during the Socratic Seminar. Collect student note-catchers at the end of the discussion to assess the quality of note-taking during the podcast homework assignment.

Ways to Gain/Maintain Attention (Primacy): *How will you gain and maintain students' attention? Consider* <u>need</u>, <u>novelty</u>, *meaning, or emotion.*

Explain how discussion sections work in college settings. Emphasize how college courses often require students to come to group discussions with notes prepared from independent reading/research. This lesson structure is designed to help prepare students for this type of rigorous high school and college-level coursework.

Ask students if they listen to podcasts or talk radio. If they do, encourage them to share. Describe a podcast or two you enjoy and explain how this medium can help us hone our listening skills, which will also be critical for success in lecture-style college classes.

Content Chunks: *How will you divide and teach the content to engage students' brains?*

Lesson Segment 1: Listen Responsively to a Speaker and Frame Inquiries

- **Activity 1: Active Listening With Podcasts**

Distribute a graphic organizer that provides students with space to demonstrate their thinking in multiple ways. You might carve out spaces for students to sketch or visually represent thinking, record key quotes and ideas, and generate their own questions. Explain that they will be using this resource to jot their ideas as they listen to a podcast. Students will benefit from seeing a model completed organizer. Explain how sketching and diagramming is yet another way to capture and organize our ideas as we listen, since this strategy may be novel for some students.

Now that students have their organizers, direct them to a podcast episode that maps to your unit of study. You can find excellent high-interest audio material for middle school ELA courses via The Allusionist, Reply All, This I Believe, StarTalk Radio, and Stuff You Missed in History Class to name a few. It's ideal if students can listen to the podcast for homework as a flipped assignment. This way they can stop, start, and relisten as many times as they'd like. Remind them to take thoughtful notes using the organizer in preparation for a class discussion.

Lesson Segment 2: Incorporate Related Evidence and Inquiries During Class Discussion

- **Activity 1: Pair-Share**

Ask students to take out their graphic organizers, stand, and pair-share with a partner. What were their big takeaways from the podcast? What surprised or interested them? What questions arose?

- **Activity 2: Socratic Seminar**

Now that students have had an opportunity to generate some initial ideas, conduct a traditional Socratic Seminar where half the class speaks first in the inner circle while the outer circle takes notes, and then the two groups switch. Encourage students to share the questions they created while listening to the podcast.

- **Activity 3: Debrief**

Have students answer the following questions:

- What is it like to learn new information from a podcast? What seems valuable? What was challenging about this experience?
- What went well about the discussion? What could be improved?
- Do you plan to explore additional podcasts on your own? Why or why not?

Brain-Compatible Strategies: *Which will you use to deliver content?*

__X__	Brainstorming/Discussion	_____	Music/Rhythm/Rhyme/Rap
__X__	Drawing/Artwork	_____	Project/Problem-Based Learning
_____	Field Trips	__X__	Reciprocal Teaching/Cooperative Learning
_____	Games		
__X__	Graphic Organizers/Semantic Maps/Word Webs	_____	Role Plays/Drama/Pantomimes/Charades
_____	Humor	_____	Storytelling
_____	Manipulatives/Experiments/Labs/Models	__X__	Technology
		_____	Visualization/Guided Imagery
_____	Metaphors/Analogies/Similes	_____	Visuals
_____	Mnemonic Devices	_____	Work Study/Apprenticeships
__X__	Movement	__X__	Writing/Journals

Literary Texts That Teach Story Elements and Skills

Beginning, Middle, and End

Thomas' Snowsuit by Robert Munsch

How Many Days to America by Eve Bunting

Pink and Say by Patricia Polacco

Jumanji by Chris Van Allsburg

The Harmonica by Tony Johnston

Love You Forever by Robert Munsch

Cloudy With a Chance of Meatballs by Judi Barrett

The Story of Ruby Bridges by Robert Coles

Mr. Lincoln's Way by Patricia Polacco

Sir Cumference and the First Round Table by Cindy Neuschwander

Cause and Effect

Abiyoyo by Pete Seeger

Why Mosquitoes Buzz in People's Ears by Verna Aardema

Alexander and the Terrible, Horrible, No Good, Very Bad Day by Judith Viorst

The Tiny Seed by Eric Carle

Sierra (Spirit of the Cimmaron) by Kathleen Duey

Why I Will Never, Ever Have Enough Time to Read This Book by Remy Charlip

Old Henry by Joan W. Blos

The Grumpy Morning by Pamela Duncan Edwards

The Stray Dog by Marc Simont

The Gingerbread Boy by Paul Galdon

Character Traits

The Sweetest Fig by Chris Van Allsburg

Alexander and the Terrible, Horrible, No Good, Very Bad Day by Judith Viorst

Emmanuel's Dream by Laurie Ann Thompson

The Talking Eggs by Robert D. San Souci

Wilma Unlimited by Kathleen Krull and David Diaz

The War With Grandpa by Robert Kimmel Smith

Hatchet by Gary Paulsen

Just a Dream by Chris Van Allsburg

Thank You, Mr. Falker by Patricia Polacco

Chester by Melanie Watt

Compare and Contrast Two Texts

Cinderella by RH Disney

Cinder-Elly by Frances Minters

The Three Little Pigs by Stephen Kellogg

The Three Little Wolves and the Big Bad Pig by Eugene Trivizas

Mufaro's Beautiful Daughters by John Steptoe

The Gospel Cinderella by Joyce Carol Thomas

Little Red Riding Hood by James Marshall

Honestly, Red Riding Hood Was Rotten by Trisha Speed Shaskan

The Princess and the Pea by Hans Christian Anderson

The Princess and the Pizza by Mary Jane Auch

My Lucky Day by Keiko Kasza

The Wolf's Chicken Stew by Keiko Kasza

Figurative Language (Similes, Alliteration, Personification, Idioms)

Zero Is the Leaves on the Tree by Betsy Franco

A Turkey for Thanksgiving by Eve Bunting

Snowflake Bentley by Jacqueline Briggs Martin

Scarecrow by Cynthia Rylant

Stellaluna by Jannell Cannon

Bad Boys by Margie Palatini and Henry Cole

The Lonely Scarecrow by Tim Preston

The Z Was Zapped by Chris Van Allsburg

The Great Fuzz Frenzy by Janet Stevens

Four Famished Foxes and Fosdyke by Pamela Duncan Edwards

The Giving Tree by Shel Silverstein

Owl Moon by Jane Yolen

Crash, Bang, Boom by Peter Spier

Monkey Business by Wallace Edwards

Ounce, Dice, Trice by Alastair Reid

Apples to Oregon by Deborah Hopkinson

Inferences

Yo, Yes by Chris Raschka

Alexander Who Used to Be Rich Last Sunday by Judith Viorst

Basket Moon by Mary Lyn Ray and Barbara Cooney

How Many Days to America by Eve Bunting

Hattie and the Fox by Mem Fox and Patricia Mullins

Hug by Jez Alborough

Encounter by Jane Yolen

Tar Beach by Faith Ringgold

The *Garden of Abdul Gasazi* by Chris Van Allsburg

The Polar Express by Chris Van Allsburg

Plot

Freedom Song by Sally M. Walker

Probuditi by Chris Van Allsburg

Jacob's New Dress by Sarah and Ian Hoffman

Jack's Worry by Sam Zuppardi

Nugget and Fang by Tammi Sauer

Ferdinand by Munro Leaf

Millions of Cats by Wanda Gag

Mr. Lincoln's Way by Patricia Polacco

Umbrella by Taro Yashima

The Emperor and the Kite by Jane Yolen

Point of View

Stellaluna by Janell Cannon

The True Story of the Three Little Pigs by Jon Scieszka

Mr. Lincoln's Way by Patricia Polacco

Hey Little Ant by Phillip and Hannah Hoose

Two Bad Ants by Chris Van Allsburg

Seven Blind Mice by Ed Young

I Am the Dog I Am the Cat by Donald Hall

School's First Day of School by Adam Rex

The Day the Crayons Quit by Drew Daywalt

The Day the Crayons Came Home by Drew Daywalt

Problem and Solution

New Shoes by Susan Lynn Myer

Lilly's Purple Plastic Purse by Kevin Henkes

Caps for Sale by Esphyr Slobodkina

Jamaica's Find by Juanita Havill

The Little Engine That Could by Watty Piper

A Bad Case of Stripes by David Shannon

Ira Sleeps Over by Bernard Waber

Where the Wild Things Are by Maurice Sendak

The Rough Face Girl by David Shannon

Swimmy by Leo Lionni

Sensory Texts for Writing

Chicken Cheeks by Michael Ian Black

Tangerine by Edward Bloor

What You Know First by Patricia MacLachlan

Saturday and Teacakes by Lester Laminack

Nothing Ever Happens on 90th Street by Roni Schotter

The Friend by Sarah Stewart

The Silver Sun by Nancy Springer

Pinduli by Jannell Cannon

When I Was Young in the Mountains by Cynthia Rylant

All the Places to Love by Patricia MacLachlan

Fireflies by Julie Brinckloe

Structure of the Text

If You Give a Mouse a Cookie by Laura Joffe Numeroff

The Cake That Mack Ate by Rose Robart

Watch the Stars Come Out by Riki Levinson

A House for Hermit Crab by Eric Carle

There Was an Old Lady That Swallowed a Fly by Lucille Colandro

Mushroom in the Rain by Mirra Ginsburg

This Is the Teacher by Rhonda Greene

Max's Dragon Shirt by Rosemary Wells

Tops and Bottoms by Janet Stevens

Summary and Synthesis

Thundercake by Patricia Polacco

Enemy Pie by Derek Munson

The Magic Fish by Freya Littledale

Annie and the Wild Animals by Jan Brett

Just the Two of Us by Will Smith

Thomas' Snowsuit by Robert Munsch

Interrupting Chicken by David Ezra Stein

Miss Rumphius by Barbara Cooney

Weslandia by Paul Fleischman

Because Amelia Smiled by David Ezra Stein

Theme/Author's Central Message

Just the Two of Us by Will Smith

The Tin Forest by Helen Ward

Mr. Peabody's Apples by Madonna

Three Hens and a Peacock by Lester Laminack

The Giving Tree by Shel Silverstein

Thundercake by Patricia Polacco

Miss Malarkey Leaves No Reader Behind by Kevin O'Malley

Thank You, Mr. Faulker by Patricia Polacco

Compiled by Simone Philp Willingham

Reading Websites

Brain Pop—Movies that teach grammar and reading skills. It also provides interactive quizzes. This site is perfect for mini-lessons (Grades 3–6).

http://puzzlemaker.discoveryeducation.com/—A puzzle generation tool for teachers, students, and parents. Create and print customized word search, criss-cross, math puzzles, and more using your own word lists.

Edmodo.com—An easy way to get your students connected so they can safely collaborate, get and stay organized, and access assignments. You can even create online quizzes with this tool.

Flocabulary.com—Hundreds of interactive songs and quizzes that engage and reinforce ELA concepts and skills.

IXL—A comprehensive K–12 curriculum where students can practice specific literary skills based on what was taught in the classroom.

Moby Max—Provides personalized and blended learning to help students learn using a complete and comprehensive K–8 curriculum for 27 subjects, including reading, phonics, language, vocabulary, spelling, writing, and social studies.

Raz-Kids—Leveled text resources (Pre-K–6) that provide opportunities for instruction and practice.

Reading A-Z—Leveled text resources (Pre-K–6) that provide opportunities for instruction and practice.

Spellingcity.com—Teachers can plug in spelling words and students can practice them through a variety of fun, interactive learning games.

Vocabulary A-Z—An online resource teachers can use to select vocabulary words and build custom lesson plans or choose premade lessons. The product offers a variety of ways to support vocabulary learning in the classroom with a database of more than 16,000 words, premade vocabulary lists and lessons, and customizable five-day lesson plans.

Vocabulary/Spelling City—A game-based program designed to help differentiate and customize lessons for learners at every skill level. Helps reinforce vocabulary and spelling instruction to help students keep up, catch up, or stay ahead. Helps manage center rotations during small group instruction.

Writing A-Z—Provides interactive writing opportunities for students in Grades K–5.

www.getepic.com—Movies that teach grammar and reading skills. It also provides interactive quizzes. This site is perfect for mini-lessons (Grades K–2).

5

25 Sample Mathematics Lessons

MATHEMATICS GRADES K–2 LESSON 1

Embedded Numbers

Lesson Objective(s): *What do you want students to know and be able to do?*

Analyze embedded numbers to 10.

Assessment (Traditional/Authentic): *How will you know students have mastered essential learning?*

Students will use number bonds to show embedded numbers.

Ways to Gain/Maintain Attention (Primacy): *How will you gain and maintain students' attention? Consider need, novelty, meaning, or emotion.*

The *finding hidden numbers* activity is novel.

Content Chunks: *How will you divide and teach the content to engage students' brains?*

Lesson Segment 1: Analyze Embedded Numbers 1–10.

- **Activity 1: Math Finger Flash**

Say, *Watch carefully as I quickly show some fingers. I will hide them and then when I snap, say the number of fingers you saw.* Flash five fingers for two to three seconds and then hide them. *Ready?* (snap) *How many did you see?* 5. Repeat several times with other numbers.

- **Activity 2: Egg Carton Fill**

Have students use egg cartons and any generic counters to take turns filling a designated number of egg carton slots. Partner A fills a number of slots and Partner B shares *how the numbers are hiding.* Any number cards will work, numbered 0-12. For example, for six counters, five and one, four and two, three and three or six and zero could be *hiding.* Take turns repeating the process.

- **Activity 3: Egg Carton Number Bonds**

Continue to use egg cartons and counters to take turns filling a number of egg carton slots. Each time a carton is filled with a particular number, fill in the number bond. Write the total in the largest circle and the counters that are *hiding* in the smaller circles. See *Number Bonds* below.

Brain-Compatible Strategies: *Which will you use to deliver content?*

X	Brainstorming/Discussion	
_____	Drawing/Artwork	
_____	Field Trips	
_____	Games	
X	Graphic Organizers/Semantic Maps/Word Webs	
_____	Humor	
X	Manipulatives/Experiments/Labs/Models	
_____	Metaphors/Analogies/Similes	
_____	Mnemonic Devices	
_____	Movement	

_____	Music/Rhythm/Rhyme/Rap
_____	Project/Problem-Based Learning
X	Reciprocal Teaching/Cooperative Learning
_____	Role Plays/Drama/Pantomimes/Charades
_____	Storytelling
_____	Technology
_____	Visualization/Guided Imagery
X	Visuals
_____	Work Study/Apprenticeships
_____	Writing/Journals

Number Bonds

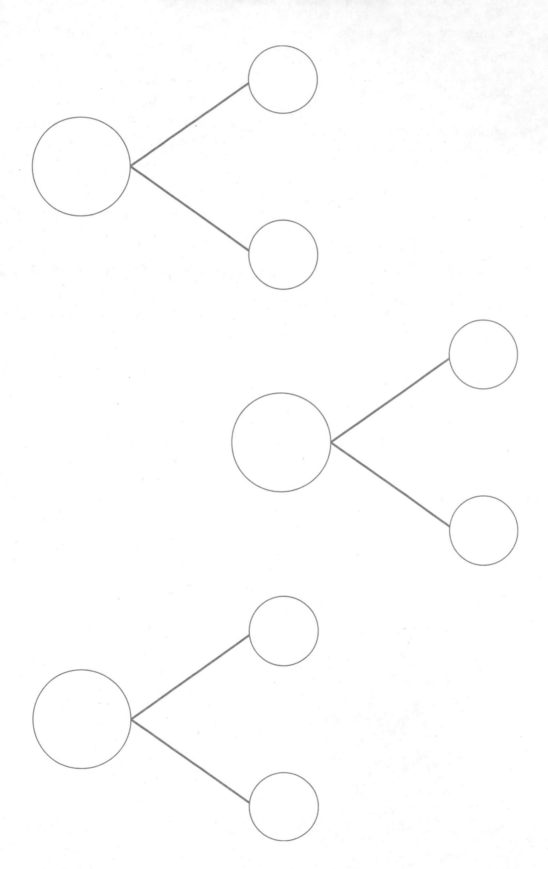

MATHEMATICS GRADES K–2 LESSON 2

Position Words

Lesson Objective(s): *What do you want students to know and be able to do?*

Identify the positions on, above, and below.

Assessment (Traditional/Authentic): *How will you know students have mastered essential learning?*

Have students touch the toy that is on the box and point to the toy below the box. Repeat with similar directions. See *Kindergarten MLP2 Assessment* in plan.

Ways to Gain/Maintain Attention (Primacy): *How will you gain and maintain students' attention? Consider <u>need</u>, novelty, meaning, or emotion.*

Have students look at the table and ask what items are on it. Have a wide assortment of toys to choose from.

Content Chunks: *How will you divide and teach the content to engage students' brains?*

Lesson Segment 1: Identify Positions *On, Above, Below*

- **Activity 1: Attribute Blocks**

Pass out attribute blocks to groups of students. Ask students to place a red shape with four sides *below* a blue shape with three sides. Demonstrate. Repeat with several different shapes. Have students place a three-sided shape *on* their chairs. Repeat with other shapes. Have students place a red shape *above* their heads. Repeat with other shapes.

- **Activity 2: Location Problem**

Introduce this problem. *Mr. Law asked Michael to put away a few of his things. He told Michael to put his blue shoes below the table. He said to put his yellow book on the table. Then he said to put the red artwork he made on the wall above the table. Where did Michael put these things?*

We will use one red, one yellow, and one blue 1" color tile to learn words that tell where things are.

Ask students to stand and hold their three color tiles. Have them put their yellow tile on their chairs. Demonstrate by pointing to the yellow tile on the chair. Have students put the red tile on their desk. Have them point to the red tile on their desks. Have students put the blue tile on the floor below the chair. Point to the blue tile.

Caution: Watch for confusion between the meanings of *on* and *next to*. Items that are close are not *on* them. When referring to *on, above,* and *below*, the reference is to the locations of things that go up and down.

• Activity 3: Chair in the Middle

Have students sit in a circle with a chair in the middle. Have several small toys for use. Ask volunteers to pick a friend to demonstrate placing a toy *on, above,* or *below* the chair.

Brain-Compatible Strategies: *Which will you use to deliver content?*

__X__	Brainstorming/Discussion	_____	Music/Rhythm/Rhyme/Rap
_____	Drawing/Artwork	__X__	Project/Problem-Based Learning
_____	Field Trips	__X__	Reciprocal Teaching/Cooperative Learning
_____	Games		
_____	Graphic Organizers/Semantic Maps/Word Webs	_____	Role Plays/Drama/Pantomimes/Charades
__X__	Humor	_____	Storytelling
__X__	Manipulatives/Experiments/Labs/Models	_____	Technology
		_____	Visualization/Guided Imagery
_____	Metaphors/Analogies/Similes	__X__	Visuals
_____	Mnemonic Devices	_____	Work Study/Apprenticeships
__X__	Movement	_____	Writing/Journals

Assessment

Image source: https://pixabay.com/en/users/openclipartvectors-30363/

MATHEMATICS GRADES K–2 LESSON 3

Subtraction

Lesson Objective(s): *What do you want students to know and be able to do?*

Relate subtraction as a symbolic sentence that connects to concrete representation.

Assessment (Traditional/Authentic): *How will you know students have mastered essential learning?*

Assess the writing station work and observe the music and drama station activities.

Ways to Gain/Maintain Attention (Primacy): *How will you gain and maintain students' attention? Consider need, novelty, meaning, or emotion.*

Have up to ten items on a table. Ask *Student A* to examine the items on the table and then leave the area. Then have *Student B* remove two items from the table. *Student A* returns and is asked questions such as: *What happened? How many are missing? What were the items? How many items are left?*

Content Chunks: *How will you divide and teach the content to engage students' brains?*

Lesson Segment 1: Relate Subtraction to Concrete Representation

- **Activity 1: Drama Station**

Use drama to act out *take away* situations. Have classroom items on a tray for student use. Student A has 4 pencils and gives 2 of them to Student B. How many does Student A have left? Students change roles. Have all students rotate acting *take away* situations.

- **Activity 2: Musical Subtraction**

Use nine chairs, whiteboard, crayons, and music. Starting with 11 students, one is at the board (students rotate) and writes 10 – ___ = ___. Begin the music as students play the classic game of musical chairs. Complete the subtraction sentence to match each round of play.

- **Activity 3: Writing Station**

Who left the train? Use masking tape, cube blocks, and paper. Partner A forms a subtraction sentence with the cubes and masking tape. Partner B writes the number sentence on paper. Alternate turns.

$$10 - 2 = 8$$

Brain-Compatible Strategies: *Which will you use to deliver content?*

__X__	Brainstorming/Discussion	__X__	Music/Rhythm/Rhyme/Rap
_____	Drawing/Artwork	__X__	Project/Problem-Based Learning
_____	Field Trips	_____	Reciprocal Teaching/Cooperative Learning
__X__	Games		
_____	Graphic Organizers/Semantic Maps/Word Webs	__X__	Role Plays/Drama/Pantomimes/Charades
__X__	Humor	_____	Storytelling
__X__	Manipulatives/Experiments/Labs/Models	_____	Technology
		_____	Visualization/Guided Imagery
_____	Metaphors/Analogies/Similes	__X__	Visuals
_____	Mnemonic Devices	_____	Work Study/Apprenticeships
__X__	Movement	__X__	Writing/Journals

Shapes

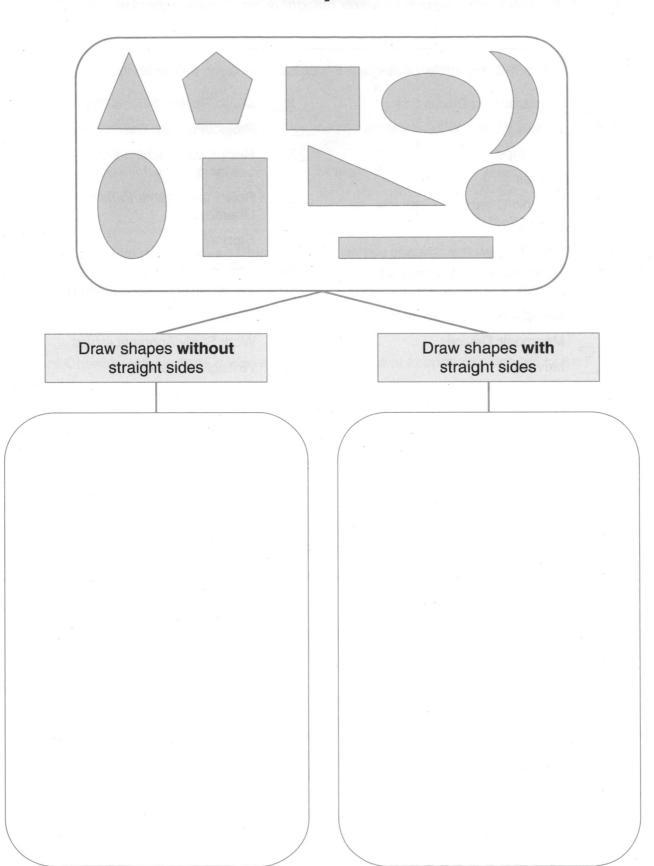

Draw shapes **without** straight sides

Draw shapes **with** straight sides

MATHEMATICS GRADES K–2 LESSON 5

Rectangles

Lesson Objective(s): *What do you want students to know and be able to do?*

Partition rectangles into equal shares or parts.

Assessment (Traditional/Authentic): *How will you know students have mastered essential learning?*

Have students assess the understanding of *Make Equal Parts* found in the plan.

Ways to Gain/Maintain Attention (Primacy): *How will you gain and maintain students' attention? Consider need, <u>novelty</u>, <u>meaning</u>, or emotion.*

Play the video and sing the song *1 Quarter*. https://www.youtube.com/watch?v=ryGvCNDoAR0

Content Chunks: *How will you divide and teach the content to engage students' brains?*

Lesson Segment 1: Fractions

Student's early understanding of fractions is usually based on the area model for partitioning the whole. Experiment with this model by partitioning rectangles into two and four equal parts. While working, words such as halves, fourths, and quarters arise. Additional math skills like geometric properties and spatial reasoning increase.

- **Activity 1: Color Tile Rectangles**

Have students use color tiles to build different sized rectangles showing halves and fourths. Which ones show halves and fourths? Discuss with your group. Roll a die and make a rectangle that size. Show one equal part by making it a different color than the rest of the rectangle.

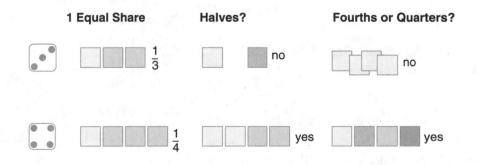

- ### Activity 2: Fraction Circle Creations

Have students use fraction circles to show halves and fourths and make up stories to go with the models.

- ### Activity 3: Geoboard Stories

Have students use geoboards to show halves and fourths. Describe the equal shares as types of food such as pizza or candy, etc.

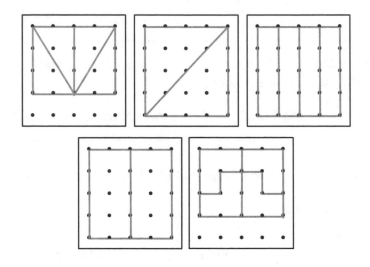

Brain-Compatible Strategies: *Which will you use to deliver content?*

__X__	Brainstorming/Discussion	__X__	Music/Rhythm/Rhyme/Rap
__X__	Drawing/Artwork	_____	Project/Problem-Based Learning
_____	Field Trips	__X__	Reciprocal Teaching/Cooperative Learning
_____	Games		
_____	Graphic Organizers/Semantic Maps/Word Webs	_____	Role Plays/Drama/Pantomimes/Charades
_____	Humor	__X__	Storytelling
__X__	Manipulatives/Experiments/Labs/Models	__X__	Technology
		_____	Visualization/Guided Imagery
_____	Metaphors/Analogies/Similes	__X__	Visuals
_____	Mnemonic Devices	_____	Work Study/Apprenticeships
_____	Movement	_____	Writing/Journals

Make Equal Parts

Use the spinner template, color tile paper, a pencil, and a paper clip. Spin and create a rectangle with that number of equal parts.

—COLOR TILE GRID PAPER—

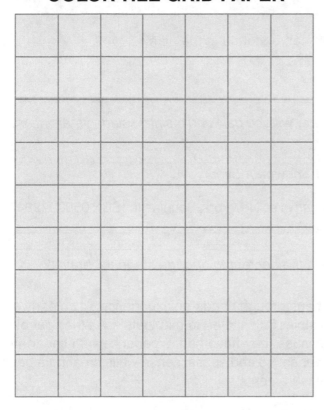

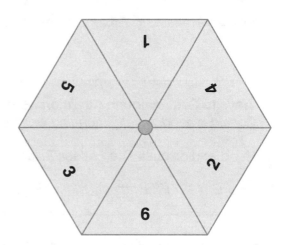

MATHEMATICS GRADES K–2 LESSON 6

Measurement (Nonstandard Units)

Lesson Objective(s): *What do you want students to know and be able to do?*

Estimate and measure length using nonstandard units.

Assessment (Traditional/Authentic): *How will you know students have mastered essential learning?*

Assess *Measuring Blocks. Measuring Blocks* can be found in the plan.

Ways to Gain/Maintain Attention (Primacy): *How will you gain and maintain students' attention? Consider need, _novelty_, _meaning_, or emotion.*

Read and discuss *The Fattest, Tallest, Biggest Snowman Ever.*

Ling, B. (1997). The fattest, tallest, biggest snowman ever. New York: Scholastic. ISBN 0590972847

Content Chunks: *How will you divide and teach the content to engage students' brains?*

Children make connections about measurement through hands-on experience. At an early age, nonstandard units are used because they are simpler for children to manipulate. As they get older, children are able to transition to using rulers because they have had experience with linear measurement. Estimating lengths incorporates number sense and spatial sense while creating a beginning foundation of reference points for linear measurements.

Lesson Segment 1: Measure Using Nonstandard Units

- **Activity 1: Miss Sven**

Tell students that Miss Sven's class is making pencil boxes. Have them determine how long the boxes should be. Have students find out how long their pencils are so Miss Sven can design the boxes.

- **Activity 2: Pattern Blocks**

Have students work in pairs to use two kinds of pattern blocks to measure how long their pencil is. Have them first make an estimate of how long. Have students write the estimate and draw the measurement with one pattern block. Caution students to line the end of the pencil with the end of the pattern block. Have them write the estimate and draw the measurement with the other pattern block. Discuss why the two measurements differ.

- **Activity 3: Rods and Cubes**

Have students work in groups to measure their pencil again, this time using Cuisenaire® Rods. First have students use a large shape, such as the yellow hexagon. Then have them use a smaller shape, such as the green triangle. Point out that their measurements differ depending on the size of the shape they use.

   Have students work in pairs to measure classroom objects with 2-cm Color Cubes. Students should make an estimate, measure the object, and compare the estimate to the actual measurement.

- **Activity 4: Measuring Blocks**

Complete the *Measuring Blocks* activity found in the plan.

Brain-Compatible Strategies: *Which will you use to deliver content?*

X	Brainstorming/Discussion	____	Music/Rhythm/Rhyme/Rap
X	Drawing/Artwork	**X**	Project/Problem-Based Learning
____	Field Trips	**X**	Reciprocal Teaching/Cooperative Learning
____	Games		
____	Graphic Organizers/Semantic Maps/Word Webs	____	Role Plays/Drama/Pantomimes/Charades
____	Humor	**X**	Storytelling
X	Manipulatives/Experiments/Labs/Models	____	Technology
		____	Visualization/Guided Imagery
____	Metaphors/Analogies/Similes	**X**	Visuals
____	Mnemonic Devices	____	Work Study/Apprenticeships
____	Movement	____	Writing/Journals

Measuring Blocks

Use pattern blocks to measure each length.

green
triangle

orange
square

blue parallelogram
(rhombus)

tan rhombus

red
trapezoid

yellow
hexagon

1.

2.

3. side of math book

4. pencil

5. your hand

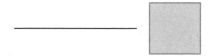

6. your shoe

Image source for scissores: https://pixabay.com/en/users/clker-free-vector-images-3736/

Image source for crayon: https://pixabay.com/en/users/loritheladybug7-2244945/

MATHEMATICS GRADES K–2 LESSON 7

Equal Shares

Lesson Objective(s): *What do you want students to know and be able to do?*

Create equal shares in composite shapes as halves.

Assessment (Traditional/Authentic): *How will you know students have mastered essential learning?*

Observe creation of composite shapes described as halves.

Ways to Gain/Maintain Attention (Primacy): *How will you gain and maintain students' attention? Consider need, novelty, meaning, or emotion.*

Have students consider what shapes can be made with tangram pieces.

Read Tompart, A. (1997). *Grandfather Tang's Story.* Oklahoma: Dragonfly Books. ISBN 0-517-88558-1

Content Chunks: *How will you divide and teach the content to engage students' brains?*

Lesson Segment 1: Create Equal Shares in Composite Shapes

- **Activity 1: Tangram Shapes**

Using tangram pieces, explore ways to compose new shapes. Start with two of the smallest triangles. Ask students, *What shapes can be made?* Circulate as students' work. Choose students to share these shapes:

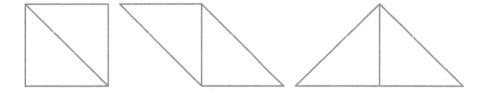

For each, ask students to name the shape, tell how many parts are in the shape, and determine if the parts are equal. Tell students that we can say these shapes are made of two equal shares, or parts, called halves. Note that the halves are the same size and same shape. Record discussion on paper or whiteboard and have students draw the shapes.
https://ideas.gstboces.org/programs/tangrams/printables.cfm

- **Activity 2:** *Give Me Half*

Either read or watch *Give Me Half.* http://www.youtube.com/watch?v=hVaxiJB6Fls. Murphy, S.J. (1996). *Give Me Half.* NY: Harper Collins. ISBN 9780060258740

● **Activity 3: Other Shapes?**

Ask students the following question: *Can other shapes be used to make halves?* Have them use a triangle and parallelogram to make a shape. Ask, *Are they halves?* Have them discuss with a partner or group. Help them determine that the shapes are different shapes and the sizes are not the same, therefore, they are not halves. Repeat with other shapes.

Brain-Compatible Strategies: *Which will you use to deliver content?*

X	Brainstorming/Discussion	____	Music/Rhythm/Rhyme/Rap
X	Drawing/Artwork	____	Project/Problem-Based Learning
____	Field Trips	**X**	Reciprocal Teaching/Cooperative Learning
____	Games		
____	Graphic Organizers/Semantic Maps/Word Webs	____	Role Plays/Drama/Pantomimes/Charades
____	Humor	**X**	Storytelling
X	Manipulatives/Experiments/Labs/Models	**X**	Technology
		____	Visualization/Guided Imagery
____	Metaphors/Analogies/Similes	____	Visuals
____	Mnemonic Devices	____	Work Study/Apprenticeships
____	Movement	____	Writing/Journals

MATHEMATICS GRADES K–2 LESSON 8

Composite Shapes

Lesson Objective(s): *What do you want students to know and be able to do?*

Create equal shares in composite shapes as thirds.

Assessment (Traditional/Authentic): *How will you know students have mastered essential learning?*

Observe creation of composite shapes described as thirds.

Ways to Gain/Maintain Attention (Primacy): *How will you gain and maintain students' attention? Consider need, novelty, <u>meaning</u>, or emotion.*

Ask students if they know what shapes can be made with pattern blocks.

Content Chunks: *How will you divide and teach the content to engage students' brains?*

Lesson Segment 1: Create Equal Shares in Pattern Block Halves

- **Activity 1: Pattern Block Halves**

Using pattern blocks, explore ways to compose new shapes. Start with a yellow hexagon. Placing it under a document camera works well. Ask students the following questions:

- What smaller polygon would cover the hexagon?
- Is there one that would cover half of it? Demonstrate that two trapezoids will cover the hexagon.
- How many trapezoids make a hexagon?
- Are they equal shares?
- Are they the same size and shape?
- How many halves are in the hexagon?

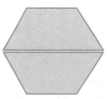

Repeat with a blue rhombus covering it with two green equilateral triangles.

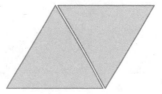

Lesson Segment 2: Create Equal Shares in Pattern Block Thirds

- **Activity 1: Pattern Block Thirds**

Tell students that we will try a different one. Use a red trapezoid. Again, using a document camera works well. Cover the trapezoid with three shapes. Ask students the following:

- What shape was able to cover it?
- Are the shapes equal in size?
- How many equal shares compose the trapezoid?

Repeat with the hexagon.

- **Activity 2: Colorful Creations**

Have students use the pattern block paper to create shapes with three equal pieces. Encourage creativity and allow students that need a challenge to color outside the lines. See *Pattern Block Paper* in the plan.

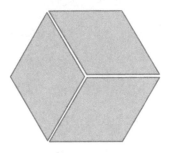

Brain-Compatible Strategies: *Which will you use to deliver content?*

__X__	Brainstorming/Discussion	_____	Music/Rhythm/Rhyme/Rap
__X__	Drawing/Artwork	_____	Project/Problem-Based Learning
_____	Field Trips	_____	Reciprocal Teaching/Cooperative Learning
_____	Games		
_____	Graphic Organizers/Semantic Maps/Word Webs	_____	Role Plays/Drama/Pantomimes/Charades
_____	Humor	_____	Storytelling
__X__	Manipulatives/Experiments/Labs/Models	_____	Technology
		_____	Visualization/Guided Imagery
_____	Metaphors/Analogies/Similes	__X__	Visuals
_____	Mnemonic Devices	_____	Work Study/Apprenticeships
_____	Movement	_____	Writing/Journals

Pattern Block Paper

MATHEMATICS GRADES K–2 LESSON 9

Addition

Lesson Objective(s): *What do you want students to know and be able to do?*

Use addition to design a beaded necklace with a budget of $1.

Assessment (Traditional/Authentic): *How will you know students have mastered essential learning?*

Students will make a necklace worth $1 or less.

Ways to Gain/Maintain Attention (Primacy): *How will you gain and maintain students' attention? Consider <u>need</u>, <u>novelty</u>, meaning, or emotion.*

Students need to add to make the necklace and should consider if making jewelry seems possible.

Content Chunks: *How will you divide and teach the content to engage students' brains?*

Lesson Segment 1: Using Addition for a Real-World Purpose

- **Activity 1: Jewelry Decision Time**

After brainstorming with their groups, have students choose a word or words for a necklace they will make. It could be a name of a friend, family member, or sports team. It can be one of their favorite things. Have students use the chart below to estimate if the name of the necklace will cost $1 or less.

A	B	C	D	E	F	G	H	I	J	K	L	M
10¢	11¢	12¢	13¢	10¢	11¢	12¢	13¢	10¢	11¢	12¢	13¢	10¢
N	O	P	Q	R	S	T	U	V	W	X	Y	Z
11¢	12¢	13¢	10¢	9¢	8¢	7¢	6¢	5¢	4¢	3¢	2¢	1¢

- **Activity 2: Actual Cost**

Provide cubes, sticky dots, and string and have students make the necklace if it is $1 or less. Have them write a letter on a sticky dot and attach it to each cube.

M y   d o g   R o v e r

10¢+2¢   + 13¢+12¢+12¢   +   9¢ +12¢+5¢+10¢+9¢ = 94¢

• Activity 3: Tell Me

Have students write a journal entry about why the name for the necklace was chosen and how estimation and addition were used to find the total cost. Have them draw a picture of their necklaces.

Brain-Compatible Strategies: *Which will you use to deliver content?*

__X__	Brainstorming/Discussion	_____	Music/Rhythm/Rhyme/Rap
__X__	Drawing/Artwork	__X__	Project/Problem-Based Learning
_____	Field Trips	__X__	Reciprocal Teaching/Cooperative Learning
_____	Games		
__X__	Graphic Organizers/Semantic Maps/Word Webs	_____	Role Plays/Drama/Pantomimes/ Charades
_____	Humor	_____	Storytelling
__X__	Manipulatives/Experiments/Labs/ Models	_____	Technology
		_____	Visualization/Guided Imagery
_____	Metaphors/Analogies/Similes	__X__	Visuals
_____	Mnemonic Devices	_____	Work Study/Apprenticeships
_____	Movement	__X__	Writing/Journals

MATHEMATICS GRADES 3–5 LESSON 1

Multiplication

Lesson Objective(s): *What do you want students to know and be able to do?*

Use the meaning of repeated addition to calculate multiplication problems.

Assessment (Traditional/Authentic): *How will you know students have mastered essential learning?*

Observe calculations of repeated addition as multiplication in *Pattern Block Spinner* game.

Ways to Gain/Maintain Attention (Primacy): *How will you gain and maintain students' attention? Consider need, <u>novelty</u>, <u>meaning</u>, or emotion.*

Play the video *Three is a Magic Number*. https://www.youtube.com/watch?v=aU4pyiB-kq0

Content Chunks: *How will you divide and teach the content to engage students' brains?*

Lesson Segment 1: Use Repeated Addition to Calculate Multiplication Problems

- **Activity 1: Multiplication**

Explain the concept to students with the following problem:

The total of equal groups of objects is called multiplication. The symbol ($\times$) means to multiply. The numbers multiplied are the factors. Point out that addition and subtraction are analogous. They are simply inverse operations, as are multiplication and division. Multiplication is a faster way of adding.

The class could order square pizzas. If 6 pizzas were ordered, how many sides would there be?

Find <u>6</u> pizzas of <u>4</u> sides

One way: $4 + 4 + 4 + 4 + 4 + 4 = 24$

Another way: Write a multiplication sentence.

$$\underbrace{6}_{\text{factor}} \overset{\text{\# of pizzas}}{\times} \underbrace{4}_{\text{factor}} \overset{\text{\# of sides}}{=} \underbrace{\underline{24}}_{\text{product}} \overset{\text{total}}{}$$

find the unknown or missing value

So <u>6</u> groups of <u>4</u> is <u>24</u>. The unknown is 24 sides.

● **Activity 2: Pattern Block Work Mats**

Set up four work mats or stations. At each of the four work mats or stations, there is one type of pattern block.

 Work mat 1: 6 green triangles

 Work mat 2: 5 blue rhombi

 Work mat 3: 4 yellow hexagons

 Work mat 4: 3 red trapezoids

 At each work mat, have students write a multiplication sentence for the pattern block sides in their journals.

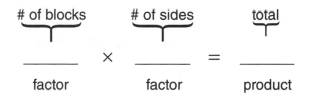

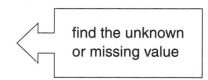
find the unknown or missing value

Example for 2 orange squares

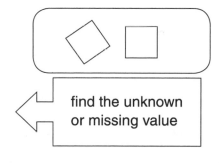
find the unknown or missing value

● **Activity 3: Pattern Block Spinning**

Have students use the pattern block spinner, a six-sided die, game markers, and a 100 chart according to the following directions: Spin the spinner, roll the die. Multiply those two together. Triangle (3) × die side (4) = 12. Move 12 spaces on the hundred chart. Alternate turns. The first one to 100 wins! *Pattern Block Spinner* and *100 Chart* are both in the plan.

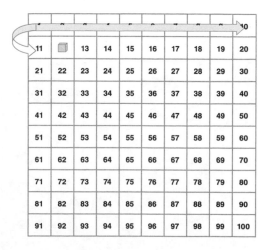

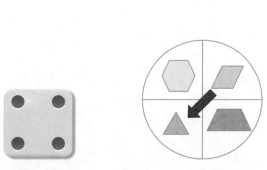

Image source for die: Pixabay.com/OpenClipart-Vectors

Brain-Compatible Strategies: *Which will you use to deliver content?*

X	Brainstorming/Discussion		Music/Rhythm/Rhyme/Rap
	Drawing/Artwork	**X**	Project/Problem-Based Learning
	Field Trips	**X**	Reciprocal Teaching/Cooperative Learning
X	Games		
	Graphic Organizers/Semantic Maps/Word Webs		Role Plays/Drama/Pantomimes/Charades
	Humor		Storytelling
X	Manipulatives/Experiments/Labs/Models	**X**	Technology
			Visualization/Guided Imagery
X	Metaphors/Analogies/Similes	**X**	Visuals
	Mnemonic Devices		Work Study/Apprenticeships
	Movement	**X**	Writing/Journals

100 Chart

1	2	3	4	5	6	7	8	9	10
11	12	13	14	15	16	17	18	19	20
21	22	23	24	25	26	27	28	29	30
31	32	33	34	35	36	37	38	39	40
41	42	43	44	45	46	47	48	49	50
51	52	53	54	55	56	57	58	59	60
61	62	63	64	65	66	67	68	69	70
71	72	73	74	75	76	77	78	79	80
81	82	83	84	85	86	87	88	89	90
91	92	93	94	95	96	97	98	99	100

Pattern Block Spinner

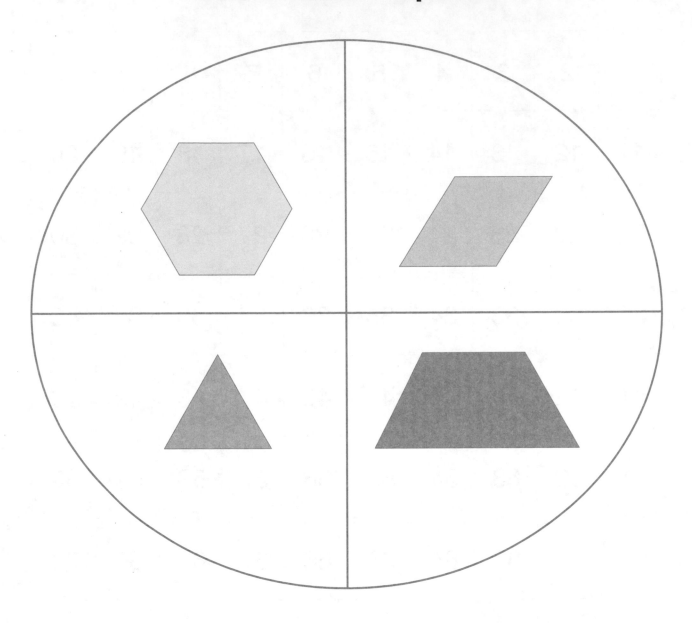

MATHEMATICS GRADES 3–5 LESSON 2

Partitioning Shapes

Lesson Objective(s): *What do you want students to know and be able to do?*

Partition shapes into parts with equal areas.

Assessment (Traditional/Authentic): *How will you know students have mastered essential learning?*

Assess students' demonstration of partitioning shapes in *Shapes in Shapes* found in the plan.

Ways to Gain/Maintain Attention (Primacy): *How will you gain and maintain students' attention? Consider need, novelty, meaning, or <u>emotion</u>.*

Ask students if both of these were pizzas you wanted to eat and you were very hungry, which would you rather eat?

Elicit that they are the same size, but discuss the reasoning for preferences.

Content Chunks: *How will you divide and teach the content to engage students' brains?*

Lesson Segment 1: Partition Shapes Into Parts With Equal Areas

- **Activity 1: Pattern Block Models**

A set of Pattern Blocks consists of blocks in six geometric, color-coded shapes, referred to as green triangles, orange squares, blue parallelograms, tan rhombuses, red trapezoids, and yellow hexagons.

    The relationships among the side measures and among the angle measures make it very easy to fit the blocks together to make tiling patterns that completely cover a flat surface.

Green triangle Orange square Blue parallelogram Tan rhombus Red trapezoid Yellow hexagon

    Have students use pattern blocks to create concrete models. Have them start with a hexagon. Using pattern blocks of the same shape, have them visualize how smaller shapes can fill the area. Ask what shape can fill the hexagon.

- **Activity 2: Triangles**

Starting with triangles, ask students how many it takes to fill a parallelogram/rhombus or trapezoid. Have them draw a representation of shapes the triangles made in their journals. Ask the following questions:

How many were used to make a trapezoid? 3. So 1 Δ is 1 of 3 equal parts.

That is a *unit fraction* written $\frac{1}{3}$

How many were used to make a parallelogram/rhombus? 2. So 1 Δ is 1 of 2 equal parts.

That is a *unit fraction* written $\frac{1}{2}$

- **Activity 3: Challenge**

Have students use a hexagon *and* a trapezoid. Ask them what fraction of the hexagon and trapezoid a trapezoid represents. What fraction of the hexagon and trapezoid does a triangle represent?

Complete *Shapes in Shapes* found in the plan.

Brain-Compatible Strategies: *Which will you use to deliver content?*

__X__	Brainstorming/Discussion	_____	Music/Rhythm/Rhyme/Rap
__X__	Drawing/Artwork	__X__	Project/Problem-Based Learning
_____	Field Trips	__X__	Reciprocal Teaching/Cooperative Learning
_____	Games		
_____	Graphic Organizers/Semantic Maps/Word Webs	_____	Role Plays/Drama/Pantomimes/Charades
_____	Humor	_____	Storytelling
__X__	Manipulatives/Experiments/Labs/Models	_____	Technology
		__X__	Visualization/Guided Imagery
_____	Metaphors/Analogies/Similes	__X__	Visuals
_____	Mnemonic Devices	_____	Work Study/Apprenticeships
_____	Movement	_____	Writing/Journals

Shapes in Shapes

Use pattern blocks of equal size to partition the shape. Determine the number of equal pieces. Write the fraction for one piece.

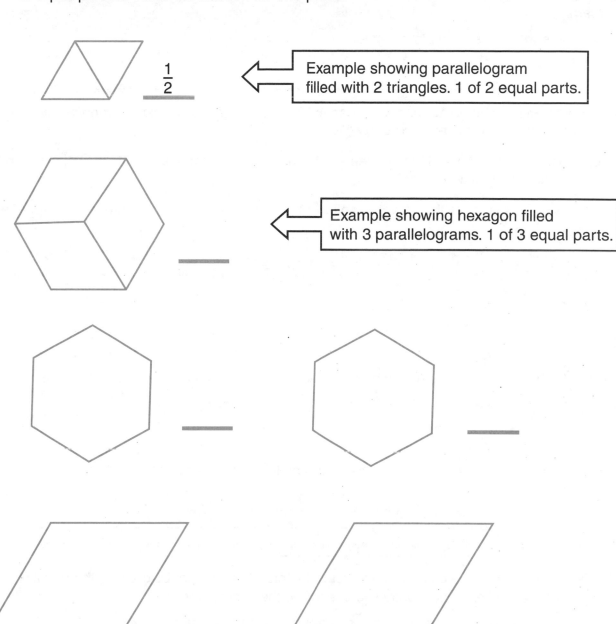

$\frac{1}{2}$ ____ ⟵ Example showing parallelogram filled with 2 triangles. 1 of 2 equal parts.

____ ⟵ Example showing hexagon filled with 3 parallelograms. 1 of 3 equal parts.

MATHEMATICS GRADES 3–5 LESSON 3

Line Plots

Lesson Objective(s): *What do you want students to know and be able to do?*

Create line plots from data sets.

Assessment (Traditional/Authentic): *How will you know students have mastered essential learning?*

Students will assess line plots created from sticky note data.

Ways to Gain/Maintain Attention (Primacy): *How will you gain and maintain students' attention? Consider need, novelty, meaning, or* <u>emotion</u>.

Inform the class that we will have a team color for the end-of-the-year event. The color with the most votes will be our team color.

Have students vote for their favorite color between red, orange, yellow, green, blue, purple, pink, or black.

red	orange	yellow	green	blue	purple	pink	black

Record the data in journals.

Content Chunks: *How will you divide and teach the content to engage students' brains?*

Lesson Segment 1: Create a Line Plot From Team Color Data

- **Activity 1: Line Plot**

Draw and label a line plot. Include all the values of the data. Give the line plot a title.

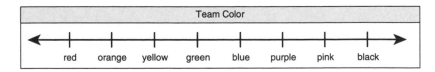

Draw an X above the color for each vote. Complete the line plot by drawing the remaining Xs. An X is placed above the horizontal line every time the data occurs.

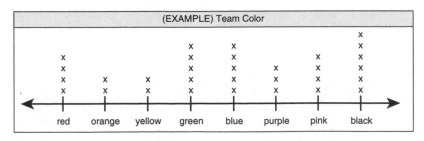

- **Activity 2: Line Plot Analysis**

Ask students the following questions:

1. What color was chosen most?

2. What color was chosen least?

3. Are any conclusions drawn from the data?

4. What's the difference between the highest number of Xs and the lowest number of Xs?

5. How is the line plot similar and different from graphs previously learned?

- **Activity 3: Original Line Plots**

Each student is given a sticky note and asked to write their initials on it to create data sets on the board. Examples: shoe size, number of letters in first name, favorite pizza topping, etc. Students record the data for each set in journals.

Students work in groups or partners to create their own line plot from any data set gathered with construction paper, markers, computer programs such as *Word,* etc. Each group or partner writes to analyze the line plot and interpret the data.

Brain-Compatible Strategies: *Which will you use to deliver content?*

X	Brainstorming/Discussion	___	Music/Rhythm/Rhyme/Rap
X	Drawing/Artwork	**X**	Project/Problem-Based Learning
___	Field Trips	**X**	Reciprocal Teaching/Cooperative Learning
___	Games		
X	Graphic Organizers/Semantic Maps/Word Webs	___	Role Plays/Drama/Pantomimes/Charades
___	Humor	___	Storytelling
X	Manipulatives/Experiments/Labs/Models	**X**	Technology
		___	Visualization/Guided Imagery
___	Metaphors/Analogies/Similes	**X**	Visuals
___	Mnemonic Devices	___	Work Study/Apprenticeships
X	Movement	**X**	Writing/Journals

MATHEMATICS GRADES 3–5 LESSON 4

Prime and Composite Numbers

Lesson Objective(s): *What do you want students to know and be able to do?*

Identify prime and composite numbers.

Assessment (Traditional/Authentic): *How will you know students have mastered essential learning?*

Observation of student's 100 chart in Lesson Segment 2, Activity 1.

Ways to Gain/Maintain Attention (Primacy): *How will you gain and maintain students' attention? Consider need, novelty meaning, or emotion.*

View *Prime Number's Song for Kids.* http://youtube.com/watch?v=f_Nc1mz7O0M

Content Chunks: *How will you divide and teach the content to engage students' brains?*

Lesson Segment 1: Identify Prime and Composite Numbers

- **Activity 1: Grouping Items**

Explain the following to students:

A *prime number* is a whole number that can only be divided evenly by 1 or itself.

A *composite number* is a whole number that can be divided evenly by at least one number other than 1 or itself. Place items on a table in groups. Example: 3 erasers, 12 pencils, 5 math books, 8 bottles of glue. Have students look at the items placed on the table. Ask can they be grouped equally in more than one way. Have volunteers group them.

- **Activity 2: Counters**

Have students place 7 counters on their desk. Ask what are equal ways to group the counters.

7 – ▢ ▢ ▢ ▢ ▢ ▢ ▢ 7 groups of 1.

7 ▢▢▢▢▢▢▢ 1 group of 7.

Tell students that these numbers are also known as the factors. 7: 1, 7

Have students place 18 counters on their desk. Ask what are equal ways to group the counters.

18 – ☐ ☐ ☐ ☐ ☐ ☐ ☐ ☐ ☐ ☐ ☐ ☐ ☐ ☐ ☐ ☐ ☐ ☐ 18 groups of 1

18 – ☐☐ ☐☐ ☐☐ ☐☐ ☐☐ ☐☐ ☐☐ ☐☐ ☐☐ 9 groups of 2

18 – ☐☐☐ ☐☐☐ ☐☐☐ ☐☐☐ ☐☐☐ ☐☐☐ 6 groups of 3

18 – ☐☐☐☐☐☐ ☐☐☐☐☐☐ ☐☐☐☐☐☐ 3 groups of 6

18 – ☐☐☐☐☐☐☐☐☐ ☐☐☐☐☐☐☐☐☐ 2 groups of 9

18 – ☐☐☐☐☐☐☐☐☐☐☐☐☐☐☐☐☐☐ 1 group of 18

These are also known as the factors. 18: 1, 2, 3, 6, 9, 18

- **Activity 3: Dice Game**

Have students use two six-sided dice to create two-digit numbers according to the following procedure: Use counters to group numbers equally as many ways as possible. Identify the two-digit number as prime or composite in a graphic organizer based on its factors or groups. Roll one die again and move that many spaces on the game board. The first player to the finish line wins the game.
   https://www.timvandevall.com/templates/blank-board-game-template/
   http://www.everythingesl.net/downloads/tchart.pdf

- **Activity 4: 100 Chart**

Have students use a 100 chart. Sieve of Eratosthenes gives a simple method of finding prime numbers. Demonstrate to students.

1. Cross 1 out.

2. Then starting from 2, circle 2 and then cross out every multiple of 2.

3. Then starting from 3, circle 3 and then cross out every multiple of 3.

4. Then starting from 5, circle 5 and then cross out every multiple of 5.

5. Then starting from 7, circle 7 and then cross out every multiple of 7.

6. Do the same with all the other primes that are known. The numbers that are crossed are not primes because they are multiples of other numbers. The numbers that are circled are primes. They have no divisors apart from themselves and one.

7. Make a list of the prime numbers in your journal.

https://www.montanamath.org/lessons/100chart.pdf

Brain-Compatible Strategies: *Which will you use to deliver content?*

__X__	Brainstorming/Discussion		__X__	Music/Rhythm/Rhyme/Rap
__X__	Drawing/Artwork		_____	Project/Problem-Based Learning
_____	Field Trips		__X__	Reciprocal Teaching/Cooperative Learning
__X__	Games			
__X__	Graphic Organizers/Semantic Maps/Word Webs		_____	Role Plays/Drama/Pantomimes/Charades
_____	Humor		_____	Storytelling
__X__	Manipulatives/Experiments/Labs/Models		__X__	Technology
			_____	Visualization/Guided Imagery
_____	Metaphors/Analogies/Similes		__X__	Visuals
_____	Mnemonic Devices		_____	Work Study/Apprenticeships
__X__	Movement		__X__	Writing/Journals

MATHEMATICS GRADES 3–5 LESSON 5

Perimeter

Lesson Objective(s): *What do you want students to know and be able to do?*

Calculate the perimeter of a rectangle and square.

Assessment (Traditional/Authentic): *How will you know students have mastered essential learning?*

Observation of student work during the lesson.

Ways to Gain/Maintain Attention (Primacy): *How will you gain and maintain students' attention? Consider need, novelty, meaning, or emotion.*

View and sing the *Perimeter Song* at https://www.youtube.com/watch?v–n5ULJ_kcFzl

Content Chunks: *How will you divide and teach the content to engage students' brains?*

Lesson Segment 1: Calculate the Perimeter of a Rectangle

- **Activity 1: Perimeter**

Perimeter of a rectangle is found by adding the side lengths or by using the formula $P = (2 \times l) + (2 \times w)$, where l is the length and w is the width. Demonstrate with the problem below.

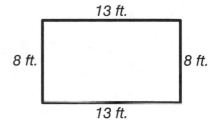

$P = (2 \times l) + (2 \times w)$ **write the formula**

$P = (2 \times 13) + (2 \times 8)$ **$l = 13$ ft. and w is 8 ft.**

$P = 26 + 16$ **multiply**

$P = 42$ ft.   **add**

The perimeter of the rectangle is 42 ft.

- **Activity 2: World Cup**

There were 32 soccer teams in the 2018 *FIFA World Cup*. Ask if any of the students play or watch soccer. How far is it all the way around the outside of the field?

　Have them work in partners to figure out the perimeter.

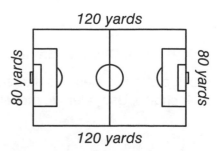

$P = (2 \times l) + (2 \times w)$ **write the formula**

$P = (2 \times 120) + (2 \times 80)$ **$l = 120$ yds. and w is 80 yds.**

$P = 240 + 160$ **multiply**

$P = 400$ yds.   **add**

The perimeter of the soccer field is 400 yds.

Lesson Segment 2: Calculate the Perimeter of a Square

- **Activity 1: Square**

A square is also a rectangle. And because it is, the same formula used above will work to find the perimeter. It also has its own formula. Demonstrate with the following problem:

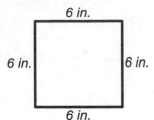

$P = 4 \times s$ ***write the formula***

$P = 4 \times (6)$ ***multiply 4 x s (6 in.)***

$P = 24$ in.

The perimeter of the square is 24 in.

- **Activity 2: Two Ways**

There is another way to find the perimeter of rectangles and squares. Ask students if they remember the song at the beginning of the lesson. (Add up the lengths around the outside.)

Using journals, have students construct arguments by comparing which formula they prefer: Adding all the sides of a square and multiplying by 4 and adding all the sides of a rectangle or by multiplying the lengths by 2 and multiplying the widths by 2 and adding them together.

- **Activity 3: What's Missing?**

Ask students what if we use the rectangle from earlier in the lesson? If we know the perimeter and 1 of the side lengths, the missing value can be found.

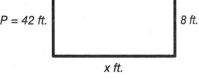

$P = 42$ ft.   ***start with the perimeter***

2 lengths of 8 = 16   ***identify the lengths known***

42 − 16 = 26   ***subtract the lengths known***

26 ÷ 2 = 13   ***divide by 2 for the other sides***

X = 13   ***missing value***

Have students work with a partner using the *work backwards* strategy to find the missing value.

1) Perimeter = 26   2) Perimeter = 24   3) Perimeter = 18

- **Activity 4: Chenille Stems**

Provide chenille stems to student pairs. Have them twist the ends together to make a rectangle of their choice. Use rulers to measure the perimeters of the rectangles.

Brain-Compatible Strategies: *Which will you use to deliver content?*

__X__	Brainstorming/Discussion	__X__	Music/Rhythm/Rhyme/Rap
__X__	Drawing/Artwork	__X__	Project/Problem-Based Learning
_____	Field Trips	__X__	Reciprocal Teaching/Cooperative Learning
_____	Games		
_____	Graphic Organizers/Semantic Maps/Word Webs	_____	Role Plays/Drama/Pantomimes/Charades
_____	Humor	_____	Storytelling
__X__	Manipulatives/Experiments/Labs/Models	__X__	Technology
		_____	Visualization/Guided Imagery
_____	Metaphors/Analogies/Similes	__X__	Visuals
_____	Mnemonic Devices	_____	Work Study/Apprenticeships
_____	Movement	__X__	Writing/Journals

MATHEMATICS GRADES 3–5 LESSON 6

Divide by Tens

Lesson Objective(s): *What do you want students to know and be able to do?*

Divide by multiples of ten.

Assessment (Traditional/Authentic): *How will you know students have mastered essential learning?*

Assessment of ticket-out-the-door.

Ways to Gain/Maintain Attention (Primacy): *How will you gain and maintain students' attention? Consider need, novelty, meaning, or <u>emotion</u>.*

Ask students to solve the following problem:

We can all go see the school musical if we can all fit. The school theater holds 220 people. Each row holds 20 seats. How many rows are there?

Content Chunks: *How will you divide and teach the content to engage students' brains?*

Lesson Segment 1: Divide by Multiples of Ten

- **Activity 1: Patterns**

Write 22 ÷ 2 and 220 ÷ 20 on the board. Point out that the numbers in the problems are similar except for the number of zeros they contain. Remind students about the patterns when multiplying

$22 \times 1 = 22$

$22 \times 10 = 220$

$22 \times 100 = 2200$

And so on.

- **Activity 2: Base Ten Blocks**

  Have students model 22 ÷ 2.

  Then divide the blocks into 2 equal groups.

  Record the answer. 22 ÷ 2 = 11

  Model 220 with base ten blocks.

  Use flats and rods to build 220.

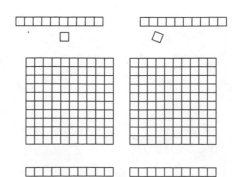

We need to divide 220 into 20 equal groups. Discuss with your group the best way to do this.

Have students walk to visually see the way groups suggest.

Lead them to exchange each flat for 10 rods and make 20 groups of 1 rod each.

Then exchange the remaining 2 rods for 20 units.

Place 1 unit with each rod.

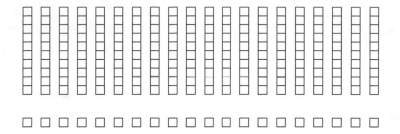

Discuss what similarities students notice.

Write 220 ÷ 20 = 11. Refer to the opening question about the theater that holds 220 people. There are 20 seats in each row. How many rows are there?

Our school has 10 classes with 18 students in each. Will the theater seat us all? Can we go?

Caution students to reread word problems to be sure they are answering correctly.

Also, it is a misconception to think that the last digits can be removed in all division problems, such as thinking that 121 ÷ 11 is the same as 12 ÷ 1.

● **Activity 3: Model It/Sketch**

Use base ten blocks in groups to model these problems.

24 ÷ 2 = _____	36 ÷ 4 = _____	18 ÷ 2 = _____
240 ÷ 20 = _____	360 ÷ 40 = _____	180 ÷ 20 = _____

Be sure that students realize this is math class, not art class and a quick sketch of the flats, rods, and units are the goal.

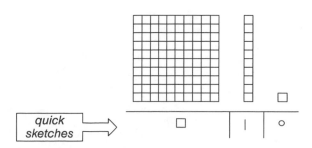

quick sketches

Continue until students understand the concept.

- **Activity 4: Ticket-out-the-door / Baseball cards**

Amanda wants to give away her baseball cards to her friends. She has 10 friends and 250 cards. How many will each friend get? Draw a quick sketch along with the problem.

Brain-Compatible Strategies: *Which will you use to deliver content?*

__X__	Brainstorming/Discussion	_____	Music/Rhythm/Rhyme/Rap
__X__	Drawing/Artwork	__X__	Project/Problem-Based Learning
_____	Field Trips	__X__	Reciprocal Teaching/Cooperative Learning
_____	Games		
_____	Graphic Organizers/Semantic Maps/Word Webs	_____	Role Plays/Drama/Pantomimes/Charades
_____	Humor	_____	Storytelling
__X__	Manipulatives/Experiments/Labs/Models	_____	Technology
		_____	Visualization/Guided Imagery
_____	Metaphors/Analogies/Similes	__X__	Visuals
_____	Mnemonic Devices	_____	Work Study/Apprenticeships
__X__	Movement	__X__	Writing/Journals

MATHEMATICS GRADES 3–5 LESSON 7

Multiplying Decimals

Lesson Objective(s): *What do you want students to know and be able to do?*

Multiply decimals by decimals.

Assessment (Traditional/Authentic): *How will you know students have mastered essential learning?*

Use traditional assessment found at https://tinyurl.com/y7jomdeg.

Ways to Gain/Maintain Attention (Primacy): *How will you gain and maintain students' attention? Consider need, novelty, meaning, or emotion.*

Read *Minnie's Diner* by Dayle Ann Dodds.

Dodds, D. A. (2007). *Minnie's diner.* Somerville, MA. Candlewick Press. 9780763617363

Content Chunks: *How will you divide and teach the content to engage students' brains?*

Lesson Segment 1: Multiply Decimals as Whole Numbers

Algorithms are sometimes easier to learn when they are described or shown in steps. Demonstrate to students as they think of multiplying decimals as a two-step process. The first step is to multiply the numbers as though there were no decimal points in the factors. The second step is to count the decimal places in the factors and then place the decimal point in the product.

- **Activity 1: Step One**

The first step in multiplying decimals is to multiply as with whole numbers. Ask students to get in groups of 3 or 4. Give each group 3 or 4 index cards, one card to each student. Have students write 1 digit on each card, 0-9. They may not repeat digits. Give each group one more index card. Have students draw a decimal point on the index card. Have students show the following:

1. *Organize your index cards to create a decimal that is greater than 1 and less than 10. Place the decimal point between appropriate digits.*

2. *Roll a 6-sided die and multiply your number by that number. Multiply as with whole numbers. Place the decimal point in the product.*

3. *Organize your index cards to create a different decimal. Place the decimal point between appropriate digits.* Repeat number 2.

After enough time to see a pattern, discuss where the decimal point continues to be in the product.

The conclusion is that the students need to count the number of decimal places in the factors, then place the decimal point so that the product has the same number of decimal places as the total number of decimal places in the factors.

● **Activity 2: Show It**

Have students use 10 × 10 grids found at https://tinyurl.com/y7z9dzwz to model the index card activity. In this version, start with a decimal less than 1. The group participates while one member colors the decimal in. Then the decimal is multiplied by 2 and the grid paper is passed to the next member to color an additional decimal and state the product.

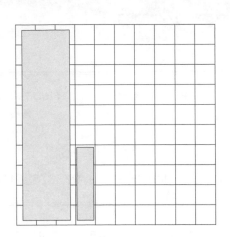 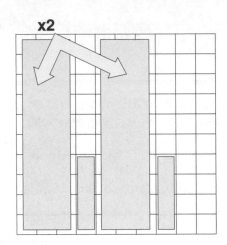

Lesson Segment 2: Multiply Decimals by Decimals

Have students move to multiplying a decimal by a decimal according to the following activity:

Consider the activities you completed with your group. The conclusion that held true for the opening activities holds true for the next.

[The conclusion is that the students need to count the number of decimal places in the factors, then place the decimal point so that the product has the same number of decimal places as the total number of decimal places in the factors.]

Let's start with 3.8 × 5.2.

What is an estimate for our answer in whole numbers? <u>20</u>

Now multiply and the product is 1976. Count the decimal places in the factors and move the decimal that many places from the right.

● **Activity 1: How Many Places?**

Write decimal by decimal multiplication problems on the board. Have pairs determine how many decimal places will be in the product. Gain speed in writing to formatively assess who might be struggling.

3.7 × 2.49 = <u>3</u> decimal places   6.15 × 4.72 = <u>4</u> decimal places   7.76 × 8 = <u>2</u> decimal places

● **Activity 2: Calculators Please**

Divide students into two teams, A and B. Distribute a write-on/wipe-off board to each team. Designate a student to be the referee and give him or her a calculator. Team A writes a decimal number between 0 and 9.99. Team B writes a decimal number between 0 and 9.99. Both teams multiply the decimal numbers together. The first team to solve the problem, write it on the write-on board, and then read it aloud receives a point after the referee checks for accuracy. Continue until both teams have 5 points.

● **Activity 3: Act It Out**

Give students a grocery store ad or a premade grocery list of produce and deli meat with prices included. Instruct student pairs to select what they will purchase. They draw each item as many times as they are purchasing on paper so the class can see the items. They must then multiply the price by the number of it they will purchase. One member of the pair shows the multiplication on the board.

$3 \times \$1.49 = \$4.47$ (or $3.7 \times \$1.49$, to make sure students relate it to real life like 3.7 lbs of tomatoes at $1.49).

$$3.7 \times \$1.49 = \$5.51 \ (5.513)$$

Brain-Compatible Strategies: *Which will you use to deliver content?*

__X__	Brainstorming/Discussion	_____	Music/Rhythm/Rhyme/Rap
__X__	Drawing/Artwork	__X__	Project/Problem-Based Learning
_____	Field Trips	__X__	Reciprocal Teaching/Cooperative Learning
__X__	Games		
__X__	Graphic Organizers/Semantic Maps/Word Webs	_____	Role Plays/Drama/Pantomimes/ Charades
_____	Humor	__X__	Storytelling
__X__	Manipulatives/Experiments/Labs/ Models	__X__	Technology
		_____	Visualization/Guided Imagery
__X__	Metaphors/Analogies/Similes	__X__	Visuals
_____	Mnemonic Devices	_____	Work Study/Apprenticeships
_____	Movement	_____	Writing/Journals

MATHEMATICS GRADES 3–5 LESSON 8

Volume of Prisms

Lesson Objective(s): *What do you want students to know and be able to do?*

Use volume of prisms knowledge to create a fish aquarium.

Assessment (Traditional/Authentic): *How will you know students have mastered essential learning?*

Assess volume calculations of an aquarium.

Ways to Gain/Maintain Attention (Primacy): *How will you gain and maintain students' attention? Consider need, _novelty_, meaning, or _emotion_.*

Ask if anyone has an aquarium. Have any of them visited the Georgia Aquarium, the largest aquarium in the world holding 6.3 million gallons of water? https://www.georgiaaquarium.org/

Content Chunks: *How will you divide and teach the content to engage students' brains?*

Lesson Segment 1: Understand Volume of Prisms by Creating an Aquarium

- **Activity 1: Aquariums**

Have students discuss any facts about aquariums. Tell them that it is recommended that for each inch of fish, an aquarium should have one gallon of water. One gallon of water is about 231 cubic inches.

Have each student create their own aquarium on paper and encourage them to make a model out of cardboard. Have them work with a group to make calculations regarding the volume of water needed.

- **Activity 2: How Much H_2O?**

Have students figure how much water would be needed for (10) 3" fish.

$$10 \times 3 = 30 \text{ gallons of } H_2O$$

$$30 \times 231 = 6{,}930 \text{ in}^3$$

Review how to calculate volume. Measure the length, width, and depth of an object in inches. To calculate the volume of a rectangular space, all you need to know are the values of its dimensions in inches. $v = l \times w \times h$.

Have students work in pairs to find the dimensions that could accommodate 30 gallons of water. Record work in journals. Discuss responses.

l	w	h	volume	size?
20"	30"	10"	6000 in³	too small
20"	36"	12"	8640 in³	too large
20"	36"	10"	7200 in³	very close

Point out the space does not need to be exact, but has to be large enough to hold the water. The size of each student's aquarium 3 will depend on the size and amount of fish put in it.

- **Activity 3: Tropical Fish**

Have students use the internet or the tropical fish chart to find the fish preferred in the aquarium.

Tropical Fish Size	
Fish Name	**Length (in.)**
Clownfish	3
Marble angelfish	6
Cherry barb	1.5
Neon dottyback	4
Goldfish	5

Record in a journal:

- What do the fish look like?
- What size fish was chosen?
- How many of each was chosen?

- **Activity 4: How Many Gallons?**

Have students use the list of fish and determine the lengths. Have them determine how many gallons of water the aquarium needs and determine how many cubic inches the aquarium tank needs to be.

- How many inches of fish were chosen?
- How many gallons of water are needed?
- How many cubic inches are needed?

- **Activity 5: Dimensions**

Have students decide on the dimensions of the tank. Have them write the volume and dimensions of the tank and think about the dimensions.

- Is it too large?
- Is it reasonable?
- Is adjusting the amount of fish or the size needed?

- **Activity 6: Report**

Have students write a journal report about the aquarium created and be sure to include the estimates that helped select the size. What choices were available in selecting the size?

- **Activity 7: Work Backwards (Optional)**

Have students create a second aquarium of a certain size and choose the kinds of fish to put in the tank. Discuss which strategy was preferred.

Brain-Compatible Strategies: *Which will you use to deliver content?*

__X__	Brainstorming/Discussion	_____	Music/Rhythm/Rhyme/Rap
__X__	Drawing/Artwork	__X__	Project/Problem-Based Learning
_____	Field Trips	__X__	Reciprocal Teaching/Cooperative Learning
_____	Games		
__X__	Graphic Organizers/Semantic Maps/Word Webs	_____	Role Plays/Drama/Pantomimes/Charades
_____	Humor	_____	Storytelling
_____	Manipulatives/Experiments/Labs/Models	__X__	Technology
		_____	Visualization/Guided Imagery
_____	Metaphors/Analogies/Similes	__X__	Visuals
_____	Mnemonic Devices	_____	Work Study/Apprenticeships
_____	Movement	__X__	Writing/Journals

MATHEMATICS GRADES 3–5 LESSON 9

Measurement

Lesson Objective(s): *What do you want students to know and be able to do?*

Use measurement concepts to create a game room floor plan.

Assessment (Traditional/Authentic): *How will you know students have mastered essential learning?*

Students will assess the measurement calculations in the game room floor plan.

Ways to Gain/Maintain Attention (Primacy): *How will you gain and maintain students' attention? Consider need, novelty, meaning, or emotion.*

Read *How Big is a Foot?* Myller, R. (1991) *How Big is a Foot?* Yearling. ISBN 0440404959

Content Chunks: *How will you divide and teach the content to engage students' brains?*

Lesson Segment 1: Use Measurement Concepts to Create a Game Room Floor

Have students visualize and talk about a time when they rearranged their bedrooms, another room in their houses, or their classroom. Have students share the reasoning for the rearrangement. They may use similar reasoning in this lesson as they use mixed numbers to figure out the furniture arrangement for a new game room.

Ask students if they had to choose a game room design between these two, would they pick option 1 or option 2.

Option 1

Option 2

- **Activity 1: Scale It**

Have students think about a model of the game room and the furniture in it using a scale of 1 foot = 1 inch. Have student practice changing the unit of feet to inches. For a 6 ½ foot table, they would use the measurement as 6 ½ inches. If a piece of furniture was 4 ½ feet by 4 feet, the model will be 4 ½ inches by 4 inches.

- **Activity 2: Design It**

Have students design the game room keeping in mind the need for adding dimensions together and comparing it with the wall-space dimensions. The need for subtracting dimensions is also a consideration. The furniture choices and specific directions are included in the *Make a Game Room Floor Plan*. Encourage students to use their journals to record their work using number sentences and inequality symbols. Let them know the design projects will be displayed.

- **Activity 3: Create It**

Hand out the *Make a Game Room Floor Plan*. The *Make a Game Room Floor Plan* is in the plan.

Brain-Compatible Strategies: *Which will you use to deliver content?*

X	Brainstorming/Discussion	____	Music/Rhythm/Rhyme/Rap
X	Drawing/Artwork	**X**	Project/Problem-Based Learning
____	Field Trips	**X**	Reciprocal Teaching/Cooperative Learning
____	Games		
____	Graphic Organizers/Semantic Maps/Word Webs	____	Role Plays/Drama/Pantomimes/Charades
____	Humor	**X**	Storytelling
X	Manipulatives/Experiments/Labs/Models	____	Technology
		X	Visualization/Guided Imagery
____	Metaphors/Analogies/Similes	**X**	Visuals
____	Mnemonic Devices	____	Work Study/Apprenticeships
____	Movement	**X**	Writing/Journals

Make a Game Room Floor Plan

Imagine that you are moving into a new home and you have a game room of the shape and size shown below. You want to plan the arrangement of your game room furniture before moving in. Use your knowledge of mixed numbers and improper fractions to make a plan.

1. Decide how you would place the furniture.

   - Make a model of the room and the furniture where 1 foot equals 1 inch.

You will use your model to try different arrangements.

   - How will you use addition and subtraction number sentences and comparisons to show if the arrangements fit?

2. Make a sketch of your chosen arrangement.

   - Identify each item and its dimensions.
   - Be sure you do not block the door or the closet.

3. Write a report about your project. Include the following:

   - What number sentences did you use?
   - How did you use comparing and ordering to find an arrangement that would work?
   - Include the sketch of your favorite arrangement.
   - Finalize your plan by coloring and decorating it.

Game Room Furniture	
TV	$5\frac{1}{2}$ feet long $3\frac{1}{2}$ feet wide
Refrigerator	$2\frac{1}{2}$ feet wide $2\frac{1}{2}$ feet deep
Gaming Table	4 feet long 4 feet wide
Recliner	$5\frac{1}{2}$ feet long $2\frac{1}{2}$ feet wide
Rug	4 feet long $2\frac{1}{2}$ feet wide

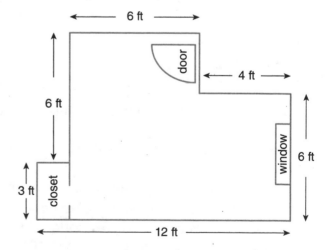

MATHEMATICS GRADES 3–5 LESSON 10

Map Locations

Lesson Objective(s): *What do you want students to know and be able to do?*

Represent map locations.

Assessment (Traditional/Authentic): *How will you know students have mastered essential learning?*

Students will assess *Map Locations on a Coordinate Plane* found in the plan.

Ways to Gain/Maintain Attention (Primacy): *How will you gain and maintain students' attention? Consider need, novelty, meaning, or emotion.*

Ask students how they find their way around places. Do they get lost at the mall? Why or why not?

Content Chunks: *How will you divide and teach the content to engage students' brains?*

Lesson Segment 1: Represent Map Locations

- **Activity 1: Treasure Map**

Read *Treasure Map.* Murphy, S.J. (2004). *Treasure map*. New York: Harper Collins. ISBN 0064467384.

- **Activity 2: Marcia's Map**

Have students use grid paper to represent locations on a map.

With a 0.5" grid paper, have students represent points of interest.

Begin with all students labeling *school* at (0,0).

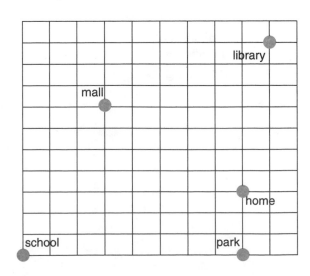

- From her school, Marcia walks 8 blocks east to the park. Move 8 blocks right.
- Then she walks 10 blocks north and turns east 1 block to the library. Move 10 blocks up and 1 block right.
- Her friend then drives her 6 blocks west and turns 3 blocks south to the mall. Move 6 blocks left and 3 blocks down.
- Marcia lives 3 blocks north of the park. Move up 3 blocks.

- ### Activity 3: Create and Rotate

Have students use grid paper to represent five locations of their choice. Have them ask three questions that classmates will answer about how to get from one location to another. When students have completed their map, have them rotate and answer one question. When the teacher signals, they move to another classmate's map and answer the second question. And when the teacher sounds a final signal, they move to another classmate's map and answer the last question remaining.

Lesson Segment 2: Represent Coordinates

- ### Activity 1: Coordinates

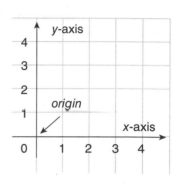

Help students become more familiar with the coordinate plane by using an ordered pair of numbers, called its coordinates. Understand that the first number indicates how far to travel right from the origin in the direction of one axis (x-axis and x-coordinate), and the second number indicates how far to travel up in the direction of the second axis (y-axis and y-coordinate).

- ### Activity 2: Mall

We will graph points in the first quadrant of the coordinate plane, and interpret coordinate points.

Using the grid paper, have students label the x-coordinates along the x-axis and y-coordinates along the y-axis. Since we are working in quadrant I with positive numbers only, remind them that the x-coordinate tells us how far to move right on the x-axis from the origin (0,0). The y-coordinate tells us how far to move up on the y-axis.

Have students label the origin as *entrance*.

- Have students write the coordinate pair and mall space name for the location stated.
- The furniture store is 3 units east and then 6 units north.
- The shoe store is 4 units east and then 2 units north.
- The toy store is 9 units to the east and then 6 units north.
- The card store is 1 unit east and 4 units north.

Have students write the coordinate pair for the location stated.

Label (5,5) as the food court.   Label (2,8) as the coffee shop.

Label (10,3) as the security office.   Label (8,9) as the hair salon.

Note: For students finding it difficult to locate the coordinate; remind them to use the phrase *crawl first and then climb.*

Many more practice activities with coordinates can be found at https://tinyurl.com/y7yocww7.

- ### Activity 3: *Treasure Hunt*

Play *Treasure Hunt* at https://www.education.com/game/treasure-map-graphing/.

Brain-Compatible Strategies: *Which will you use to deliver content?*

__X__	Brainstorming/Discussion	_____	Music/Rhythm/Rhyme/Rap
__X__	Drawing/Artwork	__X__	Project/Problem-Based Learning
_____	Field Trips	__X__	Reciprocal Teaching/Cooperative Learning
__X__	Games		
_____	Graphic Organizers/Semantic Maps/Word Webs	_____	Role Plays/Drama/Pantomimes/Charades
_____	Humor	__X__	Storytelling
__X__	Manipulatives/Experiments/Labs/Models	__X__	Technology
		_____	Visualization/Guided Imagery
_____	Metaphors/Analogies/Similes	__X__	Visuals
_____	Mnemonic Devices	_____	Work Study/Apprenticeships
__X__	Movement	_____	Writing/Journals

Map Locations on a Coordinate Plane

Dr. Graham has collected data about her patient's growth. The points show the age and the number of inches grown since each person's last birthday.

Dillon wanted to make a map of his neighborhood, so he graphed the locations of several places he visits.

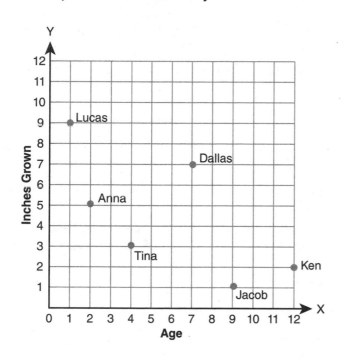

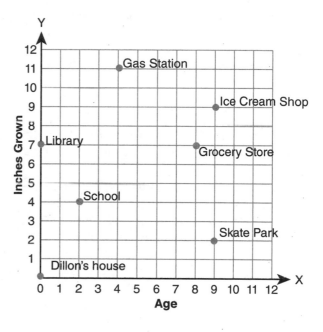

1. Who has grown the most since their last birthday?

   _____

2. What is the total number of inches grown?

   _____

3. How many more inches did Dallas grow than Ken?

   _____

1. There is a video game store halfway between the library and the grocery store. At what coordinates should Dillon graph the video game store?

   _____

2. What is the farthest place from Dillon's house?

   _____

MATHEMATICS GRADES 6–8 LESSON 1

Order of Operations

Lesson Objective(s): *What do you want students to know and be able to do?*

Find the value of expressions using order of operations.

Assessment (Traditional/Authentic): *How will you know students have mastered essential learning?*

Assess understanding of expressions written and solved in cooperative learning groups.

Ways to Gain/Maintain Attention (Primacy): *How will you gain and maintain students' attention? Consider need, novelty, meaning, or emotion.*

Ask what's the answer to $6 + 2 \times 5$? Is it 40 or 16?

Mathematicians have agreed on an order of operations so the one answer is always achieved. This mnemonic device/sentence is often used to help remember the order of operations.

PEMDAS

(**P**arentheses, **E**xponents, **M**ultiplication, **D**ivision, **A**ddition, **S**ubtraction)

Please   **E**xcuse   **M**y **D**ear   **A**unt **S**ally

Complete the work in the parentheses first, then the exponents, then all multiplication and division from left to right in the order they appear, and then all the addition and subtraction from left to right in the order they appear.

Content Chunks: *How will you divide and teach the content to engage students' brains?*

Lesson Segment 1: Comprehend the Order of Operations

- **Activity 1: Order of Operations**

A numerical expression like $3 \times 2 + 4 \times 4$ is a combination of numbers and operations with only one answer.

The order of operations tells which operation to perform first so there is only one value for an expression.

Ask students the following questions regarding: $10 - 2 + 8$:

- Does the expression contain grouping symbols? No
- Does the expression contain exponents? No
- Does the expression contain multiplication or division? No
- Does the expression contain addition or subtraction? Yes
- From what order is the expression evaluated? From left to right

$$10 - 2 + 8$$
$$10 - 2 + 8 = 8 + 8$$
$$= 16$$

Have them try another: $30 - 11 + 9$
Then give them this one: $4 + 3 \times 5$

- Does the expression contain grouping symbols? No
- Does the expression contain exponents? No
- Does the expression contain multiplication or division? If so, which one? Yes, multiplication
- What is evaluated first? 3×5
- What operation is next? Add 4 to the product.

$$4 + 3 \times 5$$
$$4 + 3 \times 5 = 4 + 15$$
$$= 19$$

Give them another: $6 + 10 \times 36$

Lesson Segment 2: Comprehend Parentheses and Exponents

Expressions inside grouping symbols, such as parentheses, are simplified first. Follow the order of operations inside parentheses. For example in the expression $8 + (4^2 + 5)$, find the value of the power, 4^2, before adding the expression inside the parentheses.

- **Activity 1: Solve It**

Have students solve the following:

$20 \div 4 + 16 \times (9 - 6)$

What is evaluated first? $(9 - 6)$

What is evaluated next? $20 \div 4$

Multiply 16 by 3 or add 5 to 16? Multiply 16 by 3.

What is the last step? Add 5 to 48

$$20 \div 4 + 16 \times (9 - 6)$$
$$20 \div 4 + 16 \times (9 - 6) = 20 \div 4 + 16 \times 3$$
$$= 5 + 16 \times 3$$
$$= 5 + 48$$
$$= 53$$

Have them try another: $5 + (8^2 - 2) \times 2$

What is evaluated first? 8^2

What is evaluated next? Subtract 2 from 64

Add 5 to 62 or multiply 62 by 2? Multiply 62 by 2.

What is the last step? Add 5 to 124.

$$5 + (8^2 - 2) \times 2$$
$$5 + (8^2 - 2) \times 2 = 5 + (64 - 2) \times 2$$
$$= 5 + 62 \times 2$$
$$= 5 + 124$$
$$= 129$$

- **Activity 2: Act It Out**

Using the following chart, have students work in groups to create stories to act out. Record each in journals.

Item	Cost
candy	$2.00
chips	$1.00
drinks	$3.00
pizza	$5.00

Example: For a group with three female students choosing drinks and one male student choosing chips:

Cost of 3 drinks	+	cost of 1 chips
3 × $3	+	1 × $1
$9	+	$1
	$10	

Brain-Compatible Strategies: *Which will you use to deliver content?*

_____	Brainstorming/Discussion	_____	Music/Rhythm/Rhyme/Rap
__X__	Drawing/Artwork	__X__	Project/Problem-Based Learning
_____	Field Trips	__X__	Reciprocal Teaching/Cooperative Learning
_____	Games		
_____	Graphic Organizers/Semantic Maps/Word Webs	__X__	Role Plays/Drama/Pantomimes/Charades
_____	Humor	__X__	Storytelling
_____	Manipulatives/Experiments/Labs/Models	_____	Technology
		_____	Visualization/Guided Imagery
_____	Metaphors/Analogies/Similes	__X__	Visuals
__X__	Mnemonic Devices	_____	Work Study/Apprenticeships
__X__	Movement	__X__	Writing/Journals

MATHEMATICS GRADES 6–8 LESSON 2

Order of Operations

Lesson Objective(s): *What do you want students to know and be able to do?*

Write and solve expressions using order of operations.

Assessment (Traditional/Authentic): *How will you know students have mastered essential learning?*

Assess understanding of expressions written and solved in cooperative learning groups.

Ways to Gain/Maintain Attention (Primacy): *How will you gain and maintain students' attention? Consider need, novelty, meaning, or emotion.*

Review numerical and variable expressions through video. http://youtube.com/watch?v=rpuS-s1o3zl

Content Chunks: *How will you divide and teach the content to engage students' brains?*

Lesson Segment 1: Solve Expressions Using Order of Operations

- **Activity 1: *PEMDAS* Review**

Discuss any thoughts from the opening video. Review the order of operations and the mnemonic device *PEMDAS*.

P	E	M D	A S
Please	Excuse	My Dear	Aunt Sally

- **Activity 2: Family Grocery List**

In pairs, have students create a chart from shared grocery ads via the newspaper, circulars, or searching local ads on the internet. Coupons must be used at least once, but be sure to match the coupon with items desired to purchase. Have them create a grocery list for a family. Round each item's cost to the nearest dollar. Spend as close to $200.00 without going over. Remind them to purchase items for the family and home and record each in journals.

Example:

Item	Cost
Chicken (per lb.)	$5.00
Bottled water (per bottle)	$2.00
Avocadoes (per bag of 6)	$3.00
Paper towels (2-pack)	$4.00
BBQ potato chips (9 oz.)	$6.00

● **Activity 3: Writing Expressions**

Have students write expressions for items on the list and have classmates use order of operations to find the value of each expression. Expressions could be made for an entire day's meals, cost of household items for the week, etc.

1 family dinner

4 × (Cost of 1 lb. of Chicken + cost of bottled water) + cost of 1 chips

$4 \times (5 + 2) + 6 =$

$$= 4 \times 7 + 6$$
$$= 28 + 6$$
$$= 34$$

Brain-Compatible Strategies: *Which will you use to deliver content?*

_____	Brainstorming/Discussion	_____	Music/Rhythm/Rhyme/Rap
__X__	Drawing/Artwork	_____	Project/Problem-Based Learning
_____	Field Trips	__X__	Reciprocal Teaching/Cooperative Learning
_____	Games		
_____	Graphic Organizers/Semantic Maps/Word Webs	_____	Role Plays/Drama/Pantomimes/Charades
_____	Humor	_____	Storytelling
_____	Manipulatives/Experiments/Labs/Models	__X__	Technology
		_____	Visualization/Guided Imagery
_____	Metaphors/Analogies/Similes	__X__	Visuals
__X__	Mnemonic Devices	_____	Work Study/Apprenticeships
_____	Movement	__X__	Writing/Journals

MATHEMATICS GRADES 6–8 LESSON 3

Order of Operations (Errors)

Lesson Objective(s): *What do you want students to know and be able to do?*

Find errors in expressions using order of operations.

Assessment (Traditional/Authentic): *How will you know students have mastered essential learning?*

Assess understanding of expressions in *I've Got It*

Ways to Gain/Maintain Attention (Primacy): *How will you gain and maintain students' attention? Consider need, novelty, meaning, or emotion.*

Sing along with the catchy tune about order of operations. http://youtube.com/watch?v=ZzeDWFhYv3E

Content Chunks: *How will you divide and teach the content to engage students' brains?*

Lesson Segment 1: Find Errors in Expressions Using Order of Operations

Using order of operations in problem-solving situations to identify errors will allow students to apply the skills learned.

- **Activity 1: What's Wrong?**

Have students determine the errors in the following problems:

Alec is finding the value of $9 - 6 + 2$.

$$9 - 6 + 2 =$$
$$= 9 - 8$$
$$= 1$$

Alec should have worked from left to right.

$$9 - 6 + 2 =$$
$$= 3 + 2$$
$$= 5$$

Arielle has several pitchers to hold juice. She has two that hold 32 ounces and three pitchers that hold 24 ounces. How much juice can the pitchers hold?

Arielle is finding the value for juice.

$$32 \times 2 + 24 \times 3 =$$
$$= 64 + 24 \times 3$$
$$= 88 \times 3$$
$$= 264$$

Arielle should have multiplied 24 and 3 then added $64 + 72$

$$32 \times 2 + 24 \times 3 =$$
$$= 64 + 24 \times 3$$
$$= 64 + 72$$
$$= 136$$

- **Activity 2: One's Wrong**

Denny is 2 years younger than Josh and Josh is 6 years older than Stephanie, who is 12 years old. Which expression is used to find Denny's age?

12 – 6 + 2

12 + 6 – 2 ⟵ **12 + 6 – 2**

Kate wants to buy four stickers and three notepads. Which expression is used to find the cost of four stickers and three notepads?

Stickers	$ .50
Notepads	$ 2.25

4($ .50) + 3($2.25) ⟵ **4($ .50) + 3($2.25)**

4($ .50) × 3($2.25)

- **Activity 3: *I've Got It***

Match the expression to the visual using the chart. Write a possible error that is commonly made.

(4 × 4) + (3 × 2)   **(2 × 3) + (4 × 4)**

2 (2 + 4 + 1 + 2)   **(3 × 2) + 1 + (2 × 2)**

Baseball Concession Stand	
Item	Price ($)
Hot dog	4
Popcorn	2
Soda	3
Water	2
Candy	1

Visual	Expression/Error
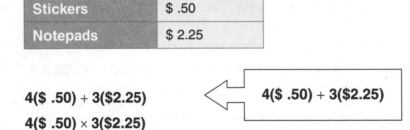	Expression
	Possible error
	Expression
	Possible error

Visual	Expression/Error	
	Expression	
	Possible error	
	Expression	
	Possible error	

Sources:
Candy and water bottle images: Pixabay.com/clker-free-vector-images-3736
Hot dog, popcorn, and soda images: Pixabay.com/ openclipart-vectors-30363/

Brain-Compatible Strategies: *Which will you use to deliver content?*

__X__	Brainstorming/Discussion	__X__	Music/Rhythm/Rhyme/Rap
__X__	Drawing/Artwork	__X__	Project/Problem-Based Learning
____	Field Trips	____	Reciprocal Teaching/Cooperative Learning
____	Games		
__X__	Graphic Organizers/Semantic Maps/Word Webs	____	Role Plays/Drama/Pantomimes/Charades
____	Humor	____	Storytelling
____	Manipulatives/Experiments/Labs/Models	__X__	Technology
		____	Visualization/Guided Imagery
____	Metaphors/Analogies/Similes	__X__	Visuals
__X__	Mnemonic Devices	____	Work Study/Apprenticeships
____	Movement	__X__	Writing/Journals

MATHEMATICS GRADES 6–8 LESSON 4

Division of Fractions

> **Lesson Objective(s):** *What do you want students to know and be able to do?*
>
> Apply and extend previous understanding of multiplication and division of fractions to divide integers.
>
> **Assessment (Traditional/Authentic):** *How will you know students have mastered essential learning?*
>
> Evaluate the answers of each *Find the Value* in the lesson.

Ways to Gain/Maintain Attention (Primacy): *How will you gain and maintain students' attention? Consider need, novelty, meaning, or emotion.*

A great white shark has 3,000 teeth. It gains and loses teeth often. What if a great white was to lose 4 teeth each day for 7 days? It would have lost 28 teeth. How could we show this situation with division? $(-28) \div (-4) = 7$ and $(-28) \div 7 = -4$.

Content Chunks: *How will you divide and teach the content to engage students' brains?*

Lesson Segment 1: Divide Integers With Different Signs

- **Activity 1: Different Signs**

In the great white shark opening problem, have students use red and yellow counters or color chip counters (virtually) to demonstrate solving it.

   $(-28) \div 7 = -4$. Show 28 negative (red) counters. Divide them into 7 groups (days). There are 4 negative counters (days) in each group.

   Color Chip counters. http://nlvm.usu.edu/en/nav/frames_asid_162_g_3_t_1.html?from=grade_g_3.html

   Point out the analogous relationships. Division is the inverse operation of multiplication. Division equations can be rewritten as multiplication equations. The rules for dividing integers are related to the rules for multiplying integers. In dividing integers, if different signs are used the quotient is negative. If the same signs are used, the quotient is positive. Work these problems together with students.

   Find $68 \div (-4) = ?$ *–17*

   Ask the following questions:

- Do the dividend and the divisor have the same sign? no
- Will the quotient be positive or negative? negative

- Find $\dfrac{-110}{11} = ?$ -10
- Do the dividend and the divisor have the same sign? no
- Will the quotient be positive or negative? negative

Activity 2: Divide Integers

Have students complete the graphic organizer *Dividing Integers* found at the end of this plan. Have them find the value of the missing number with a partner. Refer to the graphic organizer.

$-36 \div 9 = ?$ -4 $-56 \div -8 = ?$ 7 $\dfrac{-21}{3} = ?$ -7

Find the solution. A recent newspaper headline read that the total value of stocks held by Italian financial institutions dropped from \$881 billion to \$800 billion in six weeks. What was the average change in value per week? (Ask the same questions as were asked earlier.) *−13.5 billion dollars*

Lesson Segment 2: Divide integers With Same Signs

Activity 1: Same Signs

Tell students that in dividing integers if different signs are used, the quotient is negative. If the same signs are used, the quotient is positive. Have them work the following problems with a partner.

Find $-18 \div (-3) = ?$ 6

- Do the dividend and the divisor have the same sign? yes
- Will the quotient be positive or negative? positive

Find $\dfrac{-42}{-6} = ?$ 7

- Do the dividend and the divisor have the same sign? yes
- Will the quotient be positive or negative? positive

Activity 2: Find the Value

Have students find the value of the missing number. Refer them to the graphic organizer.

$-12 \div -4 = ?$ 3 $-18 \div -2 = ?$ 9 $-49 \div -7 = ?$ 7

Over the past seven days, Mr. Jones found the temperature had increased by 21°. Find the average change in temperature each day. $21 \div 7 = 3$

Research temperature changes on the internet. Discuss the changes and create equations to tell the story in the relationship of the changes in temperatures.

Examples

In January the average temperature was 55°. Two months later, the average temperature was 65°. The temperature had increased by 10°. Find the average change in temperature each month.

$$10 \div 2 = 5°$$

In July the average temperature was 85°. Four months later, the average temperature was 65°. The temperature had decreased by 20°. Find the average change in temperature each month.

$$-20 \div 4 = -5°$$

Brain-Compatible Strategies: *Which will you use to deliver content?*

X	Brainstorming/Discussion	_____	Music/Rhythm/Rhyme/Rap
_____	Drawing/Artwork	**X**	Project/Problem-Based Learning
_____	Field Trips	**X**	Reciprocal Teaching/Cooperative Learning
_____	Games		
X	Graphic Organizers/Semantic Maps/Word Webs	_____	Role Plays/Drama/Pantomimes/Charades
_____	Humor	**X**	Storytelling
X	Manipulatives/Experiments/Labs/Models	**X**	Technology
		_____	Visualization/Guided Imagery
X	Metaphors/Analogies/Similes	**X**	Visuals
_____	Mnemonic Devices	_____	Work Study/Apprenticeships
_____	Movement	_____	Writing/Journals

Dividing Integers

same signs
POSITIVE

different
signs
NEGATIVE

-63 ÷ -9 = 7

two negatives
make a
positive

63 ÷ -9 = -7

one negative
stays
negative

MATHEMATICS GRADES 6–8 LESSON 5

Angles

Lesson Objective(s): *What do you want students to know and be able to do?* Identify how vertical, adjacent, complementary, and supplementary angles are related.

Assessment (Traditional/Authentic): *How will you know students have mastered essential learning?*

Assess student's understanding in *Human Clock.*

Ways to Gain/Maintain Attention (Primacy): *How will you gain and maintain students' attention? Consider <u>need</u>, <u>novelty</u>, meaning, or emotion.*

Many careers, from engineer and architect to landscape designer, professional skateboarder, and pilot, use geometry and angles every day. Ask students if you can see all the angles in this building.

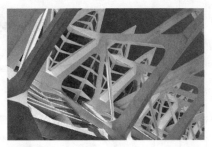

Image source: Pixabay.com/Mozart_sybilla

Content Chunks: *How will you divide and teach the content to engage students' brains?*

Lesson Segment 1: Classify Angles and Identify Vertical and Adjacent Angles

- **Activity 1: Complementary/Supplementary Angles**

Words	Models	Symbols
Two angles are complementary if the sum of their measures is 90°.		$m\angle 1 + m\angle 2 = 90°$
Two angles are supplementary if the sum of their measures is 180°.		$m\angle 3 + m\angle 4 = 180°$

Tell students the following:

If the sum of the measures of two angles is 90°, the angles are **complementary.**
If the sum of the measures of two angles is 180°, the angles are **supplementary.**
Students use what they know about angle relationships to find missing angle measures by solving algebraic equations.

Demonstrate how each angle is *complementary, supplementary,* or neither.
For each, ask, *What is the measures of the angles and what is the sum of the measures?* Point out that special relationships exist if the angles form a straight line or if they form a 90° angle.

Lesson Segment 2: Find Missing Angle Measures

- ### Activity 1: Missing Angles

Have students find the missing angle measures.
    The sum of the measures of $\angle CDF = 180°$

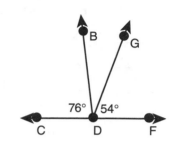

$$\angle CDB = 76°$$

$$\angle GDF = 54°$$

$$\angle BDG = ?°$$

$\angle CDB + \angle GDF + \angle BDG = 180°$ $76° + 54° + x = 180°$

$$\underline{-76° \quad -54° \quad = -130°}$$

$$x = 50°$$

Solution $\angle BDG = 50°$

Variable Let $2x$ represent the measure of $\angle CBA$.

Equation $\angle DBC = 80$

$$\angle DBA = 90°$$

$\angle DBC + \angle CBA = 90°$ $80° + 2x = 90°$

$$\underline{-80° \qquad = -80°}$$

$$\frac{2x}{2} = \frac{10}{2}$$

$$x = 5$$

Solution $\angle CBA = 10°$

- ### Activity 2: Human Clock

Have students form clock hands on the floor. Discuss how the clock hands form angles as others demonstrate. Have students create angle measures and missing angle measures for classmates to solve.

Brain-Compatible Strategies: *Which will you use to deliver content?*

__X__	Brainstorming/Discussion	_____	Music/Rhythm/Rhyme/Rap
_____	Drawing/Artwork	__X__	Project/Problem-Based Learning
_____	Field Trips	_____	Reciprocal Teaching/Cooperative Learning
_____	Games		
_____	Graphic Organizers/Semantic Maps/Word Webs	__X__	Role Plays/Drama/Pantomimes/Charades
_____	Humor	_____	Storytelling
__X__	Manipulatives/Experiments/Labs/Models	_____	Technology
		__X__	Visualization/Guided Imagery
__X__	Metaphors/Analogies/Similes	__X__	Visuals
_____	Mnemonic Devices	_____	Work Study/Apprenticeships
__X__	Movement	_____	Writing/Journals

MATHEMATICS GRADES 6–8 LESSON 6

Rational Numbers

Lesson Objective(s): *What do you want students to know and be able to do?*

Use rational approximations of irrational numbers to compare the size of irrational numbers.

Assessment (Traditional/Authentic): *How will you know students have mastered essential learning?*

Observe student interaction. Evaluate activity page *Problem-Solving Roots* at the end of the chapter.

Ways to Gain/Maintain Attention (Primacy): *How will you gain and maintain students' attention? Consider need, <u>novelty</u>, <u>meaning</u>, or emotion.*

The square base of the Great Pyramid of Giza covers 562,500 square feet. https://tinyurl.com/y87s7okl

How is the length of each side determined?

Square it or find the square root

Content Chunks: *How will you divide and teach the content to engage students' brains?*

Lesson Segment 1: Numbers

- **Activity 1: Graphic Organizer**

Ask students to create this graphic organizer in their journals. Write a list such as

$$\sqrt{10},\ 10,\ 10,\ \frac{1}{10},\ 0.01,\ -9,\ -\frac{1}{9},\ -3.171171117,\ 0.\bar{8},\ \sqrt{16}$$

Place each in the organizer.

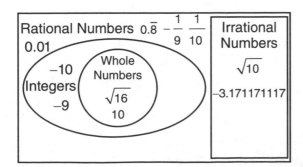
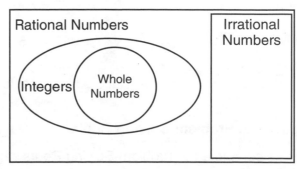

- **Activity 2: Show What You Know**

Divide students into small groups.

Use quarter-inch graph paper. https://www.waterproofpaper.com/graph-paper/grid-paper .shtml

Ask students to model fractions using the graph paper by selecting a portion of the grid to represent the whole and shading the fractional part of the whole.

Ask: *When can the fraction model be in the shape of a square?* (Only when the whole is a perfect square.) Lead students to see that, for drawing squares or laying tile or cutting fabric, only the positive *square root* makes sense.

- **Activity 3: Find It**

$\sqrt{81}$ Will the square root be positive, negative, or both? *Positive 9*

$\pm\sqrt{1.44}$ What does the plus/minus sign mean in front of the radical sign? *To find both square roots* ± 1.2

$-\sqrt{\dfrac{16}{81}}$ What does the negative sign mean? *To find the negative square root of the number* $-\dfrac{4}{9}$

Lesson Segment 2: Estimate Square Roots of Nonperfect Squares From Concrete to Abstract

- **Activity 1: Estimation**

Discuss how to estimate the square root of a nonperfect square number. Ask students to estimate the length of one side of a square that has an area of 38 square units. Using the grid paper from activity 1, cut out a square as close to 38 units. One square would be $\sqrt{36}$ and the other would be $\sqrt{49}$. The length is between 6 and 7 units.

Another way: $\sqrt{23}$

The largest perfect square less than 23 is 16. The smallest perfect square greater than 23 is 25. Find the square root of each number: $\sqrt{16} = 4$ and $\sqrt{25} = 5$.

| Write an inequality. | $16 < 23 < 25$ |
| Simplify. | $4^2 < 23 < 5^2$ |

$$\sqrt{4^2} < \sqrt{23} < \sqrt{5^2}$$

So $\sqrt{23}$ is between 4 and 5. Since 23 is closer to 25 than 16, the best estimate for $\sqrt{23}$ is 5.

- **Activity 2: Problem-Solving Roots**

Students complete the Problem-Solving Roots page found in the plan.

Brain-Compatible Strategies: *Which will you use to deliver content?*

__X__	Brainstorming/Discussion	_____	Music/Rhythm/Rhyme/Rap
__X__	Drawing/Artwork	_____	Project/Problem-Based Learning
_____	Field Trips	__X__	Reciprocal Teaching/Cooperative Learning
_____	Games		
__X__	Graphic Organizers/Semantic Maps/Word Webs	_____	Role Plays/Drama/Pantomimes/Charades
_____	Humor	_____	Storytelling
__X__	Manipulatives/Experiments/Labs/Models	__X__	Technology
		__X__	Visualization/Guided Imagery
_____	Metaphors/Analogies/Similes	_____	Visuals
_____	Mnemonic Devices	_____	Work Study/Apprenticeships
_____	Movement	__X__	Writing/Journals

Problem-Solving Roots

1. Ronaldo wants a large picture window put in the living room of his new house. The window is to be square with an area of 49 square feet. How long should each side of the window be?

2. If the area of a square is 81 square meters, how many meters long is each side?

3. A miniature portrait of LeBron James is square and has an area of 169 square centimeters. How long is each side of the portrait?

4. Codi is baking a square cake for his friend's wedding. When served to the guests, the cake will be cut into square pieces 1 inch on a side. The cake should be large enough so that each of the 121 guests gets one piece. How long should he make each side of the cake?

5. Kara has 196 marbles that she is using to make a square formation. How many marbles should be in each row?

6. Tate is planning to put a square garden with an area of 289 square feet in his backyard. What will be the length of each side of the garden?

7. Baz has 324 square paving stones that he plans to use to construct a square patio. How many paving stones will make up the width of the patio?

Find each square root.

8. $-\sqrt{400}$

9. $\sqrt{36}$

10. $\pm\sqrt{0.04}$

11. $\sqrt{\dfrac{49}{64}}$

Solve each equation.

12. $256 = s^2$

13. $t^2 = \dfrac{25}{121}$

14. $900 = y^2$

15. $l^2 = \dfrac{144}{169}$

Problem-Solving Roots Answer Key

1. Ronaldo wants a large picture window put in the living room of his new house. The window is to be square with an area of 49 square feet. How long should each side of the window be? **7 ft**

2. If the area of a square is 81 square meters, how many meters long is each side? **9m**

3. A miniature portrait of LeBron James is square and has an area of 169 square centimeters. How long is each side of the portrait? **13 cm**

4. Codi is baking a square cake for his friend's wedding. When served to the guests, the cake will be cut into square pieces 1 inch on a side. The cake should be large enough so that each of the 121 guests gets one piece. How long should he make each side of the cake? **11 in.**

5. Kara has 196 marbles that she is using to make a square formation. How many marbles should be in each row? **14 marbles**

6. Tale is planning to put a square garden with an area of 289 square feet in his backyard. What will be the length of each side of the garden? **17 ft**

7. Baz has 324 square paving stones that he plans to use to construct a square patio. How many paving stones will make up the width of the patio? **18 stones**

Find each square root.

8. $-\sqrt{400}$ **-20**

9. $\sqrt{36}$ **$.6$**

10. $\pm\sqrt{0.04}$ **± 0.2**

11. $\sqrt{\dfrac{49}{64}}$ **$\dfrac{7}{8}$**

Solve each equation.

12. $256 = s^2$ **16 or -16**

13. $t^2 = \dfrac{25}{121}$ **$\dfrac{5}{11}$ or $-\dfrac{5}{11}$**

14. $900 = y^2$ **30 or -30**

15. $l^2 = \dfrac{144}{169}$ **$\dfrac{12}{13}$ or $-\dfrac{12}{13}$**

6

25 Sample Science Lessons

SCIENCE GRADES K–2 LESSON 1

Diversity of Habitats

Lesson Objective(s): *What do you want students to know and be able to do?*

Make observations of plants and animals to compare the diversity of life in different habitats.

Assessment (Traditional/Authentic): *How will you know students have mastered essential learning?*

Students can sing "The Microscope Song." They can explain and give examples of how microscopes allow us to see microorganism (wee beasties) habitats. Students can draw, label, and create a story while observing wee beasties in a microscope. They can compare habitats.

Ways to Gain/Maintain Attention (Primacy): *How will you gain and maintain students' attention? Consider* <u>need</u>, <u>novelty</u>, *meaning, or* <u>emotion</u>.

Students will *need* to learn about microscopes in order to observe wee beasties. The *novelty* of singing songs and seeing microorganisms will add excitement to the lesson.

Content Chunks: *How will you divide and teach the content to engage students' brains?*

Lesson Segment 1: Use a Microscope to See Wee Beasties

- **Activity 1: "The Microscope Song"**

Have students sing "The Microscope Song" by Warren G. Phillips. They will identify important information and define vocabulary. Discuss how the microscope works.

- **Activity 2: Projecting Microscopes**

Using a projecting microscope (or YouTube video), have students look at a drop of pond water in order to find living things. Have students observe *wee beasties* (microorganisms), draw them, and write a story about them.

- **Activity 3: "Amoebas" Song**

Have students sing the "Amoebas" song by Warren G. Phillips, identify important information, and define vocabulary.

- **Activity 4: Amoebas Habitat Discussion**

Using whole-class discussion, have students compare the habitat of amoebas and other wee beasties to a human's environment.

Brain-Compatible Strategies: *Which will you use to deliver content?*

__X__	Brainstorming/Discussion		__X__	Music/Rhythm/Rhyme/Rap
__X__	Drawing/Artwork		_____	Project/Problem-Based Learning
_____	Field Trips		_____	Reciprocal Teaching/Cooperative Learning
_____	Games			
_____	Graphic Organizers/Semantic Maps/Word Webs		_____	Role Plays/Drama/Pantomimes/Charades
_____	Humor		__X__	Storytelling
__X__	Manipulatives/Experiments/Labs/Models		__X__	Technology
			_____	Visualization/Guided Imagery
__X__	Metaphors/Analogies/Similes		__X__	Visuals
_____	Mnemonic Devices		_____	Work Study/Apprenticeships
__X__	Movement		__X__	Writing/Journals

The Microscope Song

By Warren G. Phillips

© 2018

Sung to *It's a Small World*

Available on iTunes

In 1590 the world was changed

Zaccharias Janssen with lenses arranged

Microscopes multiplied

What was seen by the eye

And the world was magnified!

There's a small world under slides

Micro-organ-isms hide

If you look you'll find inside

All the secrets cells provide!

Leeu-wen-hoek made quite a discovery

Looked in water—saw all the wee beasties

His new world guaranteed

He's the "Father" you see

—of Mi-cros-co-py!

There's a small world under slides

Micro-organ-isms hide

If you look you'll find inside

All the secrets cells provide!

In the eyepiece there is a convex lens

An objective lens at the other end

They connect with a tube

Multiply magnitude

And you'll see the field of view!

There's a small world under slides

Micro-organ-isms hide

If you look you'll find inside

All the secrets cells provide!

Amoebas

By Warren G. Phillips

© 2018

Sung to *Jingle Bells*

Available on iTunes

Splashing to and 'fro

Amoebas like to play

In a petri dish

Dividing once a day!

I thought that there were two

Nothing less or more

I looked in the microscope

And counted up to four!

Oh! Single Cells! Single Cells!

See how they divide.

There was one the other day

And now it's multiplied!

Oh! Single Cells! Single Cells!

Nothing much to do

But swim in a Petri dish

Dividing into two!

SCIENCE GRADES K–2 LESSON 2

Sound Vibrations and the Ear

Lesson Objective(s): *What do you want students to know and be able to do?*

Plan and conduct investigations to provide evidence that vibrating materials can make sound and that sound can make materials vibrate.

Assessment (Traditional/Authentic): *How will you know students have mastered essential learning?*

Students can sing the "Sound Song." Students can explain and give examples with a visualization of sound waves and how they are perceived by the ear. They can demonstrate how sound travels through materials.

Ways to Gain/Maintain Attention (Primacy): *How will you gain and maintain students' attention? Consider need, novelty, meaning, or emotion.*

The *novelty* of singing songs will add excitement to the lesson. By seeing the demonstrations, they will find *meaning* in the lesson. Students will eventually become *emotionally* attached as they combine information from demonstrations and stories from classmates.

Content Chunks: *How will you divide and teach the content to engage students' brains?*

Lesson Segment 1: Learn How Vibrations Cause Sound and How the Human Ear Detects Sounds

- **Activity 1: Storytelling**

Discuss incidents or stories about hearing and the human ear. Relevant stories will be shared with the class.

- **Activity 2: Vibrating Tuning Fork**

Put a vibrating tuning fork into a small dish of water. Notice how the water splashes out of the dish as it vibrates. Put the end of the vibrating tuning fork on the table to hear the sound it makes (vibrating the atoms in the table).

- **Activity 3: Slinky and the Can**

Attach one end of a metal slinky to a Pringles can. Stretch out the slinky and hit the other end with a metal pen. The Pringles can will vibrate and make a sound, demonstrating sound traveling through a solid to an amplifier.

Activity 4: Pin Art Demo

Using a pin art demo, show how information can be assembled into an interpretation of the data by placing an object on the pins. This demo shows how the ear can interpret sound into something meaningful.

Activity 5: Dominoes

Set up a line of dominoes to demonstrate how sound travels from one atom to another. The line of dominoes transfers energy to each other as they fall, much like sound travels through a room. The energy is absorbed by the atoms, and the sound disperses.

Activity 6: "Sound Song"

Sing the "Sound Song" by Warren G. Phillips; identify important information and define vocabulary. Discuss how the ear works and compare to the demonstrations.

Brain-Compatible Strategies: *Which will you use to deliver content?*

X	Brainstorming/Discussion	**X**	Music/Rhythm/Rhyme/Rap
X	Drawing/Artwork	**X**	Project/Problem-Based Learning
___	Field Trips	___	Reciprocal Teaching/Cooperative Learning
___	Games		
___	Graphic Organizers/Semantic Maps/Word Webs	___	Role Plays/Drama/Pantomimes/Charades
___	Humor	**X**	Storytelling
X	Manipulatives/Experiments/Labs/Models	___	Technology
		___	Visualization/Guided Imagery
X	Metaphors/Analogies/Similes	**X**	Visuals
___	Mnemonic Devices	___	Work Study/Apprenticeships
X	Movement	___	Writing/Journals

Sound Song

By Warren G. Phillips / Derek Strohshneider

© 2018

Sung to *For What It's Worth*

Available on iTunes

When someone's makin' a sound

Well, the atoms start movin' around

They vibrate into your ear

Movin' your eardrum, and makin' you hear!

(I think it's time we) stop, listen to that sound

Resonating through us all around!

Compressions happening here

Longi-tud-inal waves will appear

Rar-e-factions appear over there

Through solids, and liquids, even through air!

(I think it's time we) stop, listen to that sound

Resonating through us all around!

The eardrum vibrates and repeats

Hammer and anvil will pound out the beats

The cochlea moves fluids around

The cilia will wave—and the brain makes a sound!

(I think it's time we) stop, listen to that sound

Resonating through us all around!

Be careful of the decibels you hear

More than 100 might be damaging your ear

The loudness can cause them to ring

You'll get tinnitus, or have trouble—can't hear anything!

(I think it's time we) stop, listen to that sound

Resonating through us all around!

SCIENCE GRADES K–2 LESSON 3

Forces of Flight

Lesson Objective(s): *What do you want students to know and be able to do?*

Plan and conduct an investigation to compare the effects of different strengths or different directions of pushes and pulls on the motion of an object.

Assessment (Traditional/Authentic): *How will you know students have mastered essential learning?*

Students can sing "The Flight Song." They can explain and give examples of how airplanes fly. Students can design and create a paper airplane. Students can make hypotheses and compare results.

Ways to Gain/Maintain Attention (Primacy): *How will you gain and maintain students' attention? Consider <u>need</u>, <u>novelty</u>, meaning, or emotion.*

Students will need to learn about airplanes and flight in order to conduct a flying experiment. The novelty of singing songs and creating paper airplanes will add excitement to the lesson.

Content Chunks: *How will you divide and teach the content to engage students' brains?*

Lesson Segment 1: Learn About Flight

- **Activity 1: Story of the Wright Family**

Tell the story of Wilbur, Orville, and Catherine Wright and their challenges in getting a plane to fly. Show pictures (or YouTube video) of original planes and attempts at flying.

- **Activity 2: "The Flight Song"**

Have students sing "The Flight Song" by Warren G. Phillips, identify important information, and define vocabulary. Discuss how the four forces work to fly an airplane.

Lesson Segment 2: Experiment With Flight

- **Activity 1: Paper Airplanes**

In groups of four to five, discuss paper airplanes, research designs, and have each group make several airplanes out of single sheets of paper. Have a paper airplane flying contest. Create contest rules, such as the farthest flight, curviest flight, most spins, etc. Have students color and decorate their entries. Formulate and write hypotheses using vocabulary as planes are tested from each group.

Brain-Compatible Strategies: *Which will you use to deliver content?*

__X__ Brainstorming/Discussion	__X__ Music/Rhythm/Rhyme/Rap
__X__ Drawing/Artwork	__X__ Project/Problem-Based Learning
_____ Field Trips	__X__ Reciprocal Teaching/Cooperative Learning
__X__ Games	
_____ Graphic Organizers/Semantic Maps/Word Webs	_____ Role Plays/Drama/Pantomimes/Charades
_____ Humor	__X__ Storytelling
__X__ Manipulatives/Experiments/Labs/Models	__X__ Technology
	_____ Visualization/Guided Imagery
_____ Metaphors/Analogies/Similes	__X__ Visuals
_____ Mnemonic Devices	_____ Work Study/Apprenticeships
__X__ Movement	__X__ Writing/Journals

The Flight Song

By Warren G. Phillips

© 2018

Sung to *Leaving on a Jet Plane*

Available on iTunes

Wilbur, Orville, and Catherine Wright

Changed the world with the first flight

Twelve-second flight in Nineteen Hundred
   Three.

The Wright Plane—first it was a glider

Then engines added thrust inside her

And wings that warped

Helped to set it free.

Chorus:

The Forces for flying straight

Lift, drag, thrust, and weight

They control the pitch, the roll, and yaw.

We're flying on an airplane

excitement I can't explain

The feeling that I get when I'm in flight.

Thrust is the force of forward motion

Taking planes across the ocean

Drag is made when atoms slow it down.

Low pressure on the top of wings

Bernoulli said would lift the things

Into the air—while weight will bring them
   down.

Chorus:

The Forces for flying straight

Lift, drag, thrust, and weight

They control the pitch, the roll and yaw.

We're flying on an airplane

Excitement I can't explain

The feeling that I get when I'm in flight.

SCIENCE GRADES K–2 LESSON 4

The Earth and Human Activity

Lesson Objective(s): *What do you want students to know and be able to do?*

Communicate solutions that will reduce the impact of humans on the land, water, air, and/or other living things in the local environment.

Assessment (Traditional/Authentic): *How will you know students have mastered essential learning?*

Students can compare an apple to the Earth. Students can sing "The Solution to Pollution" song with information and define the vocabulary.

Ways to Gain/Maintain Attention (Primacy): *How will you gain and maintain students' attention? Consider need, novelty, meaning, or emotion.*

The novelty of singing a song will add excitement to the lesson. Students will eventually become emotionally attached as they discuss possible ways to improve the environment and organize recycling in the classroom.

Content Chunks: *How will you divide and teach the content to engage students' brains?*

Lesson Segment 1: Comprehend the Earth's Fragility

- **Activity 1: Apple Demo Metaphor**

Compare the earth to an apple. Slice an apple into quarters—¾ represents the earth's waters. Identify the five oceans Atlantic / Pacific / Arctic / Indian / Southern while eating each piece.

Students recite and repeat each of the world's oceans. The remaining quarter (¼) is all of the continents.

Identify the continents with a story: **North America** *married* **South America** – *they went to* **Europe** *and got married. They had four children—all beginning with the letter A—* **Asia, Africa, Antarctica,** *and* **Australia.** Have students quiz each other on the names of the continents.

Now cut the quarter into ½. One of these two pieces of land is inhospitable. Throw the inhospitable piece away or eat it. Cut the remaining 1/8 into two pieces. (1/16) One of these pieces is livable, but not good soil (too rocky, too wet/swampy, etc.) Throw it away or eat it. Cut the remaining 1/16 into half. (1/32) One of these pieces is not useful for food (parking lots, roads, parks, remote areas). Throw it away or eat it.

The remaining piece is 1/32 of the earth. Carefully peel off the underlying layer, so that only the skin is remaining. We cannot live on the inside layer – Throw it away or eat it. The thin, flimsy piece left is the good fertile soil that is less than 5 feet thick. It supports all of the life on earth and about 7 billion people. It is also the most polluted piece! Wiggle the piece to show how fragile it is! We must protect this piece and not pollute it.

Lesson Segment 2: Formulate Environmental Solutions

● **Activity 1: "The Solution to Pollution" Song**

Students will sing "The Solution to Pollution" by Warren G. Phillips. Identify important information and define vocabulary.

● **Activity 2: Environmental Discussion**

Discuss possible ways to improve the environment and organize recycling in the classroom.

Brain-Compatible Strategies: *Which will you use to deliver content?*

__X__	Brainstorming/Discussion	__X__	Music/Rhythm/Rhyme/Rap
_____	Drawing/Artwork	_____	Project/Problem-Based Learning
_____	Field Trips	__X__	Reciprocal Teaching/Cooperative Learning
_____	Games		
_____	Graphic Organizers/Semantic Maps/Word Webs	_____	Role Plays/Drama/Pantomimes/Charades
_____	Humor	__X__	Storytelling
__X__	Manipulatives/Experiments/Labs/Models	_____	Technology
		_____	Visualization/Guided Imagery
__X__	Metaphors/Analogies/Similes	__X__	Visuals
_____	Mnemonic Devices	_____	Work Study/Apprenticeships
_____	Movement	_____	Writing/Journals

The Solution to Pollution

By Warren G. Phillips

© 2018

Sung to *Polly Wolly Doodle*
Available on iTunes

Greenhouse gases make the Earth get warm
And acid rain is fallin' from the sky
Ozone's depleting and the chemicals are leaching
While the litter is accumulating high!

Now pollution affects all the parts of the Earth
On the ground, in the water, and the air
And it's up to you and me to realize what it's worth
And begin to act and show that we care!

Save the Earth *(Save the Earth!)* — Save the Earth *(Save the Earth!)*
Be pro-active, that's the key
If you're thinkin' globally and then you're actin' locally
The planet will get better—you will see!

Now, what can I do? How can I help?
I'll reduce all the energy I waste
Re-use some things and recycling will bring
A difference in the world that I can make!

Everything we use and eat and drink and make and wear
It requires en-ergy
By conserving our resources and learning how to share
It'll help with our community!

Save the Earth *(Save the Earth!)*—Save the Earth *(Save the Earth!)*
Be pro-active, that's the key
If you're thinkin' globally and then you're actin' locally
The planet will get better—you will see!
The planet will get better—you will see!
The planet will get better—you will see!

SCIENCE GRADES K–2 LESSON 5

Properties of Materials

Lesson Objective(s): *What do you want students to know and be able to do?*

Analyze data obtained from testing different materials to determine which materials have the properties that are best suited for an intended purpose.*

Assessment (Traditional/Authentic): *How will you know students have mastered essential learning?*

Have students analyze data obtained from testing different materials to determine which materials have the properties that are best suited for an intended purpose. Students perform an experiment and give an explanation of results and then make hypotheses and compare results. Sing "The Scientific Method" song and identify steps of the scientific method.

Ways to Gain/Maintain Attention (Primacy): *How will you gain and maintain students' attention? Consider need, novelty, meaning, or emotion.*

Students will provide meaning to an experiment by analysis of results. The novelty of making soap bubbles and measuring results will add excitement to the lesson.

Content Chunks: *How will you divide and teach the content to engage students' brains?*

Lesson Segment 1: Comprehend the Scientific Method

- **Activity 1: "The Scientific Method" Song**

Have students sing "The Scientific Method" song by Warren G. Phillips and identify the six steps of the scientific method contained in the song.

- **Activity 2: Scientific Method Discussion**

Discuss and brainstorm how to conduct an experiment using the scientific method. Introduce an idea to test soap bubbles.

Lesson Segment 2: Analyze Data to Determine Properties

- **Activity 1: Soap Bubble Experiment**

Make three solutions of soap bubbles ahead of time. Let the solutions sit overnight. As an example:

  - Solution A: 5 oz. of Dawn Ultra to 1 gallon of water
  - Solution B: 10 oz. of Dawn Ultra to 1 gallon of water
  - Solution C: 15 oz. of Dawn Ultra to 1 gallon of water

* All safety procedures should be followed and are the responsibility of the teacher conducting the class.

Notice that only ONE variable changes—the amount of Dawn Ultra dish detergent—(food coloring could be added to make it more fun, but the SAME food color and the amount added to each) Give each student a straw, a ruler, and an index card. Have them make a hypothesis on the index card about which solution they think will work best and why. Ask: *How big might your bubbles be for each Solution A-B-C?*

Pour some Solution A onto one table with a group of students. Have the students put their straw into the solution and blow their largest bubble after several attempts. Measure the diameter of the bubble after it bursts, and record the number on the index card.

Pour some Solution B onto another table with a group of students. Have the students put their straw into the solution and blow their largest bubble after several attempts. Measure the diameter of the bubble after it bursts, and record the number on the index card.

Pour some Solution C onto another table with a group of students. Have the students put their straw into the solution and blow their largest bubble after several attempts. Measure the diameter of the bubble after it bursts, and record the number on the index card.

After 5 minutes, rotate groups of students from table to table, recording their largest bubble at each table on their index card.

Have students discuss the activity and reach as conclusion. Have them compare results of the hypotheses and give explanations on the index cards. Ask, *Which solution worked best when comparing all of the data?* Have students brainstorm other experiments that can be done.

Brain-Compatible Strategies: *Which will you use to deliver content?*

__X__	Brainstorming/Discussion	__X__	Music/Rhythm/Rhyme/Rap
_____	Drawing/Artwork	__X__	Project/Problem-Based Learning
_____	Field Trips	__X__	Reciprocal Teaching/Cooperative Learning
_____	Games		
_____	Graphic Organizers/Semantic Maps/Word Webs	_____	Role Plays/Drama/Pantomimes/Charades
_____	Humor	_____	Storytelling
__X__	Manipulatives/Experiments/Labs/Models	_____	Technology
		_____	Visualization/Guided Imagery
_____	Metaphors/Analogies/Similes	__X__	Visuals
_____	Mnemonic Devices	_____	Work Study/Apprenticeships
_____	Movement	__X__	Writing/Journals

The Scientific Method

By Warren G. Phillips

© 2018

Sung to *The Brady Bunch*

Available on iTunes

There's a problem, and you're trying to solve it

And you look into the science book to see

If there's any answer out there that could help you

But it's just not to be.

Now you need to use the scientific method

You should research and then come up with a hunch

Then experiment and analyze your data

Make a conclusion and you're gonna learn a bunch.

You'll learn a bunch!

You'll learn a bunch!

Because the scientific method solves your hunch!

SCIENCE GRADES 3–5 LESSON 1

The Scientific Method

Lesson Objective(s): *What do you want students to know and be able to do?*

Define a simple design problem reflecting a need or a want that includes specified criteria for success and constraints on materials, time, or cost.

Assessment (Traditional/Authentic): *How will you know students have mastered essential learning?*

Students will analyze data after repeated trials, brainstorm hypotheses, and come up with a conclusion. Write about experiences, pitfalls, and successes. Draw a picture with labels explaining their hypotheses.

Ways to Gain/Maintain Attention (Primacy): *How will you gain and maintain students' attention? Consider need, novelty, meaning, or emotion.*

The novelty of a mystery box will peak their interest. Brainstorming will help find meaning in their ability to solve problems. They will relate to the emotion of the excitement of discovery that scientists frequently encounter.

Content Chunks: *How will you divide and teach the content to engage students' brains?*

Lesson Segment 1: Comprehend the Scientific Method

- **Activity 1: "The Scientific Method" Song**

Have students sing "The Scientific Method" song (see preceding page) by Warren G. Phillips and identify the six steps of the scientific method contained in the song. They will use hand movements to identify the six steps and identify and define the vocabulary.

Lesson Segment 2: Formulate Hypotheses Based on Data

- **Activity 1: Serendipity Discussion**

Using *The People's Almanac*, *The People's Almanac II*, or a similar source, have students read brief stories about how things were discovered and invented. Discuss and brainstorm about serendipity.

- **Activity 2: Mystery Box**

Using a Mystery box (with unknown contents) have students work in groups to discern what the contents are. Provide various clues using several trials, brainstorm, explain, and draw what the contents of the box might look like. (An example is provided in the diagram below.) Another example would be to place various objects in sealed boxes and try to determine their contents by smell, weight, sounds, etc. Many other "Black box" experiments (with unknown outcomes) could be used.

While many versions of a "Mystery Box" can be used, here is a diagram of one that can be made by the teacher prior to the lesson:

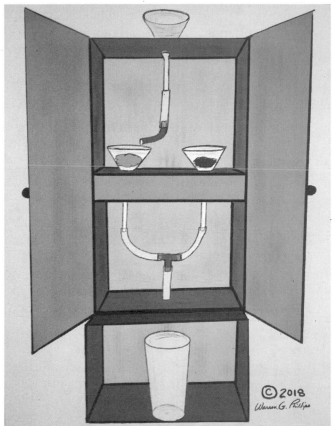

Spin the funnel quickly (so students do not notice) after pouring clear water into the funnel that contains food coloring and cotton balls. First pouring, the water trickles out red. Dump out the red water. Next pouring, the water is blue. Can be repeated several times.

Brain-Compatible Strategies: *Which will you use to deliver content?*

__X__	Brainstorming/Discussion	__X__	Music/Rhythm/Rhyme/Rap
__X__	Drawing/Artwork	__X__	Project/Problem-Based Learning
_____	Field Trips	_____	Reciprocal Teaching/Cooperative Learning
_____	Games		
_____	Graphic Organizers/Semantic Maps/Word Webs	_____	Role Plays/Drama/Pantomimes/Charades
_____	Humor	__X__	Storytelling
__X__	Manipulatives/Experiments/Labs/Models	_____	Technology
		_____	Visualization/Guided Imagery
_____	Metaphors/Analogies/Similes	__X__	Visuals
_____	Mnemonic Devices	_____	Work Study/Apprenticeships
__X__	Movement	_____	Writing/Journals

SCIENCE GRADES 3–5 LESSON 2

Coding With Glyphs

Lesson Objective(s): *What do you want students to know and be able to do?*

Generate and compare multiple solutions that use patterns to transfer information.

Assessment (Traditional/Authentic): *How will you know students have mastered essential learning?*

Students will create a glyph using interview information. They will pass on this information while introducing their classmates. They will produce a classroom display showing classmate information. They will examine subsets and create graphs or Venn diagrams of overlapping interests or traits.

Ways to Gain/Maintain Attention (Primacy): *How will you gain and maintain students' attention? Consider* <u>need</u>, <u>novelty</u>, <u>meaning</u>, *or emotion.*

Students will need to learn the interests and traits of their partners as they create their glyphs. The novelty of producing a glyph and introducing their classmates will add excitement to the lesson. As they create a glyph, they will find meaning in their project. They will eventually become emotionally attached to their classmates as they compare common interests in a Venn diagram.

Content Chunks: *How will you divide and teach the content to engage students' brains?*

Lesson Segment 1: Research Coding and Glyphs

- **Activity 1: Glyph Discussion**

Have students research information about how NASA scientists have used glyphs in the space program. Students should discuss how glyphs have been used in other situations (hieroglyphics, Morse code, etc.). Review glyph information shown on the page below.

Lesson Segment 2: Create Glyphs to Transfer Information

- **Activity 1: Creating a Code**

Have students examine and brainstorm ideas as a class to create a glyph symbol for characteristics and traits (i.e., eye color, hair color, number of siblings, favorite foods, etc.) of classmates so that they understand what information they will need to obtain to create their glyph. An example is shown below.

Write the names of each student on a craft stick and place them in a cup. Have students pick a stick from the cup and be randomly assigned a partner. Students form pairs and ask each other the information needed to make a glyph of their partner. Calm background music will provide a soothing classroom-learning atmosphere.

- **Activity 2: Drawing Glyphs**

Draw an empty face outline and place glyph symbols to represent eyes, nose, mouth, etc. (For example, # of siblings could be represented by freckles, the shape of the eyes could represent favorite foods, etc.) and develop a key to solve each glyph symbol.

- **Activity 3: Data Analysis**

Based upon the information on their glyph, have students introduce their partners to the class and hang the picture up on the wall after their presentation to display traits/interests of their classmates. Have them write a story or biography about their partner based on their glyph.

- **Activity 4: Venn Diagrams**

Create Venn diagrams comparing their Glyph codes to Morse Codes.

Brain-Compatible Strategies: *Which will you use to deliver content?*

X	Brainstorming/Discussion		**X**	Music/Rhythm/Rhyme/Rap
X	Drawing/Artwork		**X**	Project/Problem-Based Learning
____	Field Trips		**X**	Reciprocal Teaching/Cooperative Learning
____	Games			
X	Graphic Organizers/Semantic Maps/Word Webs		____	Role Plays/Drama/Pantomimes/Charades
X	Humor		____	Storytelling
X	Manipulatives/Experiments/Labs/Models		____	Technology
			____	Visualization/Guided Imagery
X	Metaphors/Analogies/Similes		**X**	Visuals
____	Mnemonic Devices		____	Work Study/Apprenticeships
X	Movement		**X**	Writing/Journals

Glyphs are pictures that display data with multiple variables. Scientists often use glyphs to record and display information. This information is usually easy to read and decipher.

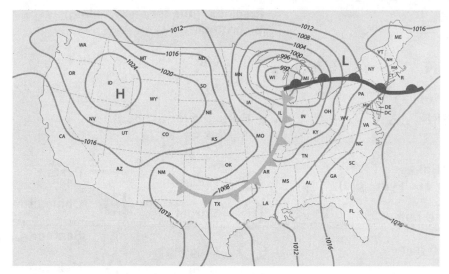

Image source: iStock.com/Rainer_Lesniewski

For example, meteorologists use glyphs on weather maps to show low pressure, high pressure, weather fronts, hurricanes, etc.

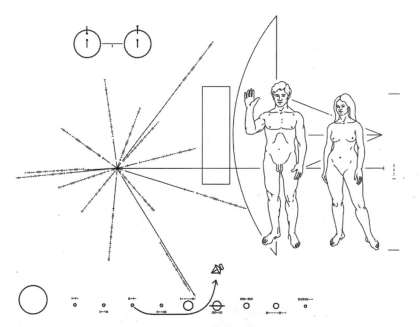

Image source: NASA Pioneer Plaque placed aboard Pioneer 10 and Pioneer 11. Designed by Frank Drake and Carl Sagan. Artwork prepared by Linda Salzman.

NASA used this glyph onboard Pioneer 11 and Pioneer 10. It is a plaque with messages designed to make contact with possible alien civilizations. The late Dr. Carl Sagan helped devise the plaques that bear the illustration of a man and a woman as well as a diagram identifying the earth's location in the galaxy. Like a message in a bottle, these plaques will journey out into interstellar space possibly to be found one day by an extraterrestrial civilization.

Your assignment is to gather information about your partner. Then, using the key below, make a biographical glyph of your partner.

Glyph Key

Face Shape

Boy

Girl

Freckles (one for each sibling)
*   brother

●   sister

Hair
(One strand for each year old)

light colored hair

dark colored hair

Short strands = Short hair
Long strands = Long hair

Eyes (Favorite Food)
(*Pick one or two*)

Pizza   Pasta

Burger   Chinese

Seafood

Chicken   Mexican

Hot Dog   Salad

Eye Color
Actual eye

Nose Color
Favorite Color

Mouth (Favorite Subject)

Science   English

Math   Geography   Reading

Nose   (Pets)

No pets   Rabbit

Dog   Hamster

Cat

Fish   Other

Ears
Like Video Games   Don't like Video games

Eyebrows (Books read per month)

0-1   2-3   4-5   6+

Necklace   (Favorite Activities)
(Pick as many as you like)

Soccer   Baseball   Computer   Gymnastics   Dance

Football   Swimming   Skateboard   Arts & Crafts

Ski/Snowboard   Music   Skating   Basketball   Tennis

Fishing   Other

SCIENCE GRADES 3–5 LESSON 3

Interpret Fossils-Archaeology

Lesson Objective(s): *What do you want students to know and be able to do?*

Analyze and interpret data from fossils to provide evidence of the organisms and the environments in which they lived long ago.

Assessment (Traditional/Authentic): *How will you know students have mastered essential learning?*

Students can sing/recite information about fossils and geological periods. They can interpret the relative age of materials from an excavation site and can replicate and describe the process of sedimentation.

Ways to Gain/Maintain Attention (Primacy): *How will you gain and maintain students' attention? Consider need, novelty, meaning, or emotion.*

Students will need to record data as they dig up various items in an excavation site. The novelty of finding items and singing songs will add excitement to the lesson. As they create a story of what they think happened, they will find meaning in their project.

Content Chunks: *How will you divide and teach the content to engage students' brains?*

Lesson Segment 1: Analyze and Interpret Fossil Data

- **Activity 1: Archaeological Hypotheses**

Have students look at various fossils (trilobites, ammonites, crinoids, etc.*), identify them, and draw/describe them. Have them interpret and hypothesize the types of environments that the life forms would have required.

- **Activity 2: "The Fossil Song"**

Have students sing "The Fossil Song" by Warren G. Phillips and identify vocabulary and important information in the song.

- **Activity 3: Archaeological Dig**

Have students dig in an area set up by you as a grid on the school grounds. As they role-play the job of an archaeologist, they will uncover various items (coins, old toys, antiques, etc.) and determine the age of the items based on the depth of the items. Have them map and label the results.

- **Activity 4: Archaeological Discussion**

Have students combine their findings and clues to help determine the sedimentation process (oldest items are at the bottom). Have them review "The Fossil Song" and information. Have them discuss the job of an archaeologist.

* A fossil sorting kit is available at Educational Innovations and other science supply companies.

Brain-Compatible Strategies: *Which will you use to deliver content?*

__X__	Brainstorming/Discussion	__X__	Music/Rhythm/Rhyme/Rap
__X__	Drawing/Artwork	__X__	Project/Problem-Based Learning
_____	Field Trips	__X__	Reciprocal Teaching/Cooperative Learning
_____	Games		
_____	Graphic Organizers/Semantic Maps/Word Webs	__X__	Role Plays/Drama/Pantomimes/Charades
_____	Humor	_____	Storytelling
__X__	Manipulatives/Experiments/Labs/Models	_____	Technology
		_____	Visualization/Guided Imagery
_____	Metaphors/Analogies/Similes	__X__	Visuals
_____	Mnemonic Devices	_____	Work Study/Apprenticeships
__X__	Movement	__X__	Writing/Journals

The Fossil Song

By Warren G. Phillips

© 2018

Sung to *I've Been Working on the Railroad*

Available on iTunes

I've been digging up these fossils

All the livelong day!

I've been digging up these fossils

They were buried in red clay!

Hardened into rocky layers

Sed-i-ment-a-ry!

And I'm hoping that I find one

Buried there for me!

In the rock I might

Find a trilobite

If the rock is from the Cambrian

Maybe an Amphibian

From the Mississippian

That would really make my day!

Looking for the bone of a reptile

Buried in a layer from the Mez-o-zo-ic

Even if it's gonna take me quite a while

Just to find a pinky toe!

Then I'd say, "Gee, I wish I could find more!

Fossils of a din-o-saur-aur-aur-aur!

Gee, I wish I could find more!

Fossils of a din-o-saur!

I've been digging up these fossils

All the livelong day!

I've been digging up these fossils

They were buried in red clay!

Hardened into rocky layers

Sed-i-ment-a-ry!

And I'm hoping that I find one

Buried there for me!

SCIENCE GRADES 3–5 LESSON 4

Germination and Photosynthesis in Plants

Lesson Objective(s): *What do you want students to know and be able to do?*

Support an argument that plants get the materials they need for growth chiefly from air and water.

Assessment (Traditional/Authentic): *How will you know students have mastered essential learning?*

Students can describe and measure plant growth. Students can see differences in the rate of growth and compare them with graphs. Students can predict future growth based on observed data.

Ways to Gain/Maintain Attention (Primacy): *How will you gain and maintain students' attention? Consider <u>need</u>, <u>novelty</u>, meaning, or <u>emotion</u>.*

Students will need to record observations to compare data as they watch seed germination and growth. The novelty of making a cartoon and singing songs will add excitement to the lesson. They will become emotionally attached as they create a comic strip of their seed experiment.

Content Chunks: *How will you divide and teach the content to engage students' brains?*

Lesson Segment 1: Compare Seeds With and Without Sunlight

- **Activity 1: Observations and Journaling**

Identify various seeds (Monocot vs. Dicot) for students and place them on a wet paper towel. Then place the towel in a plastic zip lock bag, label the contents, and keep it *away* from any light. Have students create a journal to keep a diary of observations.

   Have students observe the seeds as they germinate. Have them measure any growth and draw a picture of the growing seeds. They can make a journal entry for each day, including a prediction for tomorrow's growth.

- **Activity 2: "Photosynthesis" Song**

Have students sing the "Photosynthesis" song by Warren G. Phillips, identifying important information and vocabulary.

- **Activity 3: Seed Cartoons**

After about seven days of no light, place the plastic bags (from Activity 1) in a bright light (NOT hot) location. Have students make a prediction and observe the seeds for several more days and continue journal entries daily. Using actual observations and journal results, have students create several cartoons, as if the seeds could talk, into a comic strip.

● **Activity 4: Graphing**

After about two weeks of observations and journal entries, have students create a graph of results comparing various seeds. Use a graphing program if available.

Brain-Compatible Strategies: *Which will you use to deliver content?*

__X__	Brainstorming/Discussion	__X__	Music/Rhythm/Rhyme/Rap
__X__	Drawing/Artwork	__X__	Project/Problem-Based Learning
_____	Field Trips	__X__	Reciprocal Teaching/Cooperative Learning
_____	Games		
__X__	Graphic Organizers/Semantic Maps/Word Webs	_____	Role Plays/Drama/Pantomimes/Charades
__X__	Humor	_____	Storytelling
__X__	Manipulatives/Experiments/Labs/Models	_____	Technology
		_____	Visualization/Guided Imagery
_____	Metaphors/Analogies/Similes	__X__	Visuals
_____	Mnemonic Devices	_____	Work Study/Apprenticeships
__X__	Movement	__X__	Writing/Journals

Photosynthesis

By Warren G. Phillips

© 2018

Sung to *The Muppet Song*

Available on iTunes

The plants are making glucose

It's happenin' in the leaves!

And in plants when sunlight hits

It's photosynthesis!

They're using 6 CO_2

Add in 6 H_2O's

chlorophyll in just the right dose

makin' a glucose!

It's $C_6H_{12}O_6$

A simple sugar brew!

With energy to use

Now transpirate the 6O_2!

The plants are making glucose

It's happenin' in the leaves!

And in plants when sunlight hits

It's photosynthesis!

SCIENCE GRADES 3–5 LESSON 5

Flowers (Sexual Reproduction of Plants)

Lesson Objective(s): *What do you want students to know and be able to do?*

Construct an argument that plants and animals have internal and external structures that function to support survival, growth, behavior, and reproduction.

Assessment (Traditional/Authentic): *How will you know students have mastered essential learning?*

Students can identify, describe, and label parts of a flower. Students can dissect and label parts using a magnifying glass. Students can visualize the process of seed formation. Students can write about experiences with flowers and relate that to plant reproduction.

Ways to Gain/Maintain Attention (Primacy): *How will you gain and maintain students' attention? Consider need, novelty, meaning, or emotion.*

Students will need to learn flower parts as they dissect one. The novelty of a BrainPOP* Pollination video will add excitement to the lesson. By learning how seed formation happens, they will find meaning in the lesson. Students will eventually become emotionally attached as they visualize seed formation and create a sensory journal entry about the sight, smell, touch of past experiences with flowers.

* BrainPOP is a subscription online animated video service. It is available at https://www.brainpop.com/

Content Chunks: *How will you divide and teach the content to engage students' brains?*

Lesson Segment 1: Learn About Pollination and Parts of a Flower

- **Activity 1: BrainPOP Video**

Have students view a BrainPOP Pollination video (or YouTube video) to identify important information and define vocabulary. Have them discuss how flowers work to create seeds used for reproduction.

- **Activity 2: Flower Dissection**

Using a diagram, have students work in pairs to compare parts of a flower to a live specimen. Have them draw the parts, discuss the functions of each part, and learn about various kinds of flowers. (Obtain flowers from florists, who often are willing to save older flowers for classroom use – Lilies and gladioli are excellent for dissection).

- **Activity 3: Flower Puzzle**

Have students create a picture of a flower and flower parts that can be cut and assembled like a puzzle. Have students examine and assemble each other's puzzles.

● **Activity 4: Flower Power in Writing**

Have students write about the sight, smell, and touch of a flower using past experiences and learned information. Have them create and write a visualization describing the process from pollination to seed production using vocabulary previously learned.

Brain-Compatible Strategies: *Which will you use to deliver content?*

X	Brainstorming/Discussion	____	Music/Rhythm/Rhyme/Rap
X	Drawing/Artwork	**X**	Project/Problem-Based Learning
____	Field Trips	**X**	Reciprocal Teaching/Cooperative Learning
____	Games		
____	Graphic Organizers/Semantic Maps/Word Webs	____	Role Plays/Drama/Pantomimes/Charades
____	Humor	____	Storytelling
X	Manipulatives/Experiments/Labs/Models	**X**	Technology
		X	Visualization/Guided Imagery
____	Metaphors/Analogies/Similes	**X**	Visuals
____	Mnemonic Devices	____	Work Study/Apprenticeships
X	Movement	**X**	Writing/Journals

SCIENCE GRADES 3–5 LESSON 6

Engineering Design

Lesson Objective(s): *What do you want students to know and be able to do?*

Define a simple design problem reflecting a need or a want that includes specified criteria for success and constraints on materials, time, or cost.

Assessment (Traditional/Authentic): *How will you know students have mastered essential learning?*

Students can record data when competing in the event. Students can brainstorm and create a plan to improve results. They can compare their results to others. Students can design other events that can be accurately measured.

Ways to Gain/Maintain Attention (Primacy): *How will you gain and maintain students' attention? Consider* <u>need</u>, <u>novelty</u>, *meaning, or* <u>emotion</u>.

The novelty of a competition game will add excitement to the classroom. Students will need to measure accurately and record their results in order to compete.

Content Chunks: *How will you divide and teach the content to engage students' brains?*

Lesson Segment 1: Solve a Simple Design Problem

- **Activity 1: Paper Tower Competition**

Using 8 1/2 × 11 paper and scotch tape, groups compete to construct the tallest tower in five minutes.

Lead the class in a discussion about teamwork and communication. Discuss the construction of bridges, buildings, and tunnels. Discuss future technology such as hyperloops.

- **Activity 2: Design Team Logo Creation**

Divide students into groups and have them create a logo representing the design team. Assign a time limit (i.e., 10 minutes).

- **Activity 3: Design Project**

Set up areas around the room with ample space for construction. Meter sticks should be provided at each station for measurement. An egg (hard-boiled or raw—your choice!) will be provided to each team. Also provided are a newspaper (or construction paper) and Scotch tape. Students are provided with the following challenge:

Build the tallest freestanding structure that can support the weight of the egg at its tallest point for at least 10 seconds.

Teams will compete against one other. Student teams can report to the teacher at any time with their 10-second test, and record their height results in metrics on the board. That becomes the challenge to beat before the final time limit. (A 20- to 30-minute time limit is optimal.) Play music during the competition.

- **Activity 4: Debrief**

Compare results, successes, and failures. Discuss communication, building designs, and cooperation. Brainstorm other activities that could be tried. Have students write a reflection of their experiences and lessons learned. Recycle all materials used.

Brain-Compatible Strategies: *Which will you use to deliver content?*

__X__	Brainstorming/Discussion	__X__	Music/Rhythm/Rhyme/Rap
__X__	Drawing/Artwork	__X__	Project/Problem-Based Learning
_____	Field Trips	__X__	Reciprocal Teaching/Cooperative Learning
__X__	Games		
_____	Graphic Organizers/Semantic Maps/Word Webs	_____	Role Plays/Drama/Pantomimes/Charades
__X__	Humor	_____	Storytelling
__X__	Manipulatives/Experiments/Labs/Models	_____	Technology
		_____	Visualization/Guided Imagery
_____	Metaphors/Analogies/Similes	__X__	Visuals
_____	Mnemonic Devices	_____	Work Study/Apprenticeships
__X__	Movement	__X__	Writing/Journals

SCIENCE GRADES 3–5 LESSON 7

Respiration

Lesson Objective(s): *What do you want students to know and be able to do?*

Generate and compare multiple possible solutions to a problem based on how well each is likely to meet the criteria and constraints of the problem.

Assessment (Traditional/Authentic): *How will you know students have mastered essential learning?*

Students can record data when performing an experiment on respiration. Students can compare their results to others. Students can form a conclusion based upon observed results.

Ways to Gain/Maintain Attention (Primacy): *How will you gain and maintain students' attention? Consider* <u>need</u>*, novelty,* <u>meaning</u>*, or emotion.*

Students will need to measure accurately and record their results in order to compete. Lung capacity will provide meaning to students' lifestyles.

Content Chunks: *How will you divide and teach the content to engage students' brains?*

Lesson Segment 1: Solve the Lung Capacity Problem

- **Activity 1: Lung Capacity Discussion**

Lead the class in a discussion about lung capacity and exercise. Discuss the use of the scientific method to solve problems.

- **Activity 2: BrainPOP Video**

Watch an introductory video (BrainPOP* or YouTube) on the respiratory system and how the lungs work. Also, watch an introductory video about how to use spirometers**.

- **Activity 3: Exercise Time and Height Recordings**

Ask students to record their amount of exercise time each day and their height in centimeters. Place this information on a graph or spreadsheet.

- **Activity 4: Lung Capacity Experiment**

Using a spirometer, show students how to use the device to measure their lung capacity and how to record their lung capacity. Have students make a hypothesis about the relationship of exercise to lung capacity and height to lung capacity. Be specific with predicted numbers. Have each student

* BrainPOP is a subscription animated video web site. It is available at: https://www.brainpop.com

** Spirometers are available at many web sites. Information is available at: https://kidshealth.org/en/teens/incentive-spirometer.html

inhale using the spirometer and record the results. Wipe the mouthpiece of the spirometer after each use with an antiseptic wipe. Use a sticky note or small paper around the mouthpiece for each student to prevent the spread of germs. In groups, compare the spirometer results to the height of each student. Also, compare the spirometer results to the amount of exercise for each student. Note any relationships in the numbers and compare to the hypothesis.

- **Activity 5: "Respiration Song"**

Sing the "Respiration Song" by Warren G. Phillips. Identify important information and define vocabulary. Compare cell respiration to body respiration.

Brain-Compatible Strategies: *Which will you use to deliver content?*

__X__	Brainstorming/Discussion	__X__	Music/Rhythm/Rhyme/Rap
_____	Drawing/Artwork	__X__	Project/Problem-Based Learning
_____	Field Trips	__X__	Reciprocal Teaching/Cooperative Learning
_____	Games		
_____	Graphic Organizers/Semantic Maps/Word Webs	_____	Role Plays/Drama/Pantomimes/Charades
_____	Humor	_____	Storytelling
__X__	Manipulatives/Experiments/Labs/Models	__X__	Technology
_____	Metaphors/Analogies/Similes	_____	Visualization/Guided Imagery
_____	Mnemonic Devices	__X__	Visuals
__X__	Movement	_____	Work Study/Apprenticeships
		__X__	Writing/Journals

Respiration Song

By Warren G. Phillips / Matt Fisher

© 2018

Sung to *Zip a Dee Doo Dah*

Cell respiration happ'ning in me,

Mito-chondria's the place it will be

Breakin' the glucose—make ATP!

Gives us the power of stored energy!

Plants can use what we respire,

CO_2 and water,

Making glucose we require!

Cell respiration within my cells,

Breaking down glucose, and doing it well!

Red blood cells carry oxygen to

All the trillion cells that help make up you

Reacting with glucose, making it break—

Carbon dioxide and water it makes!

Plants can use what we respire,

CO_2 and water,

Making glucose we require!

Cell respiration within my cells,

Breaking down glucose, and doing it well!

SCIENCE GRADES 3–5 LESSON 8

Reflection and Refraction

Lesson Objective(s): *What do you want students to know and be able to do?*

Develop a model to describe that light reflecting from objects and entering the eye allows objects to be seen.

Assessment (Traditional/Authentic): *How will you know students have mastered essential learning?*

Students can predict the path of light with reflection and refraction. They can understand and draw how magnifying glasses and mirrors work and can learn "The Optics Song" and explain the lyrics.

Ways to Gain/Maintain Attention (Primacy): *How will you gain and maintain students' attention? Consider need, novelty, meaning, or emotion.*

"The Optics Song" will provide meaning behind the experiments being conducted. The novelty of using laser light and diffusion mist experiments will encourage retention of information learned.

Content Chunks: *How will you divide and teach the content to engage students' brains?*

Lesson Segment 1: Comprehend Reflection of Light

- **Activity 1: "The Optics Song"**

Have students sing "The Optics Song" by Warren G. Phillips, identify important information, and define vocabulary. Explain the lyrics, if necessary.

- **Activity 2: Ping-Pong Path**

Bounce a ping-pong ball on a table, first vertically, and then at an angle. Notice the path of the ping-pong ball and draw a diagram of its path before and after it hits the table.

- **Activity 3: Diffusion Mist**

Spray some diffusion mist* smoke into the air. Shine a laser** through the smoke to demonstrate the straight-line path of the light waves. Review "The Optics Song" lyrics.

   Attach two binder clips to the edges of a 4"x6" mirror (other small sizes will also work), so that the mirror can stand vertically. Spray diffusion mist and point the laser at the mirror to see the reflection. Have students draw a diagram of the experiment.

- **Activity 4: Mirror Deflection**

Set up several mirrors with binder clips and place them at various points on a table. Set up a target at the end of the table. As a group, have students make a hypothesis about where to place the

* Diffusion mist is available at Educational Innovations at https://www.teachersource.com.

** All safety procedures should be followed and are the responsibility of the teacher conducting the class.

mirrors so that the laser shined on one mirror will then reflect to the next mirror (and so on) until it eventually hits the target. This can lead to a fun game of "Hit the Target." Shine the laser on the first mirror to test the hypothesis and keep adjusting mirrors until the target is hit. Use diffusion mist to help with your experiment. Have students draw and explain their hypotheses.

Lesson Segment 2: Comprehend Refraction of Light

- **Activity 1: Convex Magnifying Glass**

Shine the laser through a convex magnifying glass. Now, spray diffusion mist to see the path of light as it travels through the magnifying glass. Have students notice how the path changes as you move the laser from one side of the magnifying glass to the other. Have them draw a diagram of the paths of light through a convex lens. See if they can find the focal point.

- **Activity 2: Concave Magnifying Glass**

Shine the laser through a concave magnifying glass. Now, spray diffusion mist to see the path of light as it travels through the magnifying glass. Have students notice how the path changes as you move the laser from one side of the magnifying glass to the other. Have them draw a diagram of the paths of light through a concave lens.

- **Activity 3: Jar Refraction**

Fill a large round jar (a plastic candy jar works well) with water. Place your hand inside the jar and view it from different angles. Notice the refraction of light. Place your face in front to the jar to see funny faces created as light refracts.

- **Activity 4: Laser Light**

Place a few drops of milk into the water to see the laser light easily. Shine the laser through the jar to see the light path of refraction. Have students draw and explain the results.

Brain-Compatible Strategies: *Which will you use to deliver content?*

X	Brainstorming/Discussion		X	Music/Rhythm/Rhyme/Rap
X	Drawing/Artwork		X	Project/Problem-Based Learning
	Field Trips			Reciprocal Teaching/Cooperative Learning
	Games			
	Graphic Organizers/Semantic Maps/Word Webs			Role Plays/Drama/Pantomimes/Charades
X	Humor			Storytelling
X	Manipulatives/Experiments/Labs/Models			Technology
				Visualization/Guided Imagery
	Metaphors/Analogies/Similes		X	Visuals
	Mnemonic Devices			Work Study/Apprenticeships
X	Movement			Writing/Journals

The Optics Song

By Warren G. Phillips

© 2018

Sung to *Head and Shoulders, Knees and Toes*

Available on iTunes

The sunlight shines on where we live, (where we live!)

The spectrum's made of ROY.G.BIV, (ROY. G. BIV!)

Red, Orange, Yellow, and Green and Blue

Indigo and Vi-o-let, (Violet!)

Light rays travel in straight lines, (in straight lines!)

And it happens all the time, (all the time!)

And when it hits a different medium

It refracts and it bends some, (it bends some!)

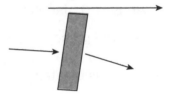

Convex lenses focus light, (focus light!)

What was "left" before is "right" (now it's right!)

Beyond the focal point, the image flips

And the image also tips (also tips!)

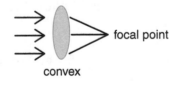

Concave lenses scatter light (scatter light!)

The scattered image isn't bright (isn't bright!)

It's blurry and the rays all move away

Refraction makes them fade away (fade away!)

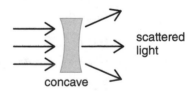

Original graphics created by
Warren G. Phillips

SCIENCE GRADES 3–5 LESSON 9

Chemical Charges and Periodic Table

Lesson Objective(s): *What do you want students to know and be able to do?*

Develop a model to describe that matter is made of particles too small to be seen.

Assessment (Traditional/Authentic): *How will you know students have mastered essential learning?*

Students can sing "The Element Song." Students can explain and give examples with positive and negative particles. Students can predict which elements may combine in a chemical interaction.

Ways to Gain/Maintain Attention (Primacy): *How will you gain and maintain students' attention? Consider need, novelty, meaning, or emotion.*

The *novelty* of singing "The Element Song" will add excitement to the lesson. By seeing the demonstrations, they will find *meaning* in the lesson. Students will eventually become *emotionally* attached as they create and organize into a periodic table.

Content Chunks: *How will you divide and teach the content to engage students' brains?*

Lesson Segment 1: Identify Positive and Negative Charges

- **Activity 1: Fun Fly Stick**

Using a Fun Fly Stick* to create a positive charge, elevate an aluminum strip to show that *likes repel*. Define and explain protons.

- **Activity 2: Electrons**

Touch the elevated aluminum strip to show that negative particles in your finger are attracted to the positive particles and neutralize the charge. Define and explain electrons.

- **Activity 3: Electrons to Electricity**

With a Genecon* hand-held generator, connect wires to light up a light bulb* with negative electrons. Relate electrons to electricity.

- **Activity 4: Uses of Electricity**

Using two Genecons* connected together, notice that by cranking one of them, the other will move. Emphasize that electricity has many uses.

* These materials can be obtained from Educational Innovations, a science supply company.

Lesson Segment 2: Create a Periodic Table

● **Activity 1: "The Element Song"**

Sing "The Element Song" by Warren G. Phillips, which organizes the first 30 elements by the number of protons in each atom. Explain atomic number and how it relates to number of protons.

● **Activity 2: Human Periodic Table**

With each student holding an element card, have students arrange themselves into a periodic table. Sing "The Element Song" again, noticing the order of each element as students sing.

Brain-Compatible Strategies: *Which will you use to deliver content?*

__X__	Brainstorming/Discussion	__X__	Music/Rhythm/Rhyme/Rap
_____	Drawing/Artwork	__X__	Project/Problem-Based Learning
_____	Field Trips	_____	Reciprocal Teaching/Cooperative Learning
_____	Games		
_____	Graphic Organizers/Semantic Maps/Word Webs	_____	Role Plays/Drama/Pantomimes/Charades
_____	Humor	_____	Storytelling
__X__	Manipulatives/Experiments/Labs/Models	_____	Technology
		_____	Visualization/Guided Imagery
_____	Metaphors/Analogies/Similes	__X__	Visuals
_____	Mnemonic Devices	_____	Work Study/Apprenticeships
__X__	Movement	_____	Writing/Journals

The Element Song

Written by Warren G. Phillips

© 2018

Sung to *The Can-Can*

Available on iTunes

(1) (2)
Hydrogen and Helium

(3) (4)
Lithium, Beryllium

(5) (6) (7)
Boron, Carbon, Nitrogen

(8) (9) (10)
Oxygen and Fluorine, Neon.

(11) (12)
Sodium, Magnesium

(13) (14)
Aluminum and Silicon

(15) (16)
Phosphorus and Sulfur,

(17) (18)
Chlorine and the noble Argon.

(19) (20) (21)
Po-tass-ium, Calcium and Scandium

(22) (23) (24)
Ti-ta-nium, Vanadium and Chromium

(25)
And Manganese,

(26) (27) (28)
And Iron, Cobalt, Nickel.

(29) (30)
Copper…….Zinc!!!

SCIENCE GRADES 6–8 LESSON 1

Density

Lesson Objective(s): *What do you want students to know and be able to do?*

Analyze data from tests to determine similarities and differences among several design solutions to identify the best characteristics of each that can be combined into a new solution to better meet the criteria for success.

Assessment (Traditional/Authentic): *How will you know students have mastered essential learning?*

Students can describe instances where density is important. They can understand the relationship between density and buoyancy. They can construct a density column and explain the results. Students can calculate the mass/volume ratio of various substances. Students can sing and explain "The Density Song."

Ways to Gain/Maintain Attention (Primacy): *How will you gain and maintain students' attention? Consider need, novelty, meaning, or emotion.*

Students will need to record data as they calculate various densities. The novelty of floating objects and singing songs will add excitement to the lesson.

Content Chunks: *How will you divide and teach the content to engage students' brains?*

Lesson Segment 1: Comprehend the Basics of Density and Buoyancy

- **Activity 1: Density BrainPOP Video**

Have students view a BrainPOP* video about density followed by a class discussion.

- **Activity 2: "The Density Song"**

Have students sing "The Density Song" by Warren G. Phillips to identify important information and define vocabulary.

- **Activity 3: Density Hypotheses**

Have students hypothesize about whether an object will float or sink in water; place various objects in the water and hypothesize reasons why it should float or sink.

- **Activity 4: Density Formula**

Using various objects, have students measure the mass and volume to determine its density. Have them compare that number to the density of water (1.0) and determine (mathematically) if it will float or sink. Have them check their results.

*BrainPOP is a subscription service with interactive animated videos about various science topics. A free trial subscription is available at https://www.brainpop.com

● **Activity 5: Density Column**

Have students construct a density column such as this one: https://sciencebob.com/a-density-experiment-you-can-drink/ and discuss the results.

Brain-Compatible Strategies: *Which will you use to deliver content?*

X	Brainstorming/Discussion		**X**	Music/Rhythm/Rhyme/Rap
___	Drawing/Artwork		**X**	Project/Problem-Based Learning
___	Field Trips		**X**	Reciprocal Teaching/Cooperative Learning
___	Games			
___	Graphic Organizers/Semantic Maps/Word Webs		___	Role Plays/Drama/Pantomimes/Charades
___	Humor		___	Storytelling
X	Manipulatives/Experiments/Labs/Models		**X**	Technology
			___	Visualization/Guided Imagery
___	Metaphors/Analogies/Similes		**X**	Visuals
___	Mnemonic Devices		___	Work Study/Apprenticeships
X	Movement		___	Writing/Journals

The Density Song

By Warren G. Phillips

© 2018

Sung to *O Christmas Tree*

Available on iTunes

Oh, density Oh, density! The mass to volume ratio!

Oh, density Oh, density! The property that's used to show

Each substance with a purity is tested with assur-ity

Oh, density Oh, density! The mass to volume ratio!

Oh, density Oh, density! Pure water has a quality!

Oh, density Oh, density! The ratio is plain to see

The mass to volume equals one, if you add salt it will have some,

More density! More density! The mass to volume ratio!

SCIENCE GRADES 6–8 LESSON 2

Cells and Cell Parts

Lesson Objective(s): *What do you want students to know and be able to do?*

Develop and use a model to describe the function of a cell as a whole and ways parts of cells contribute to the function.

Assessment (Traditional/Authentic): *How will you know students have mastered essential learning?*

Students can identify and describe cell parts. They can sing "Cells" and the "Respiration Song" and explain the vocabulary in the songs. Students can draw a model of cell parts and explain the function of each part.

Ways to Gain/Maintain Attention (Primacy): *How will you gain and maintain students' attention?* *Consider need, novelty, meaning, or emotion.*

The novelty of singing songs will add excitement to the lesson. Students will eventually become emotionally attached as they create cartoons and add humor to the process.

Content Chunks: *How will you divide and teach the content to engage students' brains?*

Lesson Segment 1: Identify Cell Parts and Functions

- **Activity 1: "Cells" Song**

Have students sing "Cells" by Warren G. Phillips and identify important information and define vocabulary.

- **Activity 2: Cell Drawing**

Have students learn and discuss cell parts and write about their functions, while drawing a model of a cell in class. Have students use microscopes to see living cells and draw what they see. Stain the cells so that students can see the nucleus and other cell parts.

- **Activity 3: Cell Cartoons**

Using actual observations of living cells, have students create several cartoons as if the cells could talk into a comic strip.

- **Activity 4: "Respiration Song"**

Have students sing the "Respiration Song" by Warren G. Phillips and identify important information and define vocabulary.

- **Activity 5: Kingdom Metaphor**

Have groups of students work together to compare cell parts to a kingdom, with descriptions and explanations of each part.

Brain-compatible Strategies: *Which will you use to deliver content?*

X	Brainstorming/Discussion	**X**	Music/Rhythm/Rhyme/Rap
X	Drawing/Artwork	**X**	Project/Problem-Based Learning
___	Field Trips	**X**	Reciprocal Teaching/Cooperative Learning
___	Games		
___	Graphic Organizers/Semantic Maps/Word Webs	___	Role Plays/Drama/Pantomimes/Charades
X	Humor	___	Storytelling
X	Manipulatives/Experiments/Labs/Models	___	Technology
		___	Visualization/Guided Imagery
X	Metaphors/Analogies/Similes	**X**	Visuals
___	Mnemonic Devices	___	Work Study/Apprenticeships
X	Movement	**X**	Writing/Journals

Cells

By Warren G. Phillips

© 2018

Sung to *Home on the Range*

Available on iTunes

Right under your skin

All around you within

Are the cells that you need to survive.

And they're spec-i-al-ized

Doing jobs that comprise

The life functions that keep you alive.

Cells, trillions of cells

Forming tissues that cooperate well

Grouped in organs that strive

To make systems that thrive

To make sure that you keep feeling swell!

Red blood cells in you

Carry oxygen to

Every cell to help make glucose break

Now that stores ener-gy

And it's called A.T.P.

That is Aden-o-sine Triphos-phate.

Cells, trillions of cells

Forming tissues that cooperate well

Grouped in organs that strive

To make systems that thrive

To make sure that you keep feeling swell!

Respiration Song

By Warren G. Phillips / Matt Fisher

© 2018

Sung to *Zip a Dee Doo Dah*

Cell respiration happ'ning in me,

Mito-chondria's the place it will be

breakin' the glucose—make ATP!

Gives us the power of stored energy!

Plants can use what we respire,

CO_2 and water,

Making glucose we require!

Cell respiration within my cells,

Breaking down glucose, and doing it well!

Red blood cells carry oxygen to

All the trillion cells that help make up you

Reacting with glucose, making it break-

Carbon dioxide and water it makes!

Plants can use what we respire,

CO_2 and water,

Making glucose we require!

Cell respiration within my cells,

Breaking down glucose, and doing it well!

SCIENCE GRADES 6–8 LESSON 3

States of Matter

Lesson Objective(s): *What do you want students to know and be able to do?*

Develop a model that predicts and describes changes in particle motion, temperature, and state of a pure substance when thermal energy is added or removed.

Assessment (Traditional/Authentic): *How will you know students have mastered essential learning?*

Students can explain and give examples of each state of matter. Using hand movements, students can represent the energy of each state of matter. Students can sing the "States of Matter" song.

Ways to Gain/Maintain Attention (Primacy): *How will you gain and maintain students' attention? Consider need, novelty, meaning, or emotion.*

The novelty of singing songs will add excitement to the lesson. By seeing examples of phase change, they will find meaning in the lesson. Students will eventually become emotionally attached as they combine movement and song to represent the phase change process.

Content Chunks: *How will you divide and teach the content to engage students' brains?*

Lesson Segment 1: Explore States of Matter

- **Activity 1: "States of Matter" Song**

Have students sing the "States of Matter" song by Warren G. Phillips. Have them identify important information and define vocabulary. Discuss examples of each state of matter. Emphasize that there are five states of matter.

- **Activity 2: Phase Changes**

Students will learn about and discuss phase changes by seeing the following examples:

- Spraying compressed air, changing it from a liquid to a gas state. Notice that the can of compressed air gets cold, indicating that it is taking energy from its environment as it switches from liquid to gas.
- Melting some chocolate bars, changing them from solid to liquid state. Notice that it requires energy from the environment to do this. Also, note that you may smell chocolate (changes to a gas!) as some of the chocolate heats up.

- Freezing water, changing from liquid to solid.
- Boiling water, changing from a liquid to gas.
- Melting ice cubes, changing them from a solid to liquid as room heat is added. Leave the puddle . . . it will evaporate as more energy is added.

- **Activity 3: States of Matter Roleplay**

Have students pantomime the states of matter. Students will use two shaking fists to represent two atoms in a solid. They maintain their position, just as atoms in a solid have a definite shape. Revolving fists indicate two atoms as a liquid (taking the shape of the container). Wiggling outstretched fists represent a gas filling its container. Opening fingers represents the heat and light given off by plasma. Clapping hands represents the collapsed atoms of Bose-Einstein.

Have students sing the "States of Matter" song while doing hand movements that represent each phase of matter.

Brain-Compatible Strategies: *Which will you use to deliver content?*

X	Brainstorming/Discussion	**X**	Music/Rhythm/Rhyme/Rap
	Drawing/Artwork	**X**	Project/Problem-Based Learning
	Field Trips	**X**	Reciprocal Teaching/Cooperative Learning
	Games		
	Graphic Organizers/Semantic Maps/Word Webs	**X**	Role Plays/Drama/Pantomimes/Charades
X	Humor		Storytelling
	Manipulatives/Experiments/Labs/Models		Technology
			Visualization/Guided Imagery
	Metaphors/Analogies/Similes	**X**	Visuals
	Mnemonic Devices		Work Study/Apprenticeships
X	Movement		Writing/Journals

States of Matter

By Warren G. Phillips

© 2018

Sung to *Battle Hymn of the Republic*

Available on iTunes

The states of matter come from atoms' energy they store (*Students vibrate fists in fixed positions*)

And it's constantly exerted as they vibrate back and forth

As the energy accumulates, the atoms vibrate more

Phase changes can occur!

Solid, Liquid, Gas and Plasma (*Students vibrate fists in fixed positions, then revolve them, then outstretch them, then open fingers*)

Solid, Liquid, Gas, and Plasma

Solid, Liquid, Gas, and Plasma

And now Bose-Einstein! (*Students clap their hands*)

Solids have less energy with atoms locked in place (*Students vibrate fists in fixed positions*)

Liquid atoms move around and take up different shapes (*Students revolve fists*)

Gaseous atoms move apart and fill up any space (*Students outstretch fists*)

And Plasma photons glow! (*Students open fists to show fingers*)

Solid, Liquid, Gas and Plasma (*Students vibrate fists in fixed positions, then revolve them, then outstretch them, then open fingers*)

Solid, Liquid, Gas, and Plasma

Solid, Liquid, Gas, and Plasma

And now Bose-Einstein! (*Students clap their hands*)

Now Einstein hypothesized another state exists *(Students clap their hands)*

And more recently a scientist has found what he had missed

A state at real cold temperatures that ar-en't in our midst

Bose found it could subsist!

Solid, Liquid, Gas, and Plasma *(Students vibrate fists in fixed positions, then revolve them, then outstretch them, then open fingers)*

Solid, Liquid, Gas, and Plasma

Solid, Liquid, Gas, and Plasma

And now Bose-Einstein! *(Students clap their hands)*

And now Bose-Einstein!

And now Bose-Einstein!

SCIENCE GRADES 6–8 LESSON 4

The Human Heart and Circulation

Lesson Objective(s): *What do you want students to know and be able to do?*

Use an argument supported by evidence for how the body is a system of interacting subsystems composed of groups of cells.

Assessment (Traditional/Authentic): *How will you know students have mastered essential learning?*

Students can identify, describe, and label parts of a human heart. Students can create a model of a heart and label parts. Students can visualize the process of circulation of blood. Students can sing the "Heart Song" and explain the lyrics.

Ways to Gain/Maintain Attention (Primacy): *How will you gain and maintain students' attention? Consider* <u>need</u>, <u>novelty</u>, <u>meaning</u>, *or* <u>emotion</u>.

Students will need to learn parts of the heart as they create a heart model. The novelty of the "Heart Song" will add excitement to the lesson. By learning how circulation happens, students will find personal meaning in the lesson. Students will eventually become emotionally attached as they visualize circulation and compare heart rates with experiments and exercise.

Content Chunks: *How will you divide and teach the content to engage students' brains?*

Lesson Segment 1: Identify Parts of the Human Heart

- **Activity 1: Heart Manipulatives**

Have students label parts of the human heart from an internet picture. Working in groups, have them use modeling clay to identify and create important parts and define vocabulary. Discuss how the heart works to pump blood throughout the body.

- **Activity 2: Pulse Rate Experiment**

Have students experiment with pulse rates. With partners, have them take a pulse rate while at rest, exercise for one minute (i.e., jump rope, jog in place, jumping jacks, etc.) Keep a journal of the type of exercise and the pulse rates for classroom comparisons (graph) and discussion.

- **Activity 3: H-E-A-R-T Acronym**

Create a mnemonic device. Have groups of students create an acronym using the letters: H - E – A –R –T using important words related to the heart. Have them draw on a poster for classroom display.

- **Activity 4: "Heart Song"**

Have students sing the "Heart Song" by Warren G. Phillips and identify important information and define vocabulary.

Lesson Segment 2: Identify the Function of Blood Circulation and Capillary Action

- **Activity 1: Coffee Stirrer Capillaries**

Use hollow coffee stirrers (or capillary tubes) and have students place the tip into red food coloring. Notice that it climbs up into the stirrer, against the force of gravity. The coffee stirrer may then be used as a pen to write a message on a piece of paper. Compare to human capillaries and explain capillary action.

- **Activity 2: Circulation Visualization**

Create a visualization. Have students describe the journey of the blood as it travels through the heart and the rest of the body. Students listen to music explaining the process of circulation using the "Heart Song" by Warren G. Phillips.

Brain-Compatible Strategies: *Which will you use to deliver content?*

X	Brainstorming/Discussion	**X**	Music/Rhythm/Rhyme/Rap
X	Drawing/Artwork	**X**	Project/Problem-Based Learning
___	Field Trips	**X**	Reciprocal Teaching/Cooperative Learning
___	Games		
___	Graphic Organizers/Semantic Maps/Word Webs	___	Role Plays/Drama/Pantomimes/Charades
___	Humor	___	Storytelling
X	Manipulatives/Experiments/Labs/Models	**X**	Technology
		X	Visualization/Guided Imagery
X	Metaphors/Analogies/Similes	**X**	Visuals
X	Mnemonic Devices	___	Work Study/Apprenticeships
X	Movement	**X**	Writing/Journals

Heart Song

By Warren G. Phillips

© 2018

Sung to *Oompa Loompa*

Available on iTunes

Lub – a – Dub, your heart is a pump

Moving your blood with valves that go
"thump."

Chambers fill and muscle cells squeeze,

Blood is pushed—along like a breeze!

All from an organ the size of a fist

Conn-ected to blood—vessels that twist.

All through the body carrying blood

Bringing some oxygen – to – cells (and
some food along with it)!

Lub – a – Dub, the organ repeats

During your lifetime, billions of beats.

A-tria and ventricles fill

Moving the blood—with never a spill!

All from an organ the size of a fist

Conn-ected to blood—vessels that twist,

All through the body carrying blood

Bringing some oxy-gen – to – cells (and
some food along with it!)

Lub – a – Dub, the cardiac beat

Heart disease may cause your defeat.

Ex-er-cise you need to include

Along with a diet of eating good foods!

SCIENCE GRADES 6–8 LESSON 5

Engineering Design—Classification

Lesson Objective(s): *What do you want students to know and be able to do?*

Define a simple design problem, reflecting a need or a want that includes specified criteria for success and constraints on materials, time, or cost.

Assessment (Traditional/Authentic): *How will you know students have mastered essential learning?*

Students can identify characteristics of objects and classify them. Students can brainstorm and create a system of organizing various types of materials. Students can compare their classification system to scientifically established ones. Students can sing the "Classification Song" and explain the lyrics.

Ways to Gain/Maintain Attention (Primacy): *How will you gain and maintain students' attention? Consider need, novelty, meaning, or emotion.*

The novelty of a classification game and song will add excitement to the lesson. By learning how important classification is, they will find personal meaning in the lesson.

Content Chunks: *How will you divide and teach the content to engage students' brains?*

Lesson Segment 1: Determine How We Classify Objects

- **Activity 1: Classifying Objects**

Place all of the students' sneakers (or gloves) in a pile in the middle of the room. Have students brainstorm ways of organizing and classifying into categories by characteristics. Divide the class into two teams. One team gets the left sneakers; the other team gets the right. Assign a secretary to write down categories as students brainstorm and compete with the other team. Assign a time limit (i.e., 15 minutes).

- **Activity 2: Categorizing Seashells**

Divide a group of random seashells (or rocks) into two piles. Divide the class into two teams. Assign a secretary to write down categories as students brainstorm and observe characteristics as they compete with the other team. Assign a time limit (i.e., 15 minutes).

Compare your seashell categories to seashell classification from a seashell identification guide. Write down the classifications seashells (or rocks) have in common.

- **Activity 3: Classification Characteristics**

Have students brainstorm in groups how you might classify all living things. Have them write down a list of characteristics that may be important.

● **Activity 4: "Classification Song"**

Sing the "Classification Song" by Warren G. Phillips and identify important information and define vocabulary. Have them compare categories and kingdoms.

Brain-Compatible Strategies: *Which will you use to deliver content?*

X	Brainstorming/Discussion	**X**	Music/Rhythm/Rhyme/Rap
___	Drawing/Artwork	**X**	Project/Problem-Based Learning
___	Field Trips	**X**	Reciprocal Teaching/Cooperative Learning
X	Games		
___	Graphic Organizers/Semantic Maps/Word Webs	___	Role Plays/Drama/Pantomimes/Charades
___	Humor	___	Storytelling
X	Manipulatives/Experiments/Labs/Models	___	Technology
		___	Visualization/Guided Imagery
___	Metaphors/Analogies/Similes	**X**	Visuals
___	Mnemonic Devices	___	Work Study/Apprenticeships
X	Movement	**X**	Writing/Journals

Classification Song

By Warren G. Phillips

© 2018

Sung to *I'm a Yankee Doodle Dandy*

Available on iTunes

Kingdom, Phylum, Class, and Order

Fam'ly, Genus, and Species.

These are the categories used by science

Cla-ssi-fying life with ease!

A scientist named Carolus Linnaeus

Made the system that we see:

Kingdom, Phylum, Class, and Order

Fam'ly, Genus, Species.

Classifying life, tax-on-omy!

These are currently the kingdoms:

Arch-a-e-bacteria,

Plant, and, Animal, and Fungi too

Protists, and Eubacteria

A scientist named Carolus Linnaeus

Made the system that we see:

Kingdom, Phylum, Class, and Order

Fam'ly, Genus, Species

Classifying life,

Classifying life,

Classifying life, tax-on-omy!

SCIENCE GRADES 6–8 LESSON 6

DNA Model

Lesson Objective(s): *What do you want students to know and be able to do?*

Develop and use a model to describe why asexual reproduction results in offspring with identical genetic information and sexual reproduction results in offspring with genetic variation.

Assessment (Traditional/Authentic): *How will you know students have mastered essential learning?*

Students can create a model of DNA molecules with complementary strands. Students can identify base pairs. Students can model and explain the process of replication.

Ways to Gain/Maintain Attention (Primacy): *How will you gain and maintain students' attention? Consider* <u>need</u>, <u>novelty</u>, *meaning, or emotion.*

Students will need to understand DNA structure to complete their model. The novelty of the "DNA" song will encourage retention of information learned.

Content Chunks: *How will you divide and teach the content to engage students' brains?*

Lesson Segment 1: Comprehend DNA Structure

- **Activity 1: Genetic Discussion**

Lead the class in a discussion about why we look like our relatives, but not exactly the same. Tell stories of identical and fraternal twins. Introduce asexual and sexual reproduction in terms of genetics and genetic variation.

- **Activity 2: BrainPOP Video**

Have students watch an introductory video (BrainPOP* or YouTube) on DNA structure and base pairs.

- **Activity 3: DNA Manipulatives**

Pass out a pipe cleaner and about 50 UV beads to each student**. Shine a light on the beads to reveal four colors. Each color bead will represent an amino acid—orange (adenine), purple (thymine), blue (cytosine), and pink (guanine).

  Have students work in pairs. When one student slides a bead onto the pipe cleaner (i.e., an orange one representing adenine), the other student will add its base pair (i.e., a purple one representing thymine). Therefore, orange (adenine) and purple (thymine) are always base pairs, and blue (cytosine) and pink (guanine) are always base pairs. While any color bead can be chosen next for the pipe cleaner, the other student with its base pair amino acid always matches it. Thus, each

* BrainPOP is a subscription animated video web site. It is available at https://www.brainpop.com

** Pipe cleaners and UV beads are available at https://www.teachersource.com

group of students is making a unique DNA strand which is complemented by the other student's DNA strand. Construction continues until both pipe cleaners are filled. A small knot can be made at each end to stop the beads from sliding.

Have students match up their DNA complementary strands, and get two more pipe cleaners to twist around their strands, representing the sugar-phosphate sides of a DNA molecule. When the strands are put into sunlight the colors appear, much like a phenotype. When the beads are placed away from light, they turn white and do not reveal the color, much like a genotype. As a final assessment, have students bring the DNA up to you. Check the complementary strand structure, while students write an explanation of the parts of the DNA molecule, phenotype and genotype, and how DNA replication occurs.

- **Activity 4: "DNA" Song**

Have students sing the "DNA" song by Warren G. Phillips and identify important information and define vocabulary. Have them explain the lyrics in terms of genotype and phenotype, and compare to the DNA strands that they constructed.

- **Activity 5: *BFF* DNA (Optional)**

Students could untwist the DNA and each student could make a bracelet out of their complementary strand. The other student could wear their complementary strand as their best friend forever (BFF). When they wear it outside in the light, they will see colors (phenotype) and notice that inside the colors disappear (genotype).

- **Activity 6: Just For Fun!**

Challenge students by having a contest to see who can spell DNA the fastest (deoxyribonucleic acid).

Brain-Compatible Strategies: *Which will you use to deliver content?*

__X__	Brainstorming/Discussion	__X__	Music/Rhythm/Rhyme/Rap
_____	Drawing/Artwork	__X__	Project/Problem-Based Learning
_____	Field Trips	__X__	Reciprocal Teaching/Cooperative Learning
__X__	Games		
_____	Graphic Organizers/Semantic Maps/Word Webs	_____	Role Plays/Drama/Pantomimes/Charades
_____	Humor	__X__	Storytelling
__X__	Manipulatives/Experiments/Labs/Models	__X__	Technology
__X__	Metaphors/Analogies/Similes	_____	Visualization/Guided Imagery
_____	Mnemonic Devices	__X__	Visuals
		_____	Work Study/Apprenticeships
__X__	Movement	__X__	Writing/Journals

DNA

By Warren G. Phillips

© 2018

Sung to *Ta-Ra-Ra Boom-De-Ay*

Available on iTunes

I made some DNA!

I just learned how today!

You take some adenine

And add some cytosine.

Thymine and guanine, too

Are added to the brew,

Then they're connected to

Long sugar molecules.

And I can hardly wait

For it to replicate:

First it's unraveling

And then assem-bl-ing.

I'll take my DNA

And find a mate today.

I'll make genetically

A brand new family tree!

My baby's DNA

It will display some day,

A handsome phenotype

And perfect genotype.

My children's DNA

It will create some day

Grandchildren that will be

Looking a lot like me!

SCIENCE GRADES 6–8 LESSON 7

Chemical Reactions

Lesson Objective(s): *What do you want students to know and be able to do?*

Analyze and interpret data on the properties of substances before and after the substances interact to determine if a chemical reaction has occurred.

Assessment (Traditional/Authentic): *How will you know students have mastered essential learning?*

Students can explain what happens in a chemical reaction. They can give examples of chemical changes, identify reactants and products of a chemical change, and understand chemical formulas.

Ways to Gain/Maintain Attention (Primacy): *How will you gain and maintain students' attention? Consider <u>need</u>, <u>novelty</u>, meaning, or emotion.*

Students will need to understand chemical change and chemical formulas to complete their experiment. The novelty of the chemical change reactions will encourage retention of information learned.

Content Chunks: *How will you divide and teach the content to engage students' brains?*

Lesson Segment 1: Analyze and Interpret Data From Chemical Reactions

- **Activity 1: BrainPOP Video**

Have students watch an introductory video (BrainPOP* or YouTube) on chemical changes, reactants, and products.

- **Activity 2: Chemical Reactant Discussion**

Discuss and brainstorm about various chemical reactions that students have seen or experienced. Make a list of various experiments and hypothesize about the reactants and products.

- **Activity 3: Chemical Reaction Experiment One**

Demonstrate a chemical reaction with the class. A great example is comparing magnesium ribbon (Mg) to aluminum shavings (Al). Examine characteristics and make a list. (They are very similar!) Note their location on the periodic table (next to each other, atomic #12 and atomic #13). Then, expose both to a flame. The aluminum melts (no chemical change) **(Al +O➔Al + O)** and the magnesium ribbon emits a bright light and large amounts of heat. (Do this experiment as a demo with goggles, forceps, and away from close proximity of students.) The magnesium combines readily with oxygen to form magnesium oxide **(Mg + O ➔MgO).** The resulting powder is **MgO**, which is a

---

* BrainPOP is a subscription online animated video service. It is available at https://www.brainpop.com/

white powder looking and acting nothing like oxygen or magnesium. A YouTube video on comparing aluminum and magnesium is available at https://www.youtube.com/watch?v=g2A5o_MJ1-k.

● **Activity 4: Chemical Reaction Experiment Two**

Have students conduct this experiment in groups of four to six.

Use a small empty water bottle and add ½ cup of vinegar. Take a balloon and stretch it out. Using a funnel, fill the balloon ½ way with baking soda. Now carefully put the neck of the balloon all the way over the neck of the bottle without letting any baking soda into the bottle. Then, lift the balloon up so that the baking soda falls from the balloon into the bottle and mixes with the vinegar. Watch and record your results as the carbon dioxide produced fills up the balloon. Details of this experiment are online at https://sciencebob.com/build-a-fizz-inflator/.

● **Activity 5: Chemical Formulas**

Analyze, explain, and have students write this chemical formula:

$$C_2H_4O_2 + NaHCO_3 \rightarrow NaC_2H_3O_2 + H_2O + CO_2$$ or, in common terms:
vinegar + baking soda → sodium acetate + water + carbon dioxide.

The carbon dioxide is the gas that fills the balloon and is a product that is chemically different than what you started with (the reactants).

● **Activity 6: Activity 2 Revisited**

Challenge students by having them review the brainstorm list (from Activity 2) and research the chemical formulas.

Note: All safety procedures should be followed and are the responsibility of the teacher conducting the class.

Brain-Compatible Strategies: *Which will you use to deliver content?*

__X__	Brainstorming/Discussion	_____	Music/Rhythm/Rhyme/Rap
_____	Drawing/Artwork	__X__	Project/Problem-Based Learning
_____	Field Trips	__X__	Reciprocal Teaching/Cooperative Learning
_____	Games		
_____	Graphic Organizers/Semantic Maps/Word Webs	_____	Role Plays/Drama/Pantomimes/Charades
_____	Humor	_____	Storytelling
__X__	Manipulatives/Experiments/Labs/Models	__X__	Technology
_____	Metaphors/Analogies/Similes	_____	Visualization/Guided Imagery
		__X__	Visuals
_____	Mnemonic Devices	_____	Work Study/Apprenticeships
__X__	Movement	_____	Writing/Journals

SCIENCE GRADES 6–8 LESSON 8

Plate Tectonics

Lesson Objective(s): *What do you want students to know and be able to do?*

Analyze and interpret data on the distribution of fossils and rocks, continental shapes, and seafloor structures to provide evidence of the past plate motions.

Assessment (Traditional/Authentic): *How will you know students have mastered essential learning?*

Students can explain the movement of the continents. Students can identify a ring of fire. Students can learn "The Volcano Song" and explain the lyrics.

Ways to Gain/Maintain Attention (Primacy): *How will you gain and maintain students' attention? Consider need, novelty, meaning, or emotion.*

Information obtained will provide meaning behind the location of earthquakes and volcanoes on the earth. The novelty of "The Volcano Song" will encourage retention of information learned.

Content Chunks: *How will you divide and teach the content to engage students' brains?*

Lesson Segment 1: Analyze Data From Plate Motions

- **Activity 1: Plate Tectonics Video**

Have students watch an introductory National Geographic plate tectonics video at:
https://video.nationalgeographic.com/video/news/101-videos/162117-news-continental-drift-101-vin. Have them discuss and brainstorm about forces at work that cause this movement.

- **Activity 2: Volcano Videos**

Visit a website showing current active volcanoes (such as: https://www.volcanodiscovery.com/erupting_volcanoes.html). Plot the locations of these volcanoes on a world map.

- **Activity 3: Seafloor Spreading Video**

View the WGBH video on seafloor spreading at https://www.youtube.com/watch?v=ZzvDlP6xd9o Discuss important ideas.

- **Activity 4: Saltine Cracker Geography**

Place students in groups of three to four. Have them use their teeth to bite saltine crackers, creating rough outlines of each of the continents. Place these crackers on a sheet of construction paper to represent a map of the earth. On the paper, label the continents and explain the concepts of seafloor spreading, the ring of fire, and continental drift.

- **Activity 5: Spaghetti Sauce/Continents**

Place a large, flat pan on the edge of a hot plate, so it will not heat evenly. Heat some spaghetti sauce on the pan slowly until it simmers.* Take one of the cracker representations from the previous activity and place the continents on the hot spaghetti sauce. Watch for slight movements, as the sauce will show slight convection due to uneven heating. Draw the continents initial position. Draw the continents again 15 minutes later.

- **Activity 6: "The Volcano Song"**

Sing "The Volcano Song" by Warren G. Phillips and identify important information and define vocabulary. Explain the lyrics.

* All safety procedures should be followed and are the responsibility of the teacher conducting the class.

Brain-Compatible Strategies: *Which will you use to deliver content?*

__X__	Brainstorming/Discussion	__X__	Project/Problem-Based Learning
__X__	Drawing/Artwork	__X__	Reciprocal Teaching/Cooperative Learning
_____	Field Trips		
_____	Games	_____	Role Plays/Drama/Pantomimes/Charades
_____	Graphic Organizers/Semantic Maps/Word Webs	_____	Storytelling
_____	Humor	__X__	Technology
__X__	Manipulatives/Experiments/Labs/Models	_____	Visualization/Guided Imagery
		__X__	Visuals
_____	Metaphors/Analogies/Similes	_____	Work Study/Apprenticeships
_____	Mnemonic Devices	_____	Writing/Journals
__X__	Music/Rhythm/Rhyme/Rap		

The Volcano Song

By Warren G. Phillips

© 2018

Sung to *She'll Be Coming Around the Mountain When She Comes*

Available on iTunes

Before the earth creates a vol-ca-no

The heat that's in the magma down below

Expands the rock which makes the pressure

'Til the magma finds a fissure

And the lava will erupt and start to flow.

If the pressure down below is really high

Then the lava will shoot way up in the sky

Making pumice full of bubbles

Forming cinder cones with troubles

'Cause the living things below are going to die.

If the pressure down below is really low

Then the lava that emerges comes out slow.

The volcano it will yield

Is what geologists call "shield"

And it's kinda flat when it begins to grow.

Now the continents are moving not too swift

But it's what they're calling "continental drift"

When the plates begin colliding

One of them begins subsiding

And the friction heats up magma where they lift.

Before the earth creates a vol-ca-no

The heat that's in the magma down below

Expands the rock which makes the pressure

'Til the magma finds a fissure

And the lava will erupt and start to flow.

SCIENCE GRADES 6–8 LESSON 9

Solar System

Lesson Objective(s): *What do you want students to know and be able to do?*

Analyze and interpret data to determine scale properties of objects in the solar system.

Assessment (Traditional/Authentic): *How will you know students have mastered essential learning?*

Students can create a model of the solar system using ratio and proportion to compare relative size and distance. Students can recite the order and relationship of planets within the solar system. Students can learn "The Solar System Song" and explain the lyrics.

Ways to Gain/Maintain Attention (Primacy): *How will you gain and maintain students' attention? Consider need, novelty, meaning, or emotion.*

The Solar System Song will provide meaning behind the activities being conducted. The novelty of creating a model of the solar system will help with comprehension of relative sizes and distances of the planets.

Content Chunks: *How will you divide and teach the content to engage students' brains?*

Lesson Segment 1: Analyze and Interpret Solar System Data

- **Activity 1: *Powers of 10* Video**

View the video "Powers of 10". The video is available at https://www.youtube.com/watch?v=0fKBhvDjuy0. Review and reflect in writing on the information obtained.

- **Activity 2: "The Solar System Song"**

Sing "The Solar System Song" by Warren G. Phillips; identify important information and define vocabulary. Explain the lyrics.

- **Activity 3: Solar System Model Calculator**

Visit the website of Solar System Model Calculator at http://thinkzone.wlonk.com/SS/SolarSystemModel.php.

   Notice that you can input the model scale or other information. Try various model scales to see the results in the model table and discuss your results. Notice that you can also enter solar system objects and choose diameter or distance from the sun. Try several different variables to see the results in the Solar System Model Table. (For example, input Earth's diameter at 1 foot and click the calculate button—notice that the Earth's diameter lists at 12 inches and Jupiter's is 131 inches) Have groups of students try various calculations until they achieve numbers that would make the "best" model for your classroom. Record those numbers in a data table and use diameter information to construct a model of each object in the solar system using scissors and construction paper. Write about your experience in a journal.

- **Activity 4: Distance Scale**

Using the same website, enter "distance from the sun." (For example, input Earth's distance at 1 foot from the sun, then click the calculate button. If you want your answer in US units, check off the US units in the data and recalculate.) The orbit radius in the Solar System Model table shows you how far apart each planet would have to be. Have groups of students try various calculations until they achieve numbers that would make the "best" model for your classroom. Then, students can create their own distance scale. Use a piece of string to demark where each of the planets would go, based upon the calculations.

Brain-Compatible Strategies: *Which will you use to deliver content?*

__X__	Brainstorming/Discussion		__X__	Music/Rhythm/Rhyme/Rap*
__X__	Drawing/Artwork		__X__	Project/Problem-Based Learning
____	Field Trips		__X__	Reciprocal Teaching/Cooperative Learning
____	Games			
____	Graphic Organizers/Semantic Maps/Word Webs		____	Role Plays/Drama/Pantomimes/Charades
____	Humor		____	Storytelling
__X__	Manipulatives/Experiments/Labs/Models		__X__	Technology
			____	Visualization/Guided Imagery
____	Metaphors/Analogies/Similes		__X__	Visuals
____	Mnemonic Devices		____	Work Study/Apprenticeships
__X__	Movement		__X__	Writing/Journals

The Solar System Song

By Warren G. Phillips

© 2018

Sung to *Oh Susannah*

Available on iTunes

The sun's a star in the Milky Way spinnin' with the galaxy

And the planets orbit 'round the sun with great velocity.

Mercury, Venus, Earth, and Mars, the inner planets go

Jupiter, Saturn, U-ran-us, Neptune, NOT Pluto!

The Solar System, eight planets 'round the sun

Ro-tating and revolving too

In orbits one by one.

Now the planets they have satellites – but we just call them moons

And comets made of rock and ice could be harbingers of doom

Ast-er-oids are rocks and dust that are floating round the sun

If gravity pulls them in to earth, a meteor they become.

The Solar System, eight planets 'round the sun

Ro-tating and revolving too

In orbits one by one.

Well scientists using telescopes have learned we're not alone

other stars in the galaxy have planets all their own.

And other galaxies have stars with planets going 'round

And maybe life exists there—just waiting to be found!

(Continued)

(Continued)

The Solar System, eight planets 'round the sun

Ro-tating and revolving too

In orbits one by one.

The sun's a star in the Milky Way spinnin' with the galaxy

And the planets orbit 'round the sun with great velocity.

Mercury, Venus, Earth, and Mars, the inner planets go

Jupiter, Saturn, U-ran-us, Neptune, NOT Pluto!

The Solar System, eight planets 'round the sun

Ro-tating and revolving too

In orbits one by one.

SCIENCE GRADES 6–8 LESSON 10

Ocean Ecosystem

Lesson Objective(s): *What do you want students to know and be able to do?*

Construct an explanation that predicts patterns of interactions among organisms across multiple ecosystems.

Assessment (Traditional/Authentic): *How will you know students have mastered essential learning?*

Students can research various organisms of an ocean ecosystem, identifying the requirements to sustain life. Students can recognize the interrelationships between organisms and explain a food web. Students can learn the "Water Wonderland" song and explain the lyrics.

Ways to Gain/Maintain Attention (Primacy): *How will you gain and maintain students' attention? Consider need, novelty, meaning, or emotion.*

The *Water Wonderland* song will provide meaning behind the activities being conducted. The novelty of creating a food web will help to understand the complexity and interactions between organisms.

Content Chunks: *How will you divide and teach the content to engage students' brains?*

Lesson Segment 1: Explain How an Ocean Ecosystem Functions

- **Activity 1: Ocean Organism Research**

Have students research an individual ocean organism using the internet, focusing on predators, prey, competition, and mutually beneficial interactions. Review and reflect on the information obtained.

- **Activity 2: Ocean Organism Drawing**

Have students draw a picture of their organism. Have them place their picture on the wall and identify the organism, thereby creating an ocean mural.

- **Activity 3: "Water Wonderland" Song**

Have students sing the "Water Wonderland" song by Warren G. Phillips and identify important information and define vocabulary. Have them explain the lyrics.

- **Activity 4: Make a Food Web**

Have students make a food web according to the following directions:

Make a card with the name of your organism (including the scientific name). Punch holes in the card and use a piece of string to hang the card around your neck. Using a ball of yarn, create a food web by connecting each organism to the other organisms that affect it (predator, prey, food source, competitor, and mutually beneficial). Pass the ball of yarn to that organism, and have that organism, in turn, connect to another organism that affects it. Continue building the web until all participants are connected. Discuss what would happen if one species were removed. What if all predators were removed? What if many other organisms were included? Students lean back with the yarn taut. Teacher cuts the string to reveal how species are dependent on each other.

Brain-Compatible Strategies: *Which will you use to deliver content?*

__X__	Brainstorming/Discussion	__X__	Music/Rhythm/Rhyme/Rap
__X__	Drawing/Artwork	__X__	Project/Problem-Based Learning
_____	Field Trips	__X__	Reciprocal Teaching/Cooperative Learning
_____	Games		
__X__	Graphic Organizers/Semantic Maps/Word Webs	__X__	Role Plays/Drama/Pantomimes/Charades
_____	Humor	_____	Storytelling
__X__	Manipulatives/Experiments/Labs/Models	_____	Technology
		_____	Visualization/Guided Imagery
_____	Metaphors/Analogies/Similes	__X__	Visuals
_____	Mnemonic Devices	_____	Work Study/Apprenticeships
__X__	Movement	_____	Writing/Journals

Water Wonderland

By Warren G. Phillips / Cyndi DiCicco

© 2018

Sung to *Winter Wonderland*

Available on iTunes

Low tide's here, birds are looking

In the sun, now we're cooking.

There's no place to hide, go along for the ride

Living in the intertidal zone.

High tide now, the waves are crashing

Against the rocks, we are smashing

Adaptations we make, to survive in this place

Floating through a water wonderland.

In the shallow ocean there are plankton.

Producers make the food, and others eat.

Light can reach the creatures that will thrive there,

Especially around the coral reef.

Further on, the open ocean

Bigger fish, they're in motion.

They swim after prey, do they sleep, do they play?

Floating through a water wonderland.

We will check out the sea floor

Where the creatures must adapt more

Bioluminescent, or live near a vent

Floating through a water wonderland.

(Continued)

(Continued)

Survival in the ocean's an adventure,

It isn't very easy you can see.

Over-fishing and pollution threaten

All the members of this whole community!

Do your part to save our ocean!

Keep it clean, that's the potion!

We can only make it better if we all just work together

Floating through a water wonderland.

SCIENCE GRADES K–8 LESSON 11

The Birthday Egg

Lesson Objective(s): *What do you want students to know and be able to do?*

Analyze data to determine if a design solution works as intended to change the speed or direction of an object with a push or a pull.

Plan and conduct an investigation to provide evidence of the effects of balanced and unbalanced forces on the motion of an object. (Recommended for Grades 6–8)

Plan an investigation to provide evidence that the change in an object's motion depends on the sum of the forces on the object and the mass of the object. (Recommended for Grades 6–8)

Assessment (Traditional/Authentic): *How will you know students have mastered essential learning?*

Students can explain the motion of the egg as it enters into the inverted milk bottle. Students can visualize the atoms and molecules involved in the Birthday Egg experiment. Students can explain with a comic strip and thought bubbles. Students can sing the "Birthday Egg Song" and identify forces involved in the experiment.

Ways to Gain/Maintain Attention (Primacy): *How will you gain and maintain students' attention?*
Consider need, novelty, meaning, or emotion.

Students will provide meaning to an experiment by analysis of results. The novelty of a birthday egg will add excitement. The personalized birthday tribute and the comic strip will add emotion to the experiment.

Content Chunks: *How will you divide and teach the content to engage students' brains?*

Lesson Segment 1: Analyze Data to Determine the Merit of Design

- **Activity 1: The Birthday Egg**

Ask students if anyone has a birthday today. If not, pick a student whose birthday is closest to today's date. Using a peeled hardboiled egg, ask the student how old (s)he is. For each year, place a wooden matchstick into the pointed end of the hardboiled egg. About 10 to 12 matchsticks work best, so a younger child can add a matchstick for good luck, one to grow on, and so forth. Explain to the class that the egg is going to jump into the milk bottle, which is held upside down over the matchsticks.

- **Activity 2: Crowded Visualization and Metaphor**

Create a visualization: Close your eyes and imagine that your classroom is empty and that there is a giant beach ball in the doorway to the next classroom. Now, imagine that all of your classmates returning from lunch start piling into the classroom. In fact, all of the *other* classrooms of students also begin to pile into your classroom, so that it is packed with kids. As they keep piling in, it is getting so crowded that they begin pushing against the walls and the beach ball. As they push the beach ball, it starts to compress and squeeze into the next classroom, which is empty. All of a sudden, the beach ball squeezes through the door, and the classmates start piling into the next classroom.

Explain that the kids in your story are like the molecules of air and that the beach ball is like the egg. When you heat the air with the matches, the molecules move farther apart. Have the students demonstrate this with their fists representing atoms. Have them vibrate their fists and move them further apart as the air is heated. Tell them that when we heat the air inside of the bottle, there will be fewer atoms because they move farther apart.

- **Activity 3: Milk Bottle Drawing**

Have students draw a picture of the inverted milk bottle. Have them draw the egg underneath it with the matchsticks pointed toward the opening in the bottle. Label the drawing.

- **Activity 4: "The Birthday Egg Song"**

Have students practice singing the "Birthday Egg Song," sung to the tune "Happy Birthday to You." Explain the lyrics and compare the bottle to the empty classroom and the egg to the beach ball. Outside of the beach ball will be the crowded area where all of the atoms will be trying to push the egg into the milk bottle.

> *Happy Birthday to you!*
>
> *This egg is for you!*
>
> *Fewer atoms in the bottle*
>
> *Make the air push it through!*

- **Activity 5: *Surprise!***

Wearing safety glasses, light the matches* and allow the large flame to enter the inverted milk bottle. This will heat the air in the bottle and the atoms will move farther apart, escaping from the bottle. After a few seconds, place the matches into the bottle and snug the egg up to the opening. Now, ask the class to sing the "Birthday Egg Song." The egg will be pushed (*opposite to gravity!*) by the outside (crowded) atoms into the bottle in a matter of seconds. Usually, the egg does not break, which indicates that it was pushed from all sides into the bottle.

Note: All safety procedures should be followed and are the responsibility of the teacher conducting the experiment.

- **Activity 6: Comic Strip Drawing**

Have students draw a picture of the experiment in comic strip format and label the drawings. Have them explain the forces involved (air pressure) and draw arrows to show the motion of the egg. Ask them to add thought bubbles to create humor and emotions.

Brain-Compatible Strategies: *Which will you use to deliver content?*

__X__	Brainstorming/Discussion	__X__	Music/Rhythm/Rhyme/Rap
__X__	Drawing/Artwork	__X__	Project/Problem-Based Learning
_____	Field Trips	__X__	Reciprocal Teaching/Cooperative Learning
_____	Games		
_____	Graphic Organizers/Semantic Maps/Word Webs	_____	Role Plays/Drama/Pantomimes/Charades
__X__	Humor	_____	Storytelling
__X__	Manipulatives/Experiments/Labs/Models	_____	Technology
		__X__	Visualization/Guided Imagery
__X__	Metaphors/Analogies/Similes	__X__	Visuals
_____	Mnemonic Devices	_____	Work Study/Apprenticeships
_____	Movement	__X__	Writing/Journals

7

25 Sample Social Studies Lessons

SOCIAL STUDIES GRADES K–2 LESSON 1

Responsibility

Lesson Objective(s): *What do you want students to know and be able to do?*

Explain that children and adults have rights and responsibilities at home, at school, in the classroom, and in the community. Have them answer the following:

1. What does responsibility look like?
2. What are my responsibilities at home and at school?
3. What would happen if I weren't responsible?

Assessment (Traditional/Authentic): *How will you know students have mastered essential learning?*

Students create an acrostic using the word *RESPONSIBILITY*.

Ways to Gain/Maintain Attention (Primacy): *How will you gain and maintain students' attention? Consider need, novelty, <u>meaning</u>, or emotion.*

Write the word *responsible* on the board and ask students to draw a picture of what they think it means to be responsible.

Content Chunks: *How will you divide and teach the content to engage students' brains?*

Lesson Segment 1: Define *Responsibility*.

- **Activity 1: Read Aloud**

Read aloud one of the two books listed below or another book related to *responsibility.*

> *If Everybody Did* by JoAnn Stover or *What If Everybody Did That?* by Ellen Javernick

- **Activity 2: T-Chart**

Have students create a T-chart that lists the responsibilities or duties they are responsible for performing at home and within the classroom. Have students discuss with a partner how performing those responsibilities helps the family or classroom operate better.

- **Activity 3: Acrostic**

Have students create an acrostic using the word *RESPONSIBILITY*.

Lesson Segment 2: Define *Irresponsibility*

- **Activity 1: Discussion**

Have students explore the implications of not being responsible by answering the question: *What would happen if I weren't responsible?*

- **Activity 2: Cartoon**

Have students create a two-panel cartoon depicting what would happen if they were not responsible at home or at school. On one side, have them draw a problem; on the other, they draw the result of the problem if they do not act responsibly in that situation.

Lesson Segment 3: Discuss Their Problems, Results, and Possible Solutions

- **Activity 1: Service Project**

Group students into groups of three to four. Working together, have each group select one problem and result to *solve.* Have students select a service project in which they can demonstrate responsibility by promoting the greater good of their local community. Projects will vary but should be relevant to the students' local community and could include collecting donations for a local shelter, making holiday cards for kids in a local shelter, or cleaning up a local park. Have students create an action plan and share with the class using a gallery walk.

Brain-Compatible Strategies: *Which will you use to deliver content?*

__X__	Brainstorming/Discussion	__X__	Project/Problem-Based Learning
__X__	Drawing/Artwork	__X__	Reciprocal Teaching/Cooperative Learning
_____	Field Trips		
_____	Games	_____	Role Plays/Drama/Pantomimes/Charades
__X__	Graphic Organizers/Semantic Maps/Word Webs	__X__	Storytelling
_____	Humor	_____	Technology
_____	Manipulatives/Experiments/Labs/Models	_____	Visualization/Guided Imagery
		__X__	Visuals
_____	Metaphors/Analogies/Similes	_____	Work Study/Apprenticeships
__X__	Mnemonic Devices	__X__	Writing/Journals
__X__	Movement		
_____	Music/Rhythm/Rhyme/Rap		

Add Your Title

Goal:

Results/Accomplishments:

Action Steps What Will Be Done?	Responsibilities Who Will Do It?	Timeline By When? (Day/Month)	Resources A. Resources Available B. Resources Needed (financial, human, political & other)
Step 1:			A. B.
Step 2:			A. B.
Step 3:			A. B.
Step 4:			A. B.
Step 5:			A. B.

Evidence of Success *(How will you know that you are making progress?)*

Evaluation Process *(How will you determine that your goal has been reached?)*

Team Action Plan

Name: _____   School: _____   Date: _____

As a result of the plan, what action am I/we going to take personally, at the school level and in the classroom?	Who will be involved?	When will this be done?	How is this to be done?	How will I/we know when I/we have achieved what we plan?
Personal level				
Whole school level				
In the classroom				

Action Plan Template

Date:	
Goal of Plan:	
Motivation:	

Timings	Action Steps

Obstacles	Responses
Resources	Actions

Additional Notes

SOCIAL STUDIES GRADES K–2 LESSON 2

Citizenship

Lesson Objective(s): *What do you want students to know and be able to do?*

Understand what makes a good citizen, why we have rules, and why we need to follow authority.

Assessment (Traditional/Authentic): *How will you know students have mastered essential learning?*

Students will complete a T-Chart drawing pictures to illustrate examples of what being a good citizen means.

Ways to Gain/Maintain Attention (Primacy): *How will you gain and maintain students' attention? Consider* <u>need</u>, *novelty,* <u>meaning</u>, *or emotion.*

Ask students what they think it means to be a good citizen. Ask them for examples of how to be a good citizen.

Content Chunks: *How will you divide and teach the content to engage students' brains?*

Lesson Segment 1: Determine What It Means to Be a Good Citizen

- **Activity 1: Read Aloud**

Read the students a book on being a good citizen such as the ones listed below.

> *Being a Good Citizen: A Book About Citizenship* by Mary Small and Stacey Previn
>
> *What If Everybody Did That?* by Ellen Javernick

Have a class discussion about the story and what characteristics are included in the story.

- **Activity 2: Good and Bad Scenarios**

Divide the students into groups of two to three. Ask them to think of a scenario and how a good citizen would respond and how a bad citizen would respond. *Example: You're at the grocery store and someone drops their wallet. What do you do?*

- **Activity 3: Skits**

Student groups will select a scenario of how a good citizen and a bad citizen would act. Students in each group will create a skit to illustrate their scenario. Have the groups present their short skits to the class. After all the groups have presented, brainstorm on the board what makes a good citizen and what makes a bad citizen.

● **Activity 4: T-Charts**

Have students complete a T-Chart drawing pictures to illustrate their examples.

Brain-Compatible Strategies: *Which will you use to deliver content?*

__X__	Brainstorming/Discussion	_____	Music/Rhythm/Rhyme/Rap
__X__	Drawing/Artwork	_____	Project/Problem-Based Learning
_____	Field Trips	__X__	Reciprocal Teaching/Cooperative Learning
	Games		
__X__	Graphic Organizers/Semantic Maps/Word Webs	__X__	Role Plays/Drama/Pantomimes/Charades
_____	Humor	__X__	Storytelling
_____	Manipulatives/Experiments/Labs/Models	_____	Technology
		_____	Visualization/Guided Imagery
_____	Metaphors/Analogies/Similes	__X__	Visuals
_____	Mnemonic Devices	_____	Work Study/Apprenticeships
_____	Movement	_____	Writing/Journals

T-Chart

SOCIAL STUDIES GRADES K–2 LESSON 3

Places I Live

Lesson Objective(s): *What do you want students to know and be able to do?*

Identify and locate the student's city, state, nation (country), and continent on a simple map or globe.

Assessment (Traditional/Authentic): *How will you know students have mastered essential learning?*

Students will create their own visual to illustrate all the places that each of them lives. Also, include their own house.

Ways to Gain/Maintain Attention (Primacy): *How will you gain and maintain students' attention? Consider <u>need</u>, novelty, meaning, or emotion.*

Hold up a treasure map and ask the class to identify it. Numerous examples can be found with a quick Google search. Discuss the purpose of a treasure map. Tell students that just like people used treasure maps to find buried treasure, we can use maps of our cities, states, countries, world, etc., to find people, places, and things that are important to us.

Content Chunks: *How will you divide and teach the content to engage students' brains?*

Lesson Segment 1: Determine Where Students Live

- **Activity 1: Visuals**

Students will study a picture of the United States and then locate where they live on the map.

Display pictures of the world, North America, the United States, your state, etc. Have a class discussion.

Ask students the following: *What do you notice? What do you think? Where do we live?*

- **Activity 2: Read Aloud**

Read a book such as *Me on the Map* by Joan Sweeney

Stop periodically throughout the book to point out the students' location on a map of your city, state, country, and the world as these locations are mentioned in the story. When the book is finished, discuss the following questions with your students:

- How can you describe your location right now? Think about some of the ways the character in the story described her location.
- What are some other types of maps you have seen that were not mentioned in the book (i.e., amusement park map, shopping mall map, etc.)?
- How are maps different from what we see or the pictures we take of certain locations?
- Why is it important for us to understand where we are in the world?

- **Activity 3: Stacked Geography**

Group students into groups of three to four. Give each group eight Styrofoam cups. Explain to the groups that they are to create a "stack" using these cups and pictures/images provided from top to bottom with the bottom cup being themselves and the top being the solar system. Provide students with images of the solar system, Earth, North America, United States, your state, your city, a picture of your school, and picture of the group (or outline symbol). These can be downloaded from clip art. Have students cut and paste one picture on each and then "stack" the cups in the order indicated.

- **Activity 4: Illustration**

Have students create their own visual to illustrate all the places that each of them lives, including their own house.

Brain-Compatible Strategies: *Which will you use to deliver content?*

X	Brainstorming/Discussion	___	Music/Rhythm/Rhyme/Rap
X	Drawing/Artwork	___	Project/Problem-Based Learning
___	Field Trips	**X**	Reciprocal Teaching/Cooperative Learning
___	Games		
___	Graphic Organizers/Semantic Maps/Word Webs	___	Role Plays/Drama/Pantomimes/Charades
___	Humor	**X**	Storytelling
X	Manipulatives/Experiments/Labs/Models	**X**	Technology
		X	Visualization/Guided Imagery
___	Metaphors/Analogies/Similes	**X**	Visuals
___	Mnemonic Devices	___	Work Study/Apprenticeships
___	Movement	___	Writing/Journals

SOCIAL STUDIES GRADES K–2 LESSON 4

Maps and Globes

Lesson Objective(s): *What do you want students to know and be able to do?*

Know the difference between a map and a globe by answering the following questions:

1. What is a map?
2. What is a globe?
3. What is the difference between a map and a globe?
4. How would you decide to use a map or a globe?

Assessment (Traditional/Authentic): *How will you know students have mastered essential learning?*

Students will examine a variety of maps and globes, and answer the question "How would you decide to use a map or a globe?" The formative performance task calls on students to choose a scenario, represent their answers through an illustration, and then explain their ideas (and why they chose them) to a small group.

- You are taking an airplane trip to Australia and want to see if you will be flying over any large bodies of water. Would you use a map or a globe? Why?
- You have been invited to a pool party and need to figure out the directions to get to the community center. Would you use a map or a globe? Why?
- You are curious about which parts of the earth have mountains. Would you use a map or a globe? Why?
- You are curious about what astronauts see when they look at Earth from their space-craft. Would you use a map or a globe? Why?
- You are taking a hike in a park you've never been to before. Would you use a map or a globe? Why?

Ways to Gain/Maintain Attention (Primacy): *How will you gain and maintain students' attention? Consider <u>need</u>, novelty, <u>meaning</u>, or emotion.*

Pose a question to the class about location, such as "How would we find the post office?" or "How would we figure out the best way to get to the grocery store?" Record students' ideas on a class chart.

Content Chunks: *How will you divide and teach the content to engage students' brains?*

Lesson Segment 1: Determine What a Map Is

- **Activity 1: World Maps**

Have students understand that maps are one way to represent the idea of place. Display two different types of world maps. Place students in groups of three to four. Have students develop a definition of the world map and list the common features they see.

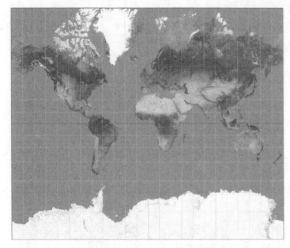

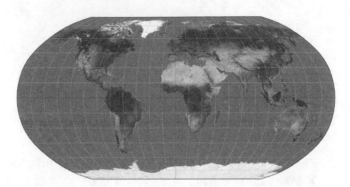

Image source: Daniel R. Strebe, 2011. Licensed under CC BY-SA 3.0: https://creativecommons.org/licenses/by-sa/3.0/ Original available at https://en.wikipedia.org/wiki/Robinson_projection#/media/File:Robinson_projection_SW.jpg

Image source: Daniel R. Strebe, 2011. Licensed under CC BY-SA 3.0: https://creativecommons.org/licenses/by-sa/3.0/ Original available at https://en.wikipedia.org/wiki/Mercator_projection#/media/ File:Mercator_projection_SW.jpg

- **Activity 2: Community Maps**

Display two different maps of your community. Have students discuss the similarities and differences between these two maps and the world maps. Have them list these on their chart.

Examples of community maps can be found at https://www.nationalgeographic.org/maps/maps-and-models.

Lesson Segment 2: Determine What a Globe Is

- **Activity 1: Globes**

Ask students *What is a globe?* Have students build on their understandings of maps by developing the idea that globes are also representations of *place.* Display two different types of globes, like a topographic globe and a political globe. Have students develop a definition of the world globe and list the common features they see.

Lesson Segment 3: Determining the Difference Between a Map and a Globe

- **Activity 1: Comparing Maps and Globes**

Lead a discussion regarding the following question: *What is the difference between a map and a globe?* Have students visualize the differences and begin making generalizations about the potential uses of maps and globes. Using the previous lists that each group made, have students create a Venn diagram comparing and contrasting the differences and similarities between maps and globes.

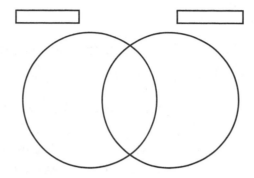

Brain-Compatible Strategies: *Which will you use to deliver content?*

__X__	Brainstorming/Discussion	_____	Music/Rhythm/Rhyme/Rap
_____	Drawing/Artwork	_____	Project/Problem-Based Learning
_____	Field Trips	__X__	Reciprocal Teaching/Cooperative Learning
_____	Games		
__X__	Graphic Organizers/Semantic Maps/Word Webs	_____	Role Plays/Drama/Pantomimes/Charades
_____	Humor	_____	Storytelling
__X__	Manipulatives/Experiments/Labs/Models	__X__	Technology
		__X__	Visualization/Guided Imagery
_____	Metaphors/Analogies/Similes	__X__	Visuals
_____	Mnemonic Devices	_____	Work Study/Apprenticeships
_____	Movement	_____	Writing/Journals

SOCIAL STUDIES GRADES K–2 LESSON 5

American Symbols

Lesson Objective(s): *What do you want students to know and be able to do?*

Identify important American symbols and explain their meaning.

Assessment (Traditional/Authentic): *How will you know students have mastered essential learning?*

Students will be graded on their participation during group research activities, their knowledge of information gathered during research, and their communication of content material.

Ways to Gain/Maintain Attention (Primacy): *How will you gain and maintain students' attention? Consider need, novelty, meaning, or emotion.*

Show several pictures of things familiar to students such as the dollar sign, the Superman "S", etc. Ask them how they were able to identify what the picture represented.

Content Chunks: *How will you divide and teach the content to engage students' brains?*

Lesson Segment 1: Identify Symbols

- **Activity 1: American Symbols**

Show several pictures of things we consider to be symbols of America such as the flag, Statue of Liberty, US Capitol, eagle, etc. Use large index cards or an interactive web whiteboard to have students draw/write down any schema that they have about US symbols. Students who are unfamiliar with this term can draw question marks on their cards.

- **Activity 2: Nonfiction Texts**

Have students preview unit content books individually or in pairs. Allow two to three minutes for students to look at a single book and then pass each book clockwise and repeat the activity. Do this three to four times and have the students talk about things they noticed. What did all the books have in common? How has their schema changed? What questions do they have?

- **Activity 3: KWHL**

Display a KWHL (Know, Want to know, How to find out, Learned) chart somewhere in the classroom. The chart can be made on a bulletin board or wall using pocket charts, chart paper, poster board, etc. Have students choose the US symbol they would like to learn more about; bald eagle, Mount Rushmore, Statue of Liberty, Liberty Bell. They will work in cooperative groups to complete the research activity.

The students will explore books about symbols to differentiate between important information and interesting facts. The students will take notes to record the big ideas that they read about in the texts. Each group will ask questions and gather additional information by looking at pictures, listening' and reading texts. The teacher will guide the students during these activities by asking probing questions, reading short stories, and assisting with recording. New questions and discoveries will continuously be added to the appropriate sections of the KWHL chart. Each time a discovery is made, the students can write down how it was discovered. Add these cards to the How section of the KWHL chart.

KWHL			
What we know	What we want to know	How we can learn more	What we learned

Brain-Compatible Strategies: *Which will you use to deliver content?*

__X__	Brainstorming/Discussion	_____	Music/Rhythm/Rhyme/Rap
__X__	Drawing/Artwork	_____	Project/Problem-Based Learning
_____	Field Trips	__X__	Reciprocal Teaching/Cooperative Learning
_____	Games		
__X__	Graphic Organizers/Semantic Maps/Word Webs	_____	Role Plays/Drama/Pantomimes/Charades
_____	Humor	__X__	Storytelling
_____	Manipulatives/Experiments/Labs/Models	__X__	Technology
		_____	Visualization/Guided Imagery
_____	Metaphors/Analogies/Similes	__X__	Visuals
_____	Mnemonic Devices	_____	Work Study/Apprenticeships
_____	Movement	__X__	Writing/Journals

SOCIAL STUDIES GRADES K–2 LESSON 6

Paul Revere

Lesson Objective(s): *What do you want students to know and be able to do?*

Discuss the life of Paul Revere and his efforts to expand people's rights and freedoms in a democracy.

(Note: The format of this lesson can be used with any historical figure by substituting other relevant literature.)

Assessment (Traditional/Authentic): *How will you know students have mastered essential learning?*

Have students draw a book cover for a book about Paul Revere.

Have students complete K-W-L chart in pairs.

Ways to Gain/Maintain Attention (Primacy): *How will you gain and maintain students' attention? Consider need, novelty, meaning, or emotion.*

Ask if anyone has heard of Paul Revere.

Find Boston and England on a map. Discuss the colonies being under the king's rule and taxes.

Content Chunks: *How will you divide and teach the content to engage students' brains?*

Lesson Segment 1: Discuss the Life of Paul Revere

- **Activity 1: Poem *The Midnight Ride of Paul Revere***

Read the poem (or parts of the poem) *The Midnight Ride of Paul Revere* by Henry Wadsworth Longfellow. (You could also project the poem and have students read along.)

- **Activity 2: K-W-L Chart**

Place students in pairs and have students complete the first column of the K-W-L chart together. As a group, have students discuss and add to the chart in the W column.

K-W-L Chart		
What we know	What we want to know	What we learned

• Activity 3: Incredible Shrinking Notes

Divide students into small groups and provide a copy of a section of the poem. This can be done by printing a copy of the poem and cutting sections apart.

Provide each group with a large sticky note and have them summarize what they have read. They may write as many notes that can fit on the large paper. Once that is complete, provide each group with a medium sticky note, and tell students to narrow down their notes. Students should be able to identify several things that may not be important to the contributions of Paul Revere. Finally, provide a small sticky note and have students record essential information that they believe should be shared about Paul Revere. (Note: You may want to begin with a full-size blank piece of paper, then reduce it to half, and then reduce it to a fourth to accommodate large handwriting.)

• Activity 4: Gallery Walk

Have students use their section of the poem and small sticky notes to create a poster for the Gallery. Hang or place each section in various places around the classroom to create stations. Group students into teams of three to five students, depending on the size of the class. Each group should start at a different station. At their first station, groups will read what is posted and one recorder should write the group's responses, thoughts, and comments on the chart paper or white-board. Having different colored markers for each group is also an option.

After three to five minutes, have the groups rotate to the next station. Students read and discuss the previous group's response and add content of their own. Repeat until all groups have visited each station. To involve all group members, you can have groups switch recorders at each station. As the teacher, it is important to monitor the stations while the students participate. You may also need to clarify or provide hints if students don't understand or misinterpret what is posted at their station. Have students go back to their first station to read all that was added to their first responses. Bring the class back together to discuss what was learned and make final conclusions about what they saw and discussed. Have students complete the last column of the K-W-L chart with their group.

Brain-Compatible Strategies: *Which will you use to deliver content?*

X	Brainstorming/Discussion	___	Music/Rhythm/Rhyme/Rap
X	Drawing/Artwork	___	Project/Problem-Based Learning
___	Field Trips	X	Reciprocal Teaching/Cooperative Learning
___	Games		
X	Graphic Organizers/Semantic Maps/Word Webs	___	Role Plays/Drama/Pantomimes/Charades
___	Humor	X	Storytelling
___	Manipulatives/Experiments/Labs/Models	___	Technology
		X	Visualization/Guided Imagery
___	Metaphors/Analogies/Similes	___	Visuals
___	Mnemonic Devices	___	Work Study/Apprenticeships
X	Movement	X	Writing/Journals

SOCIAL STUDIES GRADES K–2 LESSON 7

Martin Luther King, Jr. Day

Lesson Objective(s): *What do you want students to know and be able to do?*

Explain why we celebrate Martin Luther King, Jr. Day.

Assessment (Traditional/Authentic): *How will you know students have mastered essential learning?*

Students will understand why Martin Luther King Jr., Day is celebrated through the creation of their book.

Ways to Gain/Maintain Attention (Primacy): *How will you gain and maintain students' attention? Consider need, novelty, meaning, or emotion.*

Show students a photograph of Dr. Martin Luther King, Jr., like the one to the right from the Library of Congress: https://www.loc.gov/

Ask students the following questions:

- What do you see?
- What is something interesting you see?
- What do you think is happening?
- How do you think these people are feeling?

(Note: You might want to allow students to come forward and point out details they see. Also, by holding a blank piece of paper out from the image allows students to see details more clearly.)

Image source: Stanziola, Phil, photographer. Mayor Wagner greets Dr. & Mrs. Martin Luther King, Jr. at City Hall / World Telegram & Sun photo by Phil Stanziola. , 1964. Photograph. https://www.loc.gov/item/98503083/

Content Chunks: *How will you divide and teach the content to engage students' brains?*

Lesson Segment 1: Understand MLK's Life

- **Activity 1: Facts About MLK**

Explain to students that they will be learning about Martin Luther King, Jr. and will be creating a book about him. Read the book: *Martin Luther King, Jr. Day* by Helen Frost or any other available age-appropriate book. Use read-aloud and think-aloud strategies to have students share ideas from the book about what they think MLK was like and how he grew up.

- **Activity 2: Book Creation**

Distribute copies of the Martin Luther King, Jr. book template provided at the end of this lesson (one per student). Have students create a book about the life of Martin Luther King, Jr.

Have students fold these pages like a hamburger and cut in half.

- Have students put the pages in order and staple them together. Remind students to write their names on the front cover.
- Distribute copies of the Martin Luther King, Jr. images (one per student).
- Have students read the sentence and look at the images and decide which image matches the sentence.
- Have students cut the image out and glue on page 1 of their books.
- Allow students to write original sentences.

Allow students to draw their own images.

- **Activity 3: Think-Pair-Share**

Give students the following instructions to review what was learned:

- I'm going to give you a number—either *one* or *two*.
- Hold up that many fingers when I tell you.
- If you are a *one*, then find a *two*.
- If you are a *two*, then find a *one*.
- Think about one thing you learned about Martin Luther King, Jr.
- If you are a *one*, then tell the *two* what you learned.
- Now if you are a *two*, tell the *one* what you learned.
- Let's share!

Brain-Compatible Strategies: *Which will you use to deliver content?*

__X__	Brainstorming/Discussion	_____	Music/Rhythm/Rhyme/Rap
__X__	Drawing/Artwork	_____	Project/Problem-Based Learning
_____	Field Trips	__X__	Reciprocal Teaching/Cooperative Learning
_____	Games		
_____	Graphic Organizers/Semantic Maps/Word Webs	_____	Role Plays/Drama/Pantomimes/Charades
_____	Humor	__X__	Storytelling
__X__	Manipulatives/Experiments/Labs/Models	__X__	Technology
		_____	Visualization/Guided Imagery
_____	Metaphors/Analogies/Similes	__X__	Visuals
_____	Mnemonic Devices	_____	Work Study/Apprenticeships
_____	Movement	__X__	Writing/Journals

Martin Luther King, Jr. Day

By:

Martin Luther King, Jr. was born in Georgia long ago.

First, he went to segregated schools.

Next, he grew up to be a leader. He said segregation was wrong.

Page 3

Last, he showed people how to change laws in peaceful ways.

Page 4

Now all Americans celebrate Martin Luther King, Jr. Day.

SOCIAL STUDIES GRADES K–2 LESSON 8

Economics

Lesson Objective(s): *What do you want students to know and be able to do?*

Explain that people have economic *needs* and *wants*.

They will understand that *goods* and *services* can satisfy people's wants and that *scarcity* is the condition of not being able to have all of the goods and services that a person wants or needs.

Assessment (Traditional/Authentic): *How will you know students have mastered essential learning?*

Students will create two-sided collages with images of needs (or goods) on one side and wants (or services) on the other.

Ways to Gain/Maintain Attention (Primacy): *How will you gain and maintain students' attention? Consider* <u>need</u>, *novelty, meaning, or emotion.*

Brainstorm examples of what students say they want and need and discuss examples of goods and services.

Content Chunks: *How will you divide and teach the content to engage students' brains?*

Lesson Segment 1: Differentiate a *Want* From a *Need*

- **Activity 1: Discussion**

Ask students the following questions: *What do we want? What do we need?* Explain to students that a need is something that a person must have for health and survival, while a want is something a person would like to have. Have students identify basic needs (food, clothing, and shelter). Have students distinguish between a need and a want.

- **Activity 2: Illustrations**

Place students in groups of three to four and provide pictures from "clip art" that show various items that illustrate wants and needs. Students may also use other resources such as magazines, etc. Have students cut and paste them onto a chart paper template.

Lesson Segment 2: Differentiate *Goods* From *Services*

- **Activity 1: Discussion**

Define *goods* and *services*. Tell students that goods are objects that can satisfy people's needs and wants; services are activities that can do the same. Ask students the following questions: *How do goods and services meet our needs and wants? Identify a need or a want and determine how it could be satisfied through goods and services.*

- **Activity 2: Drawing**

Have students identify examples of goods and services. Have them (1) illustrate one good and one service related to food and one good and one service related to school and (2) determine a means by which they might acquire each of those goods and services.

Have students draw pictures and answer the following questions about goods and services.

Draw a picture of a *good* related to food. I could get this by _____ _____ _____	Draw a picture of a *service* related to food. I could get this by _____ _____ _____
Draw a picture of a *good* related to school. I could get this by _____ _____ _____	Draw a picture of a *service* related to school. I could get this by _____ _____ _____

Lesson Segment 3: Define *Scarcity*

- **Activity 1: Read Aloud**

Ask students: *What happens when there isn't enough for everyone?* Define *scarcity* as the condition of not being able to have all of the goods and services that a person wants or needs. Have students identify examples of scarcity.

Read the book *The Door Bell Rang* by Pat Hutchins. Ask students in their groups to solve the solution of scarcity by creating another ending to the story. Students should include the concepts of *wants* and *needs* as well as *goods* and *services* involved in the story. Each group will present their new ending in the form of a role play.

Brain-Compatible Strategies: *Which will you use to deliver content?*

__X__	Brainstorming/Discussion	_____	Music/Rhythm/Rhyme/Rap
__X__	Drawing/Artwork	__X__	Project/Problem-Based Learning
_____	Field Trips	__X__	Reciprocal Teaching/Cooperative Learning
_____	Games		
_____	Graphic Organizers/Semantic Maps/Word Webs	__X__	Role Plays/Drama/Pantomimes/Charades
_____	Humor	__X__	Storytelling
_____	Manipulatives/Experiments/Labs/Models	_____	Technology
		_____	Visualization/Guided Imagery
_____	Metaphors/Analogies/Similes	__X__	Visuals
_____	Mnemonic Devices	_____	Work Study/Apprenticeships
_____	Movement	_____	Writing/Journals

SOCIAL STUDIES GRADES 3–5 LESSON 1

Latitude, Longitude, Equator, Prime Meridian

Lesson Objective(s): *What do you want students to know and be able to do?*

Locate and describe the equator, prime meridian, and lines of latitude and longitude on a globe.

Assessment (Traditional/Authentic): *How will you know students have mastered essential learning?*

Students will create a mnemonic for two of the following: equator, prime meridian, latitude, or longitude.

Each should contain the characteristics and purpose of the term.

Ways to Gain/Maintain Attention (Primacy): *How will you gain and maintain students' attention? Consider need, novelty, meaning, or emotion.*

Using your classroom globe and a world map, point to the lines drawn on them. Ask students if they know why they are there. Tell them that the lines will help us find the exact place we want to go!

Content Chunks: *How will you divide and teach the content to engage students' brains?*

Lesson Segment 1: Identify Lines of Latitude, Longitude, Equator, etc.

- **Activity 1: Fruit Fun**

Engage students in the following activity:

- Pair up students and give each pair a grapefruit or orange.
- Have them put a dot with the marker at the top and the bottom. Identify these as the North and South Poles.
- Tell them to draw a line around the middle of the grapefruit or orange. Identify this as the equator.
- Explain that the equator divides the world into north and south.
- Have students draw lines around the grapefruit or orange. Identify these as lines of latitude.
- Using the same grapefruit or orange, tell students to draw a vertical line with their marker from the top to the bottom (from the North Pole to the South Pole). Identify this as the prime meridian.
- Have students draw lines around the grapefruit or orange from top to bottom going around (from the prime meridian and the North and South Pole). Identify these as lines of longitude.
- Be sure to emphasize that these are imaginary lines and must be visualized.

- **Activity 2: Imaginary Line Discussion**

Engage students in the following discussion:

- Using a classroom globe and world map, ask students why these lines are imaginary.
- Ask them why we use maps and globes at all.
- Provide each group with a globe and/or map.
- Have them locate each of the following on the globe: equator, prime meridian, latitude lines (multiple examples), and longitude lines (multiple examples).
- Have them explore these lines further by looking for countries or continents intersecting with various lines.
- Which countries or oceans does the equator cross? Which countries or oceans does the prime meridian cross? Which are crossed by the 180° line of longitude? Which locations are crossed by the 45° north latitude line?

- **Activity 3: K-W-L Chart**

Read one of the books to the class:

Latitude & Longitude: Geography 2nd Grade for Kids, from the Baby Professor series

Latitude and Longitude (Rookie Read-About Geography) by Rebecca Aberg

Using a K-W-L chart, have students fill out the K and W prior to reading. Have students complete the chart in groups upon completion of reading the book.

Brain-Compatible Strategies: *Which will you use to deliver content?*

X	Brainstorming/Discussion	___	Music/Rhythm/Rhyme/Rap
X	Drawing/Artwork	___	Project/Problem-Based Learning
___	Field Trips	**X**	Reciprocal Teaching/Cooperative Learning
___	Games		
X	Graphic Organizers/Semantic Maps/Word Webs	___	Role Plays/Drama/Pantomimes/Charades
X	Humor	**X**	Storytelling
X	Manipulatives/Experiments/Labs/Models	___	Technology
		X	Visualization/Guided Imagery
X	Metaphors/Analogies/Similes	**X**	Visuals
X	Mnemonic Devices	___	Work Study/Apprenticeships
___	Movement	___	Writing/Journals

SOCIAL STUDIES GRADES 3–5 LESSON 2

Historical Figures

Lesson Objective(s): *What do you want students to know and be able to do?*

Learn about our country's historical figures (although this lesson can be used with any historical figure).

Assessment (Traditional/Authentic): *How will you know students have mastered essential learning?*

Students will write a journal entry from the view of the historical figure.

Ways to Gain/Maintain Attention (Primacy): *How will you gain and maintain students' attention? Consider need, novelty, meaning, or emotion.*

Ask students to name some important people in their lives. What makes them important? Ask them to name some famous people and what made them famous.

Content Chunks: *How will you divide and teach the content to engage students' brains?*

Lesson Segment 1: Make Predictions About Figures

- **Activity 1: Visual Predictions**

Provide copies of biographies of historical figures that are to be studied from the media center or classroom library. Have students look at the pictures on the front of the biography. Ask the following questions:

- What do you see?
- What does this remind you of?
- When do you think this person lived? How do you know?
- How do you think this person is feeling? Why?

- **Activity 2: Factual Information**

Place students in groups of three to four. Give each group a chapter from the biography. Write the chapter titles on butcher paper and post them in the room. Have students read their chapters in small groups. Tell students to write down facts they learned from the chapter on a sticky note. Tell students to place their sticky notes on the corresponding butcher paper. Have students take a gallery walk and complete the following graphic organizer for their notes.

Brain-Compatible Strategies: *Which will you use to deliver content?*

X	Brainstorming/Discussion		____	Music/Rhythm/Rhyme/Rap
____	Drawing/Artwork		____	Project/Problem-Based Learning
____	Field Trips		**X**	Reciprocal Teaching/Cooperative Learning
____	Games			
X	Graphic Organizers/Semantic Maps/Word Webs		____	Role Plays/Drama/Pantomimes/Charades
____	Humor		**X**	Storytelling
____	Manipulatives/Experiments/Labs/Models		____	Technology
			____	Visualization/Guided Imagery
____	Metaphors/Analogies/Similes		**X**	Visuals
____	Mnemonic Devices		____	Work Study/Apprenticeships
X	Movement		**X**	Writing/Journals

Biography Research

Persons Name:

Picture:

Early Life:

Family Life:

Major Accomplishments:

3 Interesting Facts:

SOCIAL STUDIES GRADES 3–5 LESSON 3

American Indian Culture

Lesson Objective(s): *What do you want students to know and be able to do?*

Explain how early American Indian cultures developed in North America.

Assessment (Traditional/Authentic): *How will you know students have mastered essential learning?*

Students will create a graphic organizer for each early American Indian culture. The graphic organizer should include: the name of the early American Indian culture, a map showing where they lived, clothing, food, shelter, and natural resources. Have students discuss the similarities and differences between each group.

Ways to Gain/Maintain Attention (Primacy): *How will you gain and maintain students' attention? Consider need, novelty, meaning, or emotion.*

Project picture(s) of various American Indian tribes to be studied from your standards on the document camera. Ask students what they think today's lesson will be about. Ask them the following questions:

- What do you see?
- When did this take place?
- What is happening in the picture?

Content Chunks: *How will you divide and teach the content to engage students' brains?*

Lesson Segment 1: Explain Indian Culture in North America

- **Activity 1: List-Group-Label**

List-Group-Label is a vocabulary strategy that engages students in a three-step process to actively organize their understanding of content-area vocabulary and concepts. It provides students with a way to recognize the relationships between words and concepts using their prior knowledge about a topic. The list-group-label strategy can be used before and after students read.

List	Group and Label

1. List: Have students brainstorm all the words they think relate to the Indian tribes to be studied.
    a. Visually display student responses.
    b. At this point do not critique student responses. Some words may not reflect the main concept, but hopefully, students will realize this as they begin grouping the words in the next step.

2. Group: Divide your class into small groups. Each group will work to cluster the class list of words into subcategories. As groups of words emerge, challenge your students to explain their reasoning for placing words together or discarding them.

3. Label: Invite students to suggest a title or label for the groups of words they have formed. These labels should relate to their reasoning for the grouping.

- **Activity 2: Illustrated Dictionary**

Using resources provided such as textbooks or materials from the media center, have students create an illustrated dictionary of the American Indian cultures to be studied. An illustrated dictionary uses pictures, visuals, graphics, and diagrams to group words together into logical groups and allows any student to understand exactly what the word means. Each entry should include:

- The name of the early American Indian culture
- Their location and why they lived there
- How they utilized what was available in terms of
  - clothing
  - food
  - shelter
  - natural resources
- An illustration

- **Activity 3: Think, Pair, Share**

Think, Pair, Share is a collaborative learning strategy in which students work together to solve a problem or answer a question about an assigned reading. This technique requires students to (1) think individually about a topic or answer a question and (2) share ideas with classmates.

Describe the strategy and its purpose with your students and provide guidelines for discussions that will take place. Explain to students that they will (1) think individually about one of the Indian tribes in the lesson; (2) pair with a partner and discuss; and (3) share ideas with the rest of the class.

Using a student or student(s) from your classroom, model the procedure to ensure that students understand how to use the strategy. Allow time for students to ask questions that clarify their use of the technique. Once students have a firm understanding of the expectations surrounding the strategy, monitor and support students as they work through the steps below. Teachers may also ask students to write or diagram their responses while doing the Think-Pair-Share activity.

Think: Teachers begin by asking a specific higher-level question about the topic students will be discussing. Students "think" about what they know or have learned about the topic for a given amount of time (usually 1-3 minutes).

Pair: Each student should be paired with another student. Teachers may choose whether to assign pairs or let students pick their own partner. Remember to be sensitive to learners' needs (reading skills, attention skills, language skills) when creating pairs. Students share their thinking with their partner, discuss ideas, and ask questions of their partner about their thoughts on the topic (2-5 minutes).

Share: Once partners have had ample time to share their thoughts and have a discussion, teachers expand the "share" into a whole-class discussion. Allow each group to choose who will present their thoughts, ideas, and questions they had to the rest of the class. After the class "share," you may choose to have pairs reconvene to talk about how their thinking perhaps changed as a result of the "share" element.

Brain-Compatible Strategies: *Which will you use to deliver content?*

__X__	Brainstorming/Discussion	_____	Music/Rhythm/Rhyme/Rap
__X__	Drawing/Artwork	_____	Project/Problem-Based Learning
_____	Field Trips	__X__	Reciprocal Teaching/Cooperative Learning
_____	Games		
__X__	Graphic Organizers/Semantic Maps/Word Webs	_____	Role Plays/Drama/Pantomimes/Charades
_____	Humor	_____	Storytelling
_____	Manipulatives/Experiments/Labs/Models	_____	Technology
		_____	Visualization/Guided Imagery
_____	Metaphors/Analogies/Similes	__X__	Visuals
_____	Mnemonic Devices	_____	Work Study/Apprenticeships
_____	Movement	__X__	Writing/Journals

SOCIAL STUDIES GRADES 3–5 LESSON 4

The Declaration of Independence

Lesson Objective(s): *What do you want students to know and be able to do?*

Explain the development of the Declaration of Independence.

Assessment (Traditional/Authentic): *How will you know students have mastered essential learning?*

Students will complete a journal entry from the point of view of a colonist on why the Declaration of Independence was necessary.

Ways to Gain/Maintain Attention (Primacy): *How will you gain and maintain students' attention? Consider need, novelty, meaning, or emotion.*

Ask students what they think the word *independent* means? What are some things that they do that show they are independent? Would they like to be more independent at home? At school?

Content Chunks: *How will you divide and teach the content to engage students' brains?*

Lesson Segment 1: Understand the Purpose of the Declaration of Independence

- **Activity 1: Discussion**

The class discussion should include questions such as: Why do you think it was written? Was it needed? Divide students into groups of three to four students. Provide students with a copy of the Declaration of Independence. Tell each group to decide how many parts are in the document and why it is divided. Groups should also identify what they believe the purpose is of each.

- **Activity 2: Original Declarations**

Keep students in the same groups. Tell each group that they are to create their own Declaration of Independence. Remind students that their Declaration of Independence needs to contain the same sections as the original. Allow students to share and/or post around the room as a gallery walk. Debrief the activity by comparing what happened in the group (disagreements/compromises) with what happened in history. Have students complete a T-chart for their comparison.

- **Activity 3: Journal Entry**

Have student complete a journal entry from the point of view of a colonist on why the Declaration of Independence was necessary.

Brain-Compatible Strategies: *Which will you use to deliver content?*

X	Brainstorming/Discussion	____	Music/Rhythm/Rhyme/Rap
____	Drawing/Artwork	____	Project/Problem-Based Learning
____	Field Trips	**X**	Reciprocal Teaching/Cooperative Learning
____	Games		
X	Graphic Organizers/Semantic Maps/Word Webs	____	Role Plays/Drama/Pantomimes/Charades
____	Humor	____	Storytelling
____	Manipulatives/Experiments/Labs/Models	____	Technology
		____	Visualization/Guided Imagery
____	Metaphors/Analogies/Similes	**X**	Visuals
____	Mnemonic Devices	____	Work Study/Apprenticeships
X	Movement	**X**	Writing/Journals

T-Chart

SOCIAL STUDIES GRADES 3–5 LESSON 5

Colonial America

Lesson Objective(s): *What do you want students to know and be able to do?*

Compare and contrast life in the three regions of Colonial America: New England, Mid-Atlantic (Middle), and Southern colonies.

Assessment (Traditional/Authentic): *How will you know students have mastered essential learning?*

Students will write two facts about each of the regions of Colonial America and one fib. Allow students to circulate around the room reading their sentences to each other and then determining the fib.

Ways to Gain/Maintain Attention (Primacy): *How will you gain and maintain students' attention? Consider need, novelty, meaning, or emotion.*

Have students look at a variety of images of the colonies. An acrostic is a poem (or another form of writing) in which the first letter (or syllable, or word) of each line (or paragraph, or other recurring feature in the text) spells out a word, message, or the alphabet. Students will create an acrostic poem for the word *COLONIES*.

Content Chunks: *How will you divide and teach the content to engage students' brains?*

Lesson Segment 1: Understand Life in the Colonies

- **Activity 1: Flip Books**

Using classroom resources, textbooks, or media center books, students will investigate the three regions of Colonial America. Students will create a three-flap flip book for the colonies. Label the flaps—New England, Middle, and Southern. Under the top flap, have students glue a map, color, and label the colonies. On the bottom portion, have students record notes on the colonies' geography, climate, resources, economic development, culture, and population.

- **Activity 2: Report Card**

Have students evaluate each of the three colonies by assigning it a letter grade based on the impact that each had on Colonial America. Tell students to include a *teacher comment* to justify the grade they assigned.

- **Activity 3: Acrostic**

Have students create an acrostic using the word *COLONIES*.

● **Activity 4: Last Word**

Have students return to the acrostic they created at the beginning of the lesson. Tell them to add and/or make corrections to their poem based on what they now know. (Note: Students may add images to their poems.)

Brain-Compatible Strategies: *Which will you use to deliver content?*

__X__	Brainstorming/Discussion	_____	Music/Rhythm/Rhyme/Rap
__X__	Drawing/Artwork	_____	Project/Problem-Based Learning
_____	Field Trips	__X__	Reciprocal Teaching/Cooperative Learning
_____	Games		
__X__	Graphic Organizers/Semantic Maps/Word Webs	_____	Role Plays/Drama/Pantomimes/Charades
_____	Humor	_____	Storytelling
__X__	Manipulatives/Experiments/Labs/Models	_____	Technology
		_____	Visualization/Guided Imagery
_____	Metaphors/Analogies/Similes	__X__	Visuals
__X__	Mnemonic Devices	_____	Work Study/Apprenticeships
_____	Movement	__X__	Writing/Journals

Flip Book

SOCIAL STUDIES GRADES 3–5 LESSON 6

The American Revolution

Lesson Objective(s): *What do you want students to know and be able to do?*

Describe the major events of the American Revolution and their significance.

Assessment (Traditional/Authentic): *How will you know students have mastered essential learning?*

Students will be able to write how the significance of the major events of the American Revolution contributed to the success of the Revolutionary War.

Ways to Gain/Maintain Attention (Primacy): *How will you gain and maintain students' attention? Consider need, novelty, meaning, or* <u>*emotion*</u>.

Write the word *revolution* on the board. Play the Beatles song "Revolution" while beginning the lesson.

Content Chunks: *How will you divide and teach the content to engage students' brains?*

Lesson Segment 1: Define the Word *Revolution*

- **Activity 1: Revolution Discussion**

Project the word *revolution* on the document camera or write it on the board. Have the class create a classroom definition.

- **Activity 2: Flip Book**

Determine the significance of the following events in influencing the outcome of the American Revolution: Battles of Lexington and Concord, Battle of Bunker Hill, Valley Forge, Battle of Trenton, Battle of Saratoga, Battle of Yorktown, and/or others as determined by standards.

Using textbooks and other classroom resources, have students create a flipbook for the events of the American Revolution. Place one event on each page including its significance and outcome. Place events in the book in chronological order.

- **Activity 3: Acrostic Poem**

Ask students how the definition of revolution is reflected in the events included in their flip books. Students will reevaluate the class definition. They will write an acrostic poem for the word *REVOLUTION*, based on its definition and what they have learned.

Brain-Compatible Strategies: *Which will you use to deliver content?*

__X__	Brainstorming/Discussion	__X__	Music/Rhythm/Rhyme/Rap
__X__	Drawing/Artwork	_____	Project/Problem-Based Learning
_____	Field Trips	_____	Reciprocal Teaching/Cooperative Learning
_____	Games		
_____	Graphic Organizers/Semantic Maps/Word Webs	_____	Role Plays/Drama/Pantomimes/Charades
_____	Humor	__X__	Storytelling
_____	Manipulatives/Experiments/Labs/Models	_____	Technology
		_____	Visualization/Guided Imagery
_____	Metaphors/Analogies/Similes	__X__	Visuals
__X__	Mnemonic Devices	_____	Work Study/Apprenticeships
_____	Movement	__X__	Writing/Journals

SOCIAL STUDIES GRADES 3–5 LESSON 7

The American Revolution

Lesson Objective(s): *What do you want students to know and be able to do?*

Describe key individuals in the American Revolution such as King George III, George Washington, Benjamin Franklin, Abigail Adams, Martha Washington, Thomas Jefferson, Benedict Arnold, Patrick Henry, John Adams, Marquis de Lafayette, Paul Revere, Minutemen, Thomas Paine, Lord Cornwallis, and Samuel Adams.

Assessment (Traditional/Authentic): *How will you know students have mastered essential learning?*

Students will select three different key individuals in the American Revolution and create a flip book for each one.

Ways to Gain/Maintain Attention (Primacy): *How will you gain and maintain students' attention? Consider need, novelty, _meaning_, or emotion.*

Ask students to identify important people in the community, state, and the nation. Ask students what makes them important.

Content Chunks: *How will you divide and teach the content to engage students' brains?*

Lesson Segment 1: Discuss Character Traits

- **Activity 1: Word Splash**

Using classroom resources, identify key people in the American Revolution. Discuss what character traits these individuals must have possessed. Create a word splash of the character traits.

- **Activity 2: Paper Dolls**

Place students in small groups and assign each group one of the key individuals from the American Revolution. (Note: Students could work individually.) Tell each group to create a paper doll for their key individual. Have students use construction paper to assemble their paper dolls. Have them identify the contributions and roles of their individual. Have students include a symbol for their figure to hold and a nameplate. (Technology Connection: Students could use PowerPoint and/or Paint to create their key individuals.) Allow students to share their paper dolls with the class.

- **Activity 3: Letter Writing**

Discuss different points of view and contributions of the key individuals. Have students write a letter from the point of view of the key individual they were assigned.

- **Activity 4: Flip Book**

Have students select three different key individuals in the American Revolution and create a flip book for each one.

Brain-Compatible Strategies: *Which will you use to deliver content?*

X	Brainstorming/Discussion	___	Music/Rhythm/Rhyme/Rap
X	Drawing/Artwork	**X**	Project/Problem-Based Learning
___	Field Trips	**X**	Reciprocal Teaching/Cooperative Learning
___	Games		
X	Graphic Organizers/Semantic Maps/Word Webs	___	Role Plays/Drama/Pantomimes/Charades
___	Humor	___	Storytelling
___	Manipulatives/Experiments/Labs/Models	**X**	Technology
		X	Visualization/Guided Imagery
___	Metaphors/Analogies/Similes	___	Visuals
___	Mnemonic Devices	___	Work Study/Apprenticeships
___	Movement	**X**	Writing/Journals

SOCIAL STUDIES GRADES 3–5 LESSON 8

Goods and Resources

Lesson Objective(s): *What do you want students to know and be able to do?*

Learn the basic concepts of the economics of goods, resources, scarcity, and supply and demand.

Assessment (Traditional/Authentic): *How will you know students have mastered essential learning?*

Students will discuss the concepts they learned with this activity at the completion of this lesson.

Students will complete a K-W-L chart at the conclusion of the discussion.

Ways to Gain/Maintain Attention (Primacy): *How will you gain and maintain students' attention? Consider need, novelty, meaning, or emotion.*

Students will work in their cooperative groups. Groups are given one can of Play-Doh and told that the needs of their "country" are two products: snakes and donuts. They are responsible for making these goods. The definition of goods and resources are reviewed at this time.

Content Chunks: *How will you divide and teach the content to engage students' brains?*

Lesson Segment 1: Understand the Vocabulary of Economics

- **Activity 1: *Snakes* and *Donuts***

The teacher will demonstrate what a "snake" is and a "donut" and how to make them. A snake is a long, skinny piece of Play-Doh rolled out to be the length of the unsharpened pencil. Too short or too long, the snake will not be useful. A donut is similar to a snake but must be big enough to go around the Play-Doh canister. Engage students in the following activity:

1. Groups are given different colors of Play-Doh. Allow each group a practice round of one minute to make snakes. Discuss which products will be accepted and which will not. Snakes must be the length of the unsharpened pencil—no longer, no shorter.

2. Production will begin with groups producing as many snakes as they can in one minute. Compensate each group (use fake money). You can determine the amount. I usually pay $1 per snake, as long as they meet the requirement. After each round, all the Play-Doh must be placed back in the container and closed before the next round is begun. Students begin to discover that some students make the product quicker than others, so they produce the snakes, while others get the Play-Doh out or roll out. ***Specialization*** and ***productivity*** have now come in to play.

3. Have students complete a few rounds, then place some stipulations on the group. For example, each group will receive $2 for different color snakes, as long as they have their original color. *Trade* will be encouraged.

4. Complete a couple of rounds with different color snakes, then throw in another stipulation. You can choose one color that will receive even more money. For example, blue snakes will be worth $3. You may secretly want to have one group with blue Play-Doh not agree to the *voluntary exchange.*

5. Add donuts to the production. The activity continues with the addition of donuts, which are worth even more money. The groups must still continue to make snakes too. Once again, the donuts cannot be too long or too short. They must extend around the base of the container without overlapping. Each time the Play-Doh is returned to the container.

6. Change the activity by placing conditions that will help the students learn additional terms, for example, *supply and demand*. Choose a color that only one group has (*scarcity*) to be worth the most. *Opportunity cost* can also come into play when a group may decide to produce more donuts because they are worth more but find out that another group that continued to produce snakes made more money because they were able to produce them faster. (Some groups figure out that they can place the snakes back in the container without smushing the Play-Doh each time!)

7. Engage students in a whole-class discussion of the economic terms derived from the activity.

8. Have students complete a K-W-L chart regarding the concepts they learned about goods and resources during the lesson.

Brain-Compatible Strategies: *Which will you use to deliver content?*

X	Brainstorming/Discussion	___	Music/Rhythm/Rhyme/Rap
___	Drawing/Artwork	**X**	Project/Problem-Based Learning
___	Field Trips	**X**	Reciprocal Teaching/Cooperative Learning
___	Games		
X	Graphic Organizers/Semantic Maps/Word Webs	**X**	Role Plays/Drama/Pantomimes/Charades
___	Humor	___	Storytelling
X	Manipulatives/Experiments/Labs/Models	___	Technology
		___	Visualization/Guided Imagery
___	Metaphors/Analogies/Similes	**X**	Visuals
___	Mnemonic Devices	___	Work Study/Apprenticeships
___	Movement	___	Writing/Journals

SOCIAL STUDIES GRADES 6–8 LESSON 1

Military Leaders

Lesson Objective(s): *What do you want students to know and be able to do?*

Describe the roles of Abraham Lincoln, Robert E. Lee, Ulysses S. Grant, Jefferson Davis, and Thomas "Stonewall" Jackson in the Civil War.

Assessment (Traditional/Authentic): *How will you know students have mastered essential learning?*

Students will select two of the historical figures and complete a compare and contrast graphic organizer. (See template, following this lesson.)

Ways to Gain/Maintain Attention (Primacy): *How will you gain and maintain students' attention? Consider need, novelty, meaning, or emotion.*

Display a picture of several military leaders and ask students what these men have in common. Numerous images and photographs of Abraham Lincoln, Robert E. Lee, Ulysses S. Grant, Jefferson Davis, and Thomas "Stonewall" Jackson can be found online at the Library of Congress: https://www.loc.gov

Content Chunks: *How will you divide and teach the content to engage students' brains?*

Lesson Segment 1: Understand Biographical Information

- **Activity 1: Strips of Information**

Retype a selection from a biography about the historical figure and cut it into strips. (Hint: Type *he* instead of the historical figure's name.) Distribute one strip to each student. Have students circulate and read their strips to each other. Then have students predict what they will learn about the historical figure based on the sentence strips.

- **Activity 2: Character Maps**

Have students create character maps regarding historical figures. (See template, following this lesson.) Possible information to include in the maps would be actions, feelings, appearance, words, symbols, and significance.

- **Activity 3: Grading Your Figure**

Have students evaluate the historical figure's significance by assigning him a letter grade. Tell students to include a teacher comment, in writing, to justify the grade they assign.

Brain-Compatible Strategies: *Which will you use to deliver content?*

__X__	Brainstorming/Discussion	_____	Music/Rhythm/Rhyme/Rap
_____	Drawing/Artwork	_____	Project/Problem-Based Learning
_____	Field Trips	__X__	Reciprocal Teaching/Cooperative Learning
_____	Games		
__X__	Graphic Organizers/Semantic Maps/Word Webs	_____	Role Plays/Drama/Pantomimes/Charades
_____	Humor	_____	Storytelling
__X__	Manipulatives/Experiments/Labs/Models	__X__	Technology
		_____	Visualization/Guided Imagery
_____	Metaphors/Analogies/Similes	__X__	Visuals
_____	Mnemonic Devices	_____	Work Study/Apprenticeships
__X__	Movement	__X__	Writing/Journals

Compare and Contrast Chart

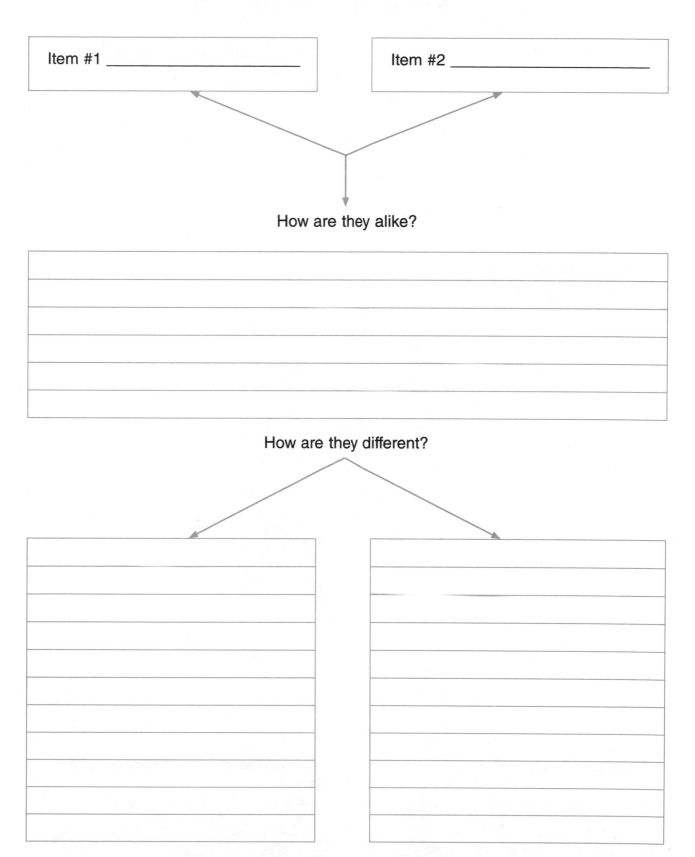

Item #1 _____

Item #2 _____

How are they alike?

How are they different?

Character Map

Character's Problem	**What do you know about the character? (Draw conclusion)**
How did the character solve the problem?	
Character Traits	**How did the character change over time?**

Character

_____
Character's Name

SOCIAL STUDIES GRADES 6–8 LESSON 2

Key Battles and Events of the Civil War

Lesson Objective(s): *What do you want students to know and be able to do?*

Identify major battles and campaigns such as Fort Sumter, Gettysburg, the Atlanta Campaign, Sherman's March to the Sea, and Appomattox Court House.

Assessment (Traditional/Authentic): *How will you know students have mastered essential learning?*

Students will complete an acrostic using the words *CIVIL WAR*. The key events must be included in the text.

Ways to Gain/Maintain Attention (Primacy): *How will you gain and maintain students' attention? Consider need, novelty, meaning, or emotion.*

Using a document camera, project photos and illustrations of the Civil War like the one to the right while playing "When Johnny Comes Marching Home Again." Ask students what they think about these photos.

Numerous Civil War-related images can be found on the Library of Congress website at https://www.loc.gov

Image source: L. Prang & Co, and Thure De Thulstrup. Battle of Shiloh / Thulstrup. United States, ca. 1888. Photograph. https://www.loc.gov/item/92500191/.

Content Chunks: *How will you divide and teach the content to engage students' brains?*

Lesson Segment 1: Identify Major Battles

- **Activity 1: Flipchart**

Project the following battles on the Smart Board, document camera, PowerPoint slide, etc.: Fort Sumter, Gettysburg, Atlanta Campaign, Sherman's March to the Sea, Appomattox Court House. Have students create an Anticipation Guide. An Anticipation Guide is a strategy that is used before reading to activate students' prior knowledge and build curiosity about a new topic.

Using classroom and media center resources, have students complete a flipchart for the major battles, events, and campaigns of the Civil War. Each flipchart should include a timeline and important facts that should be aligned with your standards.

Activity 2: I Use to Think—But Now I Know

Explain to students that the purpose of this activity is to help them reflect on their thinking about the major events of the Civil War and to identify how their ideas have changed over time. For instance, state,

When we began this study of the Civil War, you all had some initial ideas about it and what it was all about. In just a few sentences, write what it is that you used to think about these events. Take a minute to think back and then write down your response to "I used to think . . ."

Now, I want you to think about how your ideas have changed as a result of what we've been studying/doing/discussing. Again, in just a few sentences write down what you now think about the Civil War. Start your sentences with, "But now, I think . . ."

Have students share and explain their shifts in thinking. Initially, it is good to do this as a whole group so that you can probe students' thinking and push them to explain based on the facts and information they've learned. Once students become accustomed to explaining their thinking, students can share with one another in small groups or pairs.

Activity 3: Acrostic

Have students create an acrostic using the words *CIVIL WAR*.

Brain-Compatible Strategies: *Which will you use to deliver content?*

__X__	Brainstorming/Discussion	__X__	Music/Rhythm/Rhyme/Rap
_____	Drawing/Artwork	_____	Project/Problem-Based Learning
_____	Field Trips	__X__	Reciprocal Teaching/Cooperative Learning
_____	Games		
__X__	Graphic Organizers/Semantic Maps/Word Webs	_____	Role Plays/Drama/Pantomimes/Charades
_____	Humor	_____	Storytelling
_____	Manipulatives/Experiments/Labs/Models	__X__	Technology
		_____	Visualization/Guided Imagery
_____	Metaphors/Analogies/Similes	__X__	Visuals
__X__	Mnemonic Devices	_____	Work Study/Apprenticeships
_____	Movement	__X__	Writing/Journals

SOCIAL STUDIES GRADES 6–8 LESSON 3

The Lewis and Clark Expedition

Lesson Objective(s): *What do you want students to know and be able to do?*

Describe territorial expansion with emphasis on the Lewis and Clark expedition.

Assessment (Traditional/Authentic): *How will you know students have mastered essential learning?*

Students will write a journal entry as if they were accompanying Lewis and Clark on their journey.

Ways to Gain/Maintain Attention (Primacy): *How will you gain and maintain students' attention? Consider <u>need</u>, novelty, meaning, or emotion.*

Read a journal entry from Lewis and Clark's expedition to students without telling them anything about them. Have students predict what the lesson will be about.

This is the official website for the expedition. There are many resources on the site.

https://lewisandclarkjournals.unl.edu/

Content Chunks: *How will you divide and teach the content to engage students' brains?*

Lesson Segment 1: Map the Lewis and Clark Expedition

- **Activity 1: A Wagon Route**

Using a map, have students work in pairs to create a wagon route from their home to California, or from California to a state in the East.

Tell students that they may not cross rivers more than 4 to 5 times. Tell them they may not travel more than 50 to 100 miles away from major water sources.

- **Activity 2: Lewis and Clark Route**

Display a map of the actual route of Lewis and Clark on the document camera or smart board. (There a several sources such as the map and globe division of the Library of Congress) http://www.loc.gov/rr/geogmap/

Have students complete a Think-Pair-Share with another group of two students. How is their route different? The same? Students should note geography for both routes, discuss weather, supplies, etc.

- **Activity 3: Gallery Walk**

Have students brainstorm and share with the class the challenges that had to be faced during their journey. Divide the class into groups of three to four. Have students complete a gallery walk using poster size sticky notes. Write the following topics on each sticky note: *geography, weather, climate, supplies,* and *other*. Groups will rotate through each station and place as many different notes under each category. Allow three minutes per rotation. At the completion of the rotations, students will write an individual journal entry from the point of view that they are a member of the team. The writing should include the information that they have discovered on the journey including all the challenges that were faced.

Brain-Compatible Strategies: *Which will you use to deliver content?*

__X__	Brainstorming/Discussion		_____	Music/Rhythm/Rhyme/Rap
_____	Drawing/Artwork		__X__	Project/Problem-Based Learning
_____	Field Trips		__X__	Reciprocal Teaching/Cooperative Learning
_____	Games			
__X__	Graphic Organizers/Semantic Maps/Word Webs		_____	Role Plays/Drama/Pantomimes/Charades
_____	Humor		__X__	Storytelling
_____	Manipulatives/Experiments/Labs/Models		__X__	Technology
			_____	Visualization/Guided Imagery
_____	Metaphors/Analogies/Similes		__X__	Visuals
_____	Mnemonic Devices		_____	Work Study/Apprenticeships
__X__	Movement		__X__	Writing/Journals

SOCIAL STUDIES GRADES 6–8 LESSON 4

Franklin Delano Roosevelt

Lesson Objective(s): *What do you want students to know and be able to do?*

Discuss Franklin Delano Roosevelt and his efforts to expand our rights through the programs of the New Deal and fighting World War II.

Assessment (Traditional/Authentic): *How will you know students have mastered essential learning?*

Students will use research and information from the lesson and complete an acrostic using one of FDR's programs.

Ways to Gain/Maintain Attention (Primacy): *How will you gain and maintain students' attention? Consider need, novelty, meaning, or emotion.*

Project images like the one to the right depicting some posters from WWII. Discuss with students what they think each poster is promoting. Sample images can be found via the Library of Congress at https://www.loc.gov

Image source: Koerner, Henry, Artist. United We Are Strong, United We Can Win. , 1943. [Washington, D.C.: Office of War Information, #e Washington, D.C.: U.S. Government Printing Office] Photograph. https://www.loc.gov/item/2005680330/.

Content Chunks: *How will you divide and teach the content to engage students' brains?*

Lesson Segment 1: Research FDR's Programs

- **Activity 1: Research Project**

Have students research the programs created by FDR using primary sources, classroom materials, internet, and other materials from the media center.

- **Activity 2: WebQuest**

Using a guided format, place the students in small groups to complete a WebQuest for information on the policies and programs of FDR. A WebQuest is an inquiry-oriented lesson format in which most or all the information that learners work with comes from the web. The six building blocks of a WebQuest are:

- **The Introduction** orients students and captures their interest.
- **The Task** describes the activity's end product.

- **The Process** explains strategies students should use to complete the task.
- **The Resources** are the Web sites students will use to complete the task.
- **The Evaluation** measures the results of the activity.
- **The Conclusion** sums up the activity and encourages students to reflect on its process and results.

- **Activity 3: FDR Poster**

After reading about Roosevelt, place students in small groups. Assign each group one of the following:

- Civilian Conservation Corps (CCC)
- Works Progress Administration (WPA)
- Tennessee Valley Authority (TVA)
- Scrap metal
- Victory Garden
- Warm Springs
- Fireside Chat

Have groups complete a poster advertising their topic. Have students include written information and images. Allow groups to share with the class.

Have students use research and information from the lesson to complete an acrostic using one of the *FDR* programs.

- **Activity 4: Analogy**

Have students complete the analogy: Franklin Roosevelt is like ___ because ___.

Brain-Compatible Strategies: *Which will you use to deliver content?*

__X__	Brainstorming/Discussion	_____	Music/Rhythm/Rhyme/Rap
__X__	Drawing/Artwork	__X__	Project/Problem-Based Learning
_____	Field Trips	__X__	Reciprocal Teaching/Cooperative Learning
_____	Games		
_____	Graphic Organizers/Semantic Maps/Word Webs	_____	Role Plays/Drama/Pantomimes/Charades
_____	Humor	_____	Storytelling
_____	Manipulatives/Experiments/Labs/Models	__X__	Technology
		__X__	Visualization/Guided Imagery
__X__	Metaphors/Analogies/Similes	__X__	Visuals
__X__	Mnemonic Devices	_____	Work Study/Apprenticeships
_____	Movement	__X__	Writing/Journals

SOCIAL STUDIES GRADES 6–8 LESSON 5

Civil Rights Movement

Lesson Objective(s): *What do you want students to know and be able to do?*

Explain the key events of the civil rights movement including *Brown v. Board of Education* (1954), the Montgomery Bus Boycott, the March on Washington, the Civil Rights Act, and the Voting Rights Act.

Assessment (Traditional/Authentic): *How will you know students have mastered essential learning?*

Students will write a Two Minute Paper including:

- What was the most important thing you learned?
- What did you learn that you didn't know before?
- What important question(s) remain(s) unanswered?

Ways to Gain/Maintain Attention (Primacy): *How will you gain and maintain students' attention? Consider need, novelty, meaning, or _emotion_.*

Show the class images from the civil rights movement. Engage students in a discussion about what emotions they may have felt viewing the images. Ask students why they believe pictures are so important—both in the moment and in the future.

Image source: Leffler, Warren K, photographer. Civil rights march on Washington, D.C. / WKL. Washington D.C, 1963. Photograph. https://www.loc.gov/item/2003654393/.

Content Chunks: *How will you divide and teach the content to engage students' brains?*

Lesson Segment 1: Share Key Civil Rights Events

- **Activity 1: 3-2-1-Think-Pair-Share**

Have students think of three things that interest them about the civil rights movement; two things they would like to know more about; and one idea they have about the civil rights movement. Allow students to share with a partner and then the class.

- **Activity 2: Civil Right Events**

Using classroom and media center resources, have students research major events of the civil rights movement. These should be aligned with standards and include *Brown v. Board of Education* (1954), the Montgomery Bus Boycott, the March on Washington, the Civil Rights Act, and the Voting Rights Act.

Have students complete a graphic organizer for each of the events of the civil rights movement.

Each graphic organizer should contain:

- Name of the Event
- Facts
- Personal Reflection
- One Word Summary

Brown v. Board of Education	Facts
Personal Reflection	One Word Summary

- **Activity 3: Visualization**

Tell students that they are going to be transported back to the 1950s and 1960s civil rights era. During their journey, back in time, they are going to visit two important civil rights events. Have students write a journal page to describe each event and what they saw. They may pick from the following events: attending the *Brown v. Board of Education* court trial, being on the bus and watching Rosa Parks refuse to give up her seat, taking part in the March on Washington boycott, or taking part in the Montgomery Bus Boycott. Students share their journals with one another.

Brain-Compatible Strategies: *Which will you use to deliver content?*

__X__	Brainstorming/Discussion	_____	Music/Rhythm/Rhyme/Rap
_____	Drawing/Artwork	_____	Project/Problem-Based Learning
_____	Field Trips	__X__	Reciprocal Teaching/Cooperative Learning
_____	Games		
__X__	Graphic Organizers/Semantic Maps/Word Webs	_____	Role Plays/Drama/Pantomimes/Charades
_____	Humor	_____	Storytelling
_____	Manipulatives/Experiments/Labs/Models	_____	Technology
		__X__	Visualization/Guided Imagery
_____	Metaphors/Analogies/Similes	__X__	Visuals
_____	Mnemonic Devices	_____	Work Study/Apprenticeships
_____	Movement	__X__	Writing/Journals

3-2-1 Strategy

3	Label Will Appear Here
2	Label
1	Label

SOCIAL STUDIES GRADES 6–8 LESSON 6

Branches of the Federal Government

Lesson Objective(s): *What do you want students to know and be able to do?*

Organize and explain the three branches of US government as outlined by the Constitution, describe what they do, and how they relate to each other (checks and balances and separation of power) and to the states.

Assessment (Traditional/Authentic): *How will you know students have mastered essential learning?*

Students will complete a Venn diagram illustrating the three branches of government, their powers, and the system of checks and balances.

Ways to Gain/Maintain Attention (Primacy): *How will you gain and maintain students' attention? Consider need, novelty, meaning, or emotion.*

Ask students: *What if there was no government? How would our lives be different?*

Content Chunks: *How will you divide and teach the content to engage students' brains?*

Lesson Segment 1: Understand the Rationale Behind the Branches

- **Activity 1: Lecture**

Explain to students that when the Constitution was first an idea in the minds of the founding fathers, they knew that, in the best interest of the people, the United States governing power had to be split. The reason for this was because at that time the British government held near unlimited power to do as they saw fit without any barriers. Over time, the results of Britain's centralized government lead to a variety of different violations of human freedom. Because of this oppressive government, the founding fathers decided to create a more balanced and healthy government by using three branches of government to work as a cohesive whole: the judicial branch, the legislative branch, and the executive branch. Each one of the three branches of government functions very differently, yet they work together as a whole to form a powerful government that is kept within boundaries through checks and balances.

- **Activity 2: Charades**

Divide students into three groups. Give each group a copy of the US Constitution. Have the groups find the three articles that describe the branches of government. Play charades for the different branches and powers of each.

- **Activity 3: Tri-Fold Booklet**

Have students create a tri-fold booklet with pockets. Each page represents one branch of the government. Have students take notes on index cards for each branch. Label the cards for the 5Ws & H

(Who/What/When/Where/Why/How), and label one card Memory Clue. Have students place the cards in the appropriate pockets. (Technology Connection: Have students create a PowerPoint with hyperlinks for the 5Ws & H and memory clue.) Have students complete the book cover for their tri-fold including a title and illustration representing the three branches of government.

- **Activity 4: Venn Diagram**

Since *compare* and *contrast* are two terms that often come together in questions, let us look at the difference between compare and contrast. Compare and contrast are the two terms that you normally tend to use when you find similarities and yet differences between two objects or things. Have each student work with three other students (one from each of the groups in Activity 2 to compare and contrast the three branches of government and the powers of each.

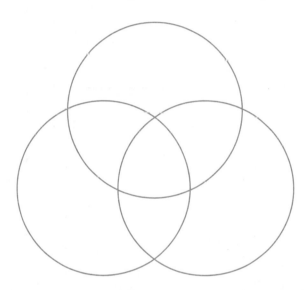

Brain-Compatible Strategies: *Which will you use to deliver content?*

_X_	Brainstorming/Discussion		____	Music/Rhythm/Rhyme/Rap
_X_	Drawing/Artwork		____	Project/Problem-Based Learning
____	Field Trips		_X_	Reciprocal Teaching/Cooperative Learning
_X_	Games			
_X_	Graphic Organizers/Semantic Maps/Word Webs		_X_	Role Plays/Drama/Pantomimes/ Charades
____	Humor		____	Storytelling
____	Manipulatives/Experiments/Labs/ Models		_X_	Technology
			____	Visualization/Guided Imagery
____	Metaphors/Analogies/Similes		_X_	Visuals
____	Mnemonic Devices		____	Work Study/Apprenticeships
____	Movement		_X_	Writing/Journals

Legislative

Judicial

Executive

Created by:

_____

SOCIAL STUDIES GRADES 6–8 LESSON 7

Compare and Contrast Two Countries

Lesson Objective(s): *What do you want students to know and be able to do?*

Compare how the location, climate, and natural resources of Brazil and Cuba affect where people live and how they trade. (This format can be used to compare any two countries.)

Note: Students have already been exposed to the concepts/vocabulary of climate, location, and natural resources.

Assessment (Traditional/Authentic): *How will you know students have mastered essential learning?*

Students will independently create a compare/contrast graphic organizer (found at the end of this lesson) and list the similarities and differences with respect to trade and population settlement in Brazil and Cuba.

Ways to Gain/Maintain Attention (Primacy): *How will you gain and maintain students' attention? Consider need, novelty, meaning, or emotion.*

Have students discuss why do you think people would choose to live in (insert local area)?

Content Chunks: *How will you divide and teach the content to engage students' brains?*

Lesson Segment 1: Compare the Location, Climate, Resources of Brazil and Cuba

- **Activity 1: Two-Column Note-Taking**

The Two-Column Note-Taking strategy encourages students to identify important information in a lecture, film, or reading and to then respond to this material. Use this strategy to prepare students to participate in a discussion or begin a writing activity. Having students take two-column notes is also an effective way to help identify students' misconceptions and questions about a topic and to evaluate students' understanding of the material.

Lead a class discussion about the climate, location, and natural resources found in their local area. Students will use two-column note-taking for discussion with the following guiding questions:

- How would you describe the climate where we live?
- How would you describe the location where we live?
- Are there any natural resources that you are aware of where we live?

As a discussion of the area where students live, have them take notes using the following procedure: The page they record notes on should be divided in half with a line or fold. The left side should be labeled *Key Ideas* and the right side should be labeled *Response*.

- **Activity 2: Primary Sources**

Have students work together in groups of four. Give them primary sources that pertain to the climate, location, and natural resources of Brazil and Cuba. The Library of Congress has document sets that are for classroom use. There are no copyright issues when using these. https://www.loc.gov/teachers/classroommaterials/primarysourcesets/

Ask students to cite evidence in order to answer the prompts:

- How did climate, location, and natural resources impact where the citizens of Brazil and Cuba settled?
- How did climate, location, and natural resources affect their trade?

As students analyze the primary sources, they will be looking for evidence to answer the two questions above. They will be keeping track of their evidence in a graphic organizer.

- **Activity 3: Appointments**

Students will work in pairs by making two appointments. Have students select two students that are not in their assigned group. Give students about six minutes to set up the two appointments and complete the assignments.

Appointment 1

Student A will have two minutes to answer the question, *How did climate, location, and natural resources impact where the citizens of Brazil lived?*, citing the evidence gathered during the collaboration activity. Student B will then have two minutes to answer the question, *How did climate, location and natural resources impact where the citizens of Cuba lived?*, citing the evidence gathered during the collaboration activity.

Appointment 2

Student A will have two minutes to answer the question, *How did climate, location, and natural resources affect Brazil's trade?* Student B will have two minutes to answer the question, *How did climate, location, and natural resources affect Cuba's trade?* The student who is listening should be adding missed information to their graphic organizer.

Brain-Compatible Strategies: *Which will you use to deliver content?*

__X__	Brainstorming/Discussion	_____	Music/Rhythm/Rhyme/Rap
_____	Drawing/Artwork	_____	Project/Problem-Based Learning
_____	Field Trips	__X__	Reciprocal Teaching/Cooperative Learning
_____	Games		
__X__	Graphic Organizers/Semantic Maps/Word Webs	_____	Role Plays/Drama/Pantomimes/Charades
_____	Humor	_____	Storytelling
_____	Manipulatives/Experiments/Labs/Models	__X__	Technology
		_____	Visualization/Guided Imagery
_____	Metaphors/Analogies/Similes	__X__	Visuals
_____	Mnemonic Devices	_____	Work Study/Apprenticeships
__X__	Movement	__X__	Writing/Journals

Compare and Contract

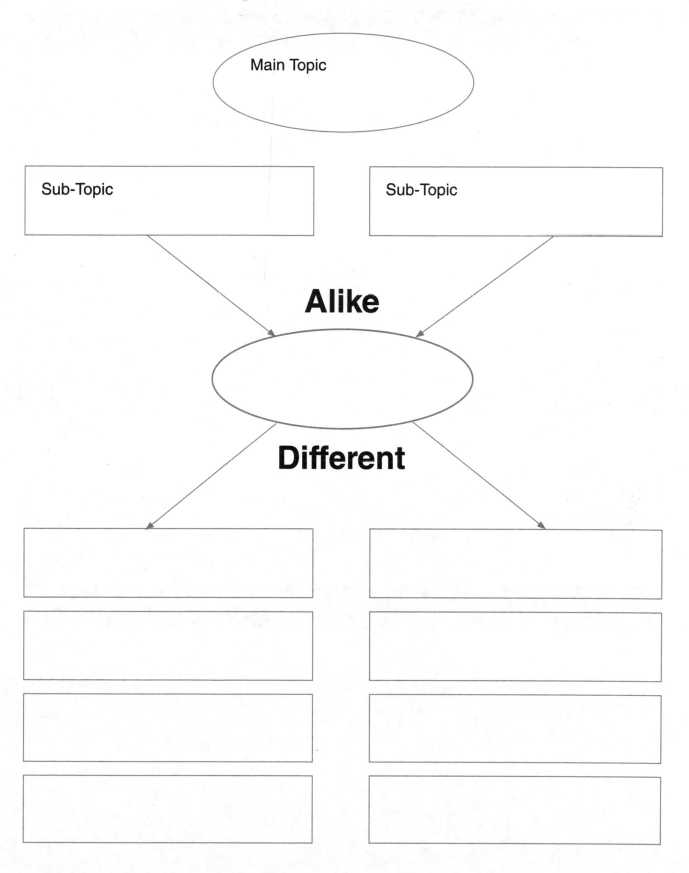

Topic: _____

Main Ideas	Details

Summary

SOCIAL STUDIES GRADES 6–8 LESSON 8

European Exploration

Lesson Objective(s): *What do you want students to know and be able to do?*

Describe European exploration in North America. (Suggested explorers include but are not limited to John Cabot, Vasco Nunez Balboa, Juan Ponce de Leon, Christopher Columbus, Henry Hudson, Jacques Cartier.)

Assessment (Traditional/Authentic): *How will you know students have mastered essential learning?*

Students will make trading cards for each explorer. The trading cards should be formatted as follows:

- front of the card—name and illustration of the explorer
- back of the card—the reasons for, obstacles to, and accomplishments of the explorer (Technology Connection: Students could use Publisher or PowerPoint to create their trading cards.)

Ways to Gain/Maintain Attention (Primacy): *How will you gain and maintain students' attention? Consider need, novelty, meaning, or emotion.*

Have students generate a *word splash* to answer the question: What is an explorer?

Word Splash is a learning tool that stimulates thinking around a topic. It can be used as a priming **activity** or a wrap-up **activity**. A **word splash** is a collection of words around a topic where the words related to the topic are arranged on a page in a variety of directions.

Content Chunks: *How will you divide and teach the content to engage students' brains?*

Lesson Segment 1: Describe European Exploration in North America

- **Activity 1: Interactive Modeling**

Tell the students that under their seat is a question about what explorers did. Students will volunteer to pull out their question and then answer it for the class. Before you put students in the hot seat, use Interactive Modeling to show them exactly how it works and what you expect them to do. Just as it does with other procedures, Interactive Modeling gives students an opportunity to observe the teacher doing what they will be doing, notice in detail what is expected of them, and practice.

- **Activity 2: *In the Hot Seat***

Place sticky notes under various desks with questions that relate to what the explorers did. (These should be questions that students can answer.) Sample questions include:

- Why might someone choose to be an explorer? What might be in it for them?
- How would you feel if you were in the middle of the ocean and had no idea how long you would be there?

- What would you do if you landed in the New World and met people you had never seen before?

Have students stand, read their question, and respond.

- **Activity 3: Presentation**

Using classroom materials and technology, have students research individual explorers as indicated by standards according to the following guidelines:

- Cut apart strips of paper with the names of the explorers and place in a basket.
- Have students draw one name and then research their explorer and record at least five facts about their explorer.
- After students have completed their research, allow students who researched the same explorers to meet.
- Tell them to create one presentation on their explorer based on all of the research.

The presentation needs to include: reasons for exploration, accomplishments of the explorer, and a memory clue (this would be something to assist their classmates in remembering the explorer, such as acrostics or acronyms). As students present, have the class complete a graphic organizer for each explorer.

- **Activity 4: Word Splash Revisited**

Have students return to the word splash they created. Ask students which words apply to each of the explorers. Encourage students to add new words.

- **Activity 5: Trading Cards**

Have students make trading cards for each explorer. (See Assessment)

Brain-Compatible Strategies: *Which will you use to deliver content?*

X	Brainstorming/Discussion	____	Music/Rhythm/Rhyme/Rap
X	Drawing/Artwork	____	Project/Problem-Based Learning
____	Field Trips	**X**	Reciprocal Teaching/Cooperative Learning
____	Games		
X	Graphic Organizers/Semantic Maps/Word Webs	____	Role Plays/Drama/Pantomimes/Charades
____	Humor	____	Storytelling
____	Manipulatives/Experiments/Labs/Models	**X**	Technology
		____	Visualization/Guided Imagery
____	Metaphors/Analogies/Similes	**X**	Visuals
X	Mnemonic Devices	____	Work Study/Apprenticeships
X	Movement	**X**	Writing/Journals

SOCIAL STUDIES GRADES 6–8 LESSON 9

Personal Money Management

> **Lesson Objective(s):** *What do you want students to know and be able to do?*
>
> Learn the value of budgeting, investing, spending, and making sound decisions regarding income, spending, and saving.
>
> Explain the principles of effective personal money management.
>
> **Assessment (Traditional/Authentic):** *How will you know students have mastered essential learning?*
>
> Students will create an individual acrostic using the words *PERSONAL MONEY MANAGEMENT.*

> **Ways to Gain/Maintain Attention (Primacy):** *How will you gain and maintain students' attention? Consider* <u>need</u>, *novelty,* <u>meaning</u>, *or emotion.*
>
> Write the words *personal finance* on the board. With an elbow partner, have students brainstorm different words or phrases that they think relate to the topic.

Content Chunks: *How will you divide and teach the content to engage students' brains?*

Lesson Segment 1: Understand Principles of Money Management

- **Activity 1: Lecture**

Explain the following information to students. Income is the starting point for personal financial management. Developing a personal financial management plan is unique to every individual. Spending and saving goals should be considered in making a realistic, workable plan. Perhaps the most important factor when first developing a financial plan should be the individual's income. Income is the money received (coming in) for labor or services, the sale of property or goods, from financial investments, or other services. Knowing monthly income allows the individual to know how much money is available to take care of expenditures (to spend). This allows the individual to maintain control of his money and helps to achieve long- and short-term financial goals.

   Glossary • *Expenditure*—an amount of money spent, as a whole or on a particular thing. • *Income*—the amount of money a person earns during a year. • *Investing*—using money in hopes of gaining more in the future by lending to businesses in exchange for a share of profits. • *Saving*—setting aside income for future use. • *Spending*—using the money a person has.

- **Activity 2: Circle Summary**

Divide students into groups of three to four. Have students complete the following *Circle Summary* activity based on what they learn regarding personal finance. All directions are on the activity listed below.

Tell students that using the five given terms to represent what Personal Finance means, they are to follow the directions below.

Directions: 1. Copy this chart onto your own paper. Make it big! 2. In the center of the circle write Personal Finance and draw a picture or symbol to represent it. 3. Write the most important fact you learned about this unit from each of the five terms related to personal finance in the middle box. 4. For each fact draw and color a picture in the first open space. 5. Write a personal response to the fact. (This reminds me of . . . I think it is fair/unfair that…)

- **Activity 3: Txt Msg Activity**

Have students complete the following activity as if they are having to explain to a friend what personal financial management is in the form of a text message. The directions and activity are attached below.

TXT MSG SUMRE Ur Job:

For example, the regular message would be:

Imagine you're sending a summary of personal finance via text message to a friend who can't save money for some reason; write up the summary in text messaging language including all appropriate abbreviations and smilies.

The text message would be:

imagin ur sendg a sumre of personl finance via txt msg 2 a friend who cant save $ for sum reson wrt ^ the sumre in txt msgn lang including all appropriate abbreviations n smilies.

Ur sumre must:

- include abbreviated words where appropriate.
- include all the key points of the definition.
- be short and to the point but at least one paragraph.
- be written in a friendly way as if you were personally involved.
- include the regular, nontext message version.

- **Activity 4: Personal Finance Mind Map**

Have students complete the activity *mapping* the important concepts studied in groups of three to four.

Whenever we learn new things, our brain makes connections to other things we already know. Have students create a visual map that shows how your brain connects the terms from a given unit. The end result will be something like a web. Tell the students to make their map look unique and artistic.

Directions:

1. Have students use one of the following activities:
   - Create a list of 20 things for Personal Money Management.
   - On a regular paper write the title of the unit in a bubble in the middle of the page.
   - Draw another bubble with one of the words from your list of 20 connected to the first bubble anywhere on the page.
   - Draw another bubble with another word. Connect it either to the first bubble or to the other word (if they are related in some way).

- Continue adding bubbles and connections until all 20 words are in a bubble and connected to some other bubble.
- Look over your map and add a second connection for each bubble. EACH BUBBLE MUST CONNECT TO AT LEAST 2 OTHER BUBBLES!

2. Write your own definitions for 10 of the 20 words from your list in a complete sentence.

3. Choose any 10 connections you made on your map and explain why you made them in 1-2 complete sentences each. (Tell how those two items are related other than "they both came from the same place.") Number these 1-10 and write the number on the connection line.

4. Consider the following when completing the final product.
   - If needed, rearrange your bubbles so connection lines can be as straight as possible.
   - Draw each bubble and word neatly using different colors throughout. (You may choose to have your colors represent certain things. If you do, be sure to include a legend showing this.)
   - Draw five pictures on your mind map which match up with either the words in the bubbles or the connections.

- **Activity 5: Acrostic**

Have students create an acrostic using the words *PERSONAL MONEY MANAGEMENT*.

Brain-Compatible Strategies: *Which will you use to deliver content?*

__X__	Brainstorming/Discussion	____	Music/Rhythm/Rhyme/Rap
__X__	Drawing/Artwork	____	Project/Problem-Based Learning
____	Field Trips	__X__	Reciprocal Teaching/Cooperative Learning
____	Games		
__X__	Graphic Organizers/Semantic Maps/Word Webs	____	Role Plays/Drama/Pantomimes/Charades
____	Humor	____	Storytelling
____	Manipulatives/Experiments/Labs/Models	____	Technology
		__X__	Visualization/Guided Imagery
__X__	Metaphors/Analogies/Similes	__X__	Visuals
__X__	Mnemonic Devices	____	Work Study/Apprenticeships
____	Movement	__X__	Writing/Journals

Circle Summary

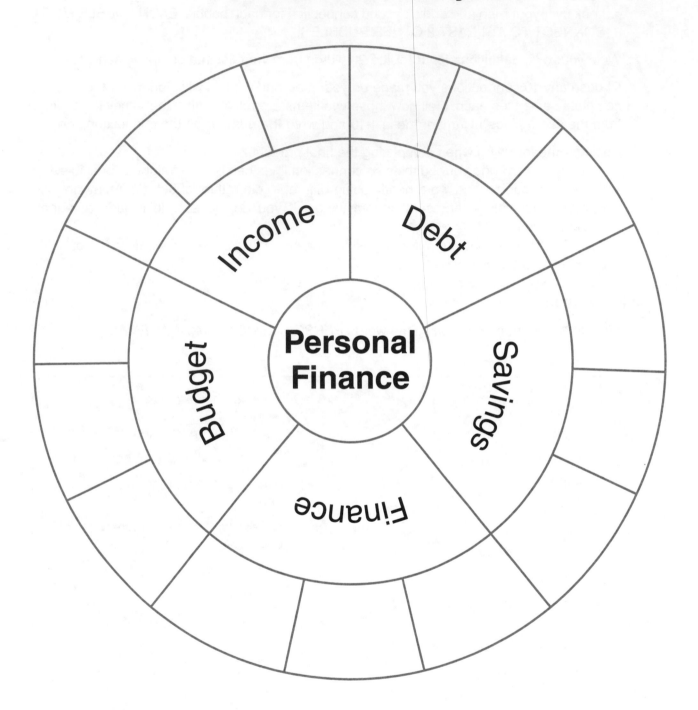

Resource

Lesson Plan Template

BRAIN-COMPATIBLE LESSON PLAN

Lesson Objective(s): *What do you want students to know and be able to do?*

Assessment (Traditional/Authentic): *How will you know students have mastered essential learning?*

Ways to Gain/Maintain Attention (Primacy): *How will you gain and maintain students' attention? Consider need, novelty, meaning, or emotion.*

Content Chunks: *How will you divide and teach the content to engage students' brains?*

Lesson Segment 1:

- **Activities:**

Lesson Segment 2:

- **Activities:**

Lesson Segment 3:

- **Activities:**

Brain-Compatible Strategies: *Which will you use to deliver content?*

_____ Brainstorming/Discussion	_____ Music/Rhythm/Rhyme/Rap
_____ Drawing/Artwork	_____ Project/Problem-Based Learning
_____ Field Trips	_____ Reciprocal Teaching/Cooperative Learning
_____ Games	
_____ Graphic Organizers/Semantic Maps/ Word Webs	_____ Role Plays/Drama/Pantomimes/ Charades
_____ Humor	_____ Storytelling
_____ Manipulatives/Experiments/Labs/ Models	_____ Technology
	_____ Visualization/Guided Imagery
_____ Metaphors/Analogies/Similes	_____ Visuals
_____ Mnemonic Devices	_____ Work Study/Apprenticeships
_____ Movement	_____ Writing/Journals

Bibliography

Allen, R. (2008). *Green light classrooms: Teaching techniques that accelerate learning.* Victoria, AUS: Hawker Brownlow.

Bender, W.N. (2017). *20 strategies for increasing student engagement.* West Palm Beach, FL. Learning Sciences International.

Cooper, N., & Garner, B. K. (2012). *Developing a learning classroom: Moving beyond management through relationships, relevance, and rigor.* Thousand Oaks, CA: Corwin.

Covey, S. (1996). *The seven habits of highly effective people.* Salt Lake City, UT: Covey Leadership Center.

Curtain-Phillips, M. (2018). *Manipulatives: The missing link in high school math.* Retrieved May 10, 2018, from http://www.mathgoodies.com/articles/manipulatives.html

Dean, C. B., Hubbell, E. R., Pitler, H., & Stone, B.J. (2012). *Classroom instruction that works: Research-based strategies for increasing student achievement.* (2nd ed.) Alexandria, VA: Association for Supervision and Curriculum Development.

Dewey, J. (1934). *Art as experience.* New York: Minion Ballet.

Ekwall, E. E., & Shanker, J. L. (1988). *Diagnosis and remediation of the disabled reader* (3rd ed.). Boston: Allyn and Bacon.

Feinstein, S. G. (2009). *Secrets of the teenage brain: Research-based strategies for reaching and teaching today's adolescents.* Thousand Oaks, CA: Corwin.

Fogarty, R. (2009). *Brain-compatible classrooms* (3rd ed.). Victoria, AUS: Hawker Brownlow.

Fulghum, R. (2004). *All I really need to know I learned in kindergarten: Uncommon thoughts on common things.* New York: Ballantine Books.

Gersten, R., Beckmann, S., Clarke, B., Foegen, A., Marsh, I., Star, J. R., & Witzel, B. (2009). *Assisting students struggling with mathematics: Response to Intervention (RtI) for elementary and middle schools* (NCEE 2009-4060). Washington, DC: National Center for Education Evaluation and Regional Assistance, Institute of Education Sciences, U.S. Department of Education.

Green, J. (2005). *The green book of songs by subject: The ultimate guide to popular music* (5th ed.). Nashville, TN. Professional Desk References.

Gregory, G. H., & Chapman, C. (2013). *Differentiated instructional strategies: One size doesn't fit all.* Thousand Oaks, CA: Corwin.

Hattie, J. (2012). *Visible learning for teachers: Maximizing impact on learning.* London and New York: Routledge, Taylor and Francis Group.

Hattie, J., Fisher, D., & Frey, N. (2017). *Visible learning for mathematics: What works best to optimize student learning.* Thousand Oaks, CA: Corwin.

Jensen, E. (1995). *Brain-based learning & teaching.* Del Mar, CA: The Brain Store.

Jensen, E. (2007). *Brain-compatible strategies* (2nd ed.). Victoria, AUS: Hawker.

Jensen, E. (2013). *Engaging students with poverty in mind.* Alexandria, VA: Association for Supervision and Curriculum Development.

Jensen, E., & Nickelsen, L. (2014). *Bringing the common core to life in K-8 classrooms.* Bloomington, IN. Solution Tree Press.

Jensen, E., & Snider, C. (2013). *Turnaround tools for the teenage brain: Helping under-performing students become lifelong learners.* San Francisco, CA: Jossey-Bass.

Konrad, M., Joseph, I. M., & Itoi, M. (2011, January). Using guided notes to enhance instruction for all students. *Intervention in School and Clinic, 46*(3), 131–140.

Lin, L. -Y., Cherng, R.-J., Chen,Y. -J., Chen, Y. -J., & Yang, H.-M. (2015, February). Effects of television exposure of developmental skills among young children. *Infant Behavior and Development, 38,* 20–26.

Mahoney, S. (2005, July/August). How to live longer. *American Association of Retired People, 48*(4B), 64–72.

Medina, J. 2008. *Brain rules: 12 principles for surviving and thriving at work, home, and school.* Seattle, WA: Pear Press.

National Research Council. (2009). *Adding it up: Helping children learn mathematics.* Washington, DC. National Academies Press.

Rosenshine, B. & Meister, C. (1994). Reciprocal teaching: *A review of the research. Review of Educational Research, 64*(4), 479–530.

Secretary's Commission on Achieving Necessary Skills (1991). *What work requires of schools: A SCANS report for America 2000.* Washington, DC: US Department of Labor.

Sheriff, K. A., & Boon, R. T. (2014, August). Effects of computer-based graphic organizers to solve one-step word problems for middle school students with mild intellectual disability: A preliminary study. *Research in Developmental Disabilities, 35*(8), 1828–1837.

Silver, D., Berckemeyer, J. C., & Baenen, J. (2015). *Deliberate optimism: Reclaiming the joy in education.* Thousand Oaks, CA: Corwin.

Sousa, D. A. (2017). *How the brain learns* (5th ed.). Thousand Oaks, CA: Corwin.

Sousa, D. A., & Pilecki, T. (2013). *From STEM to STEAM: Using brain-compatible strategies to integrate the arts.* Thousand Oaks, CA: Corwin.

Stibich, M. (2014, May 1). Retrieved July 25, 2018, from longevity.about.com.>About Health.

Tate, M.L. (2008). *Engage the brain: Graphic organizers and other visual strategies, Grade 2.* Thousand Oaks, CA. Corwin.

Tate, M.L. (2008). *Engage the brain: Graphic organizers and other visual strategies, Grade 5.* Thousand Oaks, CA: Corwin.

Tate, M.L. (2014). *Reading & language arts worksheets don't grow dendrites: 20 literacy strategies that engage the brain (2nd ed.).* Thousand Oaks, CA: Corwin.

Tate, M. L. (2014). *Shouting won't grow dendrites: 20 techniques to detour around the danger zones* (2nd ed.). Thousand Oaks, CA: Corwin.

Tate, M. L. (2016). *Worksheets don't grow dendrites: 20 instructional strategies that engage the brain* (3rd ed.). Thousand Oaks, CA: Corwin.

Wiggins, G., & McTighe, J. (2005). *Understanding by design.* Alexandria, VA: Association for Supervision and Curriculum Development.

Wiggins, G., & McTighe, J. (2008, May). Put understanding first. *Educational Leadership, 65*(19), 36–41.

Willis, J. (2006). *Research-based strategies to ignite student learning.* Alexandria, VA: Association for Supervision and Curriculum Development.

Index

Academic achievement, improvements in, 13–14

Acrostic poem activity, 305

Active listening with podcasts activity, 96

Addition lesson, 128–129

Alexander and the Terrible, Horrible, No Good, Very Bad Day, 72

All I Really Need to Know I Learned in Kindergarten, 14

American Indian culture lesson, 296–298

American Revolution lessons, 305–308

American symbols lesson, 278–279

Analogies, 19, 320

Analyzing texts lesson, 94–95

Angles, 174–176

Annotation protocol activity, 80–81

Apple tree details activity, 52

Applying the INFO formula activity, 62

Apprenticeships, 23

Aquarium activity, 152–154

Aristotle, 23

Assessment, 26–27

Attention, ways to gain/maintain student, 27–29

Attribute blocks activity, 109

Author engagement activity, 67

Backward lesson design, 26

Beginning, middle, and end activity, 49

Behavior problems, 14–15

Birthday egg lesson, 259–261

Blending hustle activity, 42

Blondie, 44

Blooming characters activity, 48

Body details activity, 52

Brain changes and teaching, 2–3

Brain-compatible lessons
  assessment, 26–27
  considering need, novelty, meaning, or emotion, 27–29
  content chunks, 29–30
  delivery strategies, 30
  lesson objectives, 25–26
  ways to gain/maintain attention, 27–29
  See also Language arts lessons; Mathematics lessons; Science lessons; Social studies lessons

Brain-compatible strategies
  benefits of, 13–16
  brainstorming and discussion, 16–17
  drawing and artwork, 17
  field trips, 16, 17
  games, 17–18
  graphic organizers, semantic maps, and word webs, 18
  humor, 18–19
  manipulatives, experiments, labs, and models, 16, 19
  metaphors, analogies, and similes, 19
  mnemonic devices, 15, 19–20
  movement, 11–12, 20
  music, rhythm, rhyme, and rap, 20
  project-based and problem-based learning, 20–21
  reciprocal teaching and cooperative learning, 21
  role plays, drama, pantomimes, and charades, 16, 21
  storytelling, 15, 21–22
  technology, 16, 22
  visualization and guided imagery, 22
  visuals, 22–23
  work study and apprenticeships, 23
  writing and journals, 23

Brain Rules 12 Principles for Surviving and Thriving at Work, Home, and School, 3

Brainstorming and discussion, 16–17, 85–86

Branches of the federal government lesson, 324–326

Building new words activity, 59

Call Me, 44

Carrey, J., 18

Cartoon activities, 265

Cell phone silhouette activity, 43–44

Cells and cell parts lesson, 229–232

Central ideas and supporting details lesson, 92–93

Chair for My Mother, A, 49

Chair in the middle activity, 110

Character development lesson, 89–91

Character maps activity, 311, 314

Character suitcase activity, 72

Character traits lesson, 72–73

Charades, 21, 324

Charlotte's Web, 49

Checker, Chubby, 33

Chemical charges and periodic table lesson, 223–225

Chemical reactions lesson, 246–247

Chunks, content, 10, 29–30

Circle summary activity, 333–334, 336

Citizenship lesson, 270–272

Civil Rights movement lesson, 321–323

Civil War, key battles and events of the, 315–316

Classification lesson, 240–242

Classifying shapes lesson, 114–116

Classroom climates, 7–8
  content taught in segments or chunks in, 10
  movement as natural part of instruction in, 11–12
  positive environment in, 8
  purposeful and relevant learning and, 9–10
  routines and procedures becoming habitual in, 9
  students challenged but remaining confident in, 12
  students engaged in conversation and, 11

Cleary, B., 58

Cleese, J., 18

Coding with glyphs lesson, 203–206

Colonial America lesson, 302–304

Comic strip drawing activity, 261

Commercial creation activity, 71

Commercials activity, 53

Compare and contrast lessons, 56–57, 74–76, 313, 327–330, 329

Compare it activity, 56–57

Composite shapes lesson, 125–127

Confidence, student, 12

Content segments and chunks, 10, 29–30

Conversations, student, 11

Cooper and garner, 16

Cooperative learning and reciprocal teaching, 21

Covey, S., 25

Creating a flipbook activity, 59

Creating an original brochure activity, 62

Crowded visualization and metaphor activity, 260
Cut it out! activity, 39

Declaration of Independence lesson, 299–301
Decoding multisyllabic words lesson, 57–59
Delivery, content, 30
Density lesson, 226–228
Descriptive details lesson, 67–69
Design project activity, 215–216
Design team logo creation activity, 215
Detail phone call metaphor activity, 44
Details and descriptive words activity, 68
Dewey, J., 17
Dice game activity, 141
Diffusion mist activity, 220
Dion, M., 63
Disney is the best activity, 53–54
Diversity of habitats lesson, 184–187
Divide by tens lesson, 146–148
Division of fractions lesson, 170–173
DNA model lesson, 243–245
Door Bell Rang, The, 290
Drama, 21
Drama station activity, 112
Drawing and artwork, 17
Drawing a plot mountain activity, 64
Drawing inferences lesson, 77–79

Earth and human activity lesson, 194–196
Economics lesson, 289–290
Egg carton fill activity, 106
Egg carton number bonds activity, 106
Electricity activity, 223
Electric Slide, The, 49
Electrons activity, 223
Embedded numbers lesson, 106–108
Emotion, 29
Endorphins, 18
Engineering design-classification lesson, 240–242
Engineering design lesson, 215–216
English language arts lessons. *See* Language arts lessons
Equal shares lesson, 123–124
European exploration lesson, 331–332
Everyday Use, 92
Exit slips, 95
Experiments, 19

Fact/opinion strips activity, 70
Factual information activity, 293
Feinstein, S. G., 20
Ferdinand who? activity, 51–52
Field trips, 16, 17
Fisher, D., 21
Fisher, M., 219
FLATS graphic organizer, 90
Flip books activity, 75, 302, 304, 305
Flipchart activity, 315
Flipgrid videos, 88
Flowers (sexual reproduction of plants) lesson, 213–214
Fly swatter activity, 33

Fogarty, R., 21
Forces of flight lesson, 191–193
Fossil data lesson, 207–209
Fractions, 117–119
    division of, 170–173
Franklin Delano Roosevelt lesson, 319–320
Frey, N., 21
Frost, H., 282
Fruit fun activity, 291
Fulghum, R., 14
Fun fly stick activity, 223

Gallery walk activities, 72, 90, 281, 317–318
Game room floor measurement lesson, 155–157
Games, 17–18
Germination and photosynthesis in plants lesson, 210–212
Gift of the Magi, The, 83
Give Me Half activity, 123
Globes and maps lesson, 275–277
Glyphs, 203–206
Goods and resources lesson, 309–310
Government branches lesson, 324–326
Grade levels, brain-friendly lessons addressing all, 14
Graphic organizers, 18, 177–179
Graphic Organizers that Engage the Brain, 65
Green, J., 20
Green Book of Songs by Subject, The, 20
Green egg rhymes, 36–37
Green Eggs and Ham, 36–37
Griffiths, M., 48
Guided imagery, 22

Happy, 43, 58
Hare and bear traits activity, 48
Hattie, J., 21
Head First activity, 64
Hey Little Ant activity, 54
High-frequency words lesson, 32–35
Historical figures lesson, 293–295
Hoose, H., 53
Hoose, P., 53
Hop on Pop, 36
How do I answer? activity, 51
How the Brain Learns, 3
Hughes, L., 80
Hula hoop it activity, 56
Human heart and circulation lesson, 237–239
Humor, 18–19
Hunter, M., 4
Hustle, The, 42
Hutchins, P., 290

Identifying informational text activity, 62
Identifying roots and affixes through metaphor activity, 58
Imaginary line discussion, 292
Incredible shrinking notes activity, 281
Inferences, 77–79
INFO anchor chart activity, 61
Inside out spelling activity, 33

Instructional changes and teaching, 3–4
Instructional strategies, 13–16
Interactive modeling activity, 331
Interpret fossils-archaeology lesson, 207–209
In the Hot Seat activity, 331–332
Irony, 83–84
It's all in the details activity, 47
I Use to Think-But Now I Know activity, 316

Jensen, E., 8
Jewelry decision time activity, 128–129

Key battles and events of the Civil War lesson, 315–316
King, M. L., Jr., 282–288
KWHL charts, 278–279
K-W-L charts, 280, 292

Labs, 19
Language arts lessons
    analyzing texts, 94–95
    central ideas and supporting details, 92–93
    character lessons, 89–91
    character traits, 72–73
    compare and contrast, 56–57, 74–76
    decoding multisyllabic words, 57–59
    descriptive details, 67–69
    drawing inferences, 77–79
    high-frequency words, 32–35
    irony, 83–84
    listening responsively, 96–97
    literary texts that teach story elements and skills for, 98–103
    main topic and details, 43–45
    opinion/point of view, 70–71
    opinion with facts, 53–55
    phonemes, 38–40
    plot structure, 64–66
    questioning, 51–52
    reading websites for, 104
    research topics, 85–86
    rhyming words, 36–37
    Socratic seminar, 80–82
    story details, 48–50
    text analysis, 87–88
    word analysis skills, 41–42
    writing, 61–63
Language Arts Worksheets Don't Grow Dendrites, 70
Latitude, longitude, equator, prime meridian lesson, 291–292
Leaf, M., 51
Let me be your substitute activity, 38–39
Letter writing activity, 307
Lewis and Clark expedition lesson, 317–318
Light refraction, 220–222
Like me? activity, 74
Line plots lesson, 138–139
Listening responsively lesson, 96–97
List-group-label activity, 296–297
Little Red Riding Hood, 56–57
Location problem activity, 109

Longfellow, H. W., 280
Lon Po Po, 57
Love You Forever, 67

Main idea and details activity, 44, 46
Main idea video activity, 43
Main topic and details lesson, 43–45
Manipulatives, 16, 19
Map locations lesson, 158–161
Maps and globes lesson, 275–277
Martin Luther King, Jr. Day lesson,
    282–288
Matching inferences activity, 77
Match my rhyme activity, 36
Mathematics lessons
    addition, 128–129
    angles, 174–176
    classifying shapes, 114–116
    composite shapes, 125–127
    divide by tens, 146–148
    division of fractions, 170–173
    embedded numbers, 106–108
    equal shares, 123–124
    line plots, 138–139
    map locations, 158–161
    measurement, 155–156
    measurement (nonstandard units),
        120–122
    multiplication, 130–132
    multiplying decimals, 149–151
    order of operations, 162–164, 165–166
    order of operations (errors), 167–169
    partitioning shapes, 135–137
    perimeter, 143–145
    position words, 109–111
    prime and composite numbers,
        140–142
    problem-solving roots, 180–181
    rational numbers, 177–179
    rectangles, 117–119
    subtraction, 112–113
    volume of prisms, 152–154
Math finger flash activity, 106
McAuliffe, C., 29
McCoy, V., 42
McTighe, J., 26
Meaning, 28–29
Measurement lesson, 155–156
Measurement (nonstandard units)
    lesson, 120–122
Medina, J., 3
Metaphors, 19
Microscopes, 184–187
Midnight Ride of Paul Revere, The, 280
Military leaders lesson, 311–314
Milk bottle drawing activity, 260
Mind map, personal finance, 334–335
Miranda, L.-M., 20
Mirror deflection activity, 220–221
Mnemonic devices, 15, 19–20
Models, 19
Money management lesson, 333–336
Movement as part of instruction,
    11–12, 20
Movie stars activity, 67
Multiplication lesson, 130–132

Multiplying decimals lesson, 149–151
Multitasking, 3
Munsch, R., 43, 66
Music, 20
Musical subtraction activity, 112
Mystery box activity, 200–201

Need, 27–28
Novelty, 28

Objectives, lesson, 25–26
Ocean ecosystem lesson, 255–258
O. Henry, 83
100 chart, 141
Opinion/point of view lesson, 70–71
Opinions and reasons activity, 70
Opinion with facts lesson, 53–55
Order of operations lesson, 162–164,
    165–166
Order of operations (errors) lesson,
    167–169

Pair-share activity, 88, 97
Pantomimes, 21
Paper dolls activity, 307
Paper tower competition activity, 215
Partitioning shapes lesson, 135–137
Partner pre-work activity, 81
Pattern block halves activities,
    125–127
Pattern block models activity, 135
Pattern block spinning activity, 131
Pattern block work mats activity, 131
Paul Revere lesson, 280–281
PEMDAS, 162–164, 165–166
Perimeter lesson, 143–145
Periodic table, 223–225
Personal money management lesson,
    333–336
Personal narrative chart activity, 67
Personal pictures activity, 67
Phonemes, 38–40
Picture it activity, 50
Ping-pong path activity, 220
Places I live lesson, 273–274
Plants, germination and photosynthesis
    in, 210–212
Plate tectonics lesson, 248–250
Plot mountain activity, 64
Plot structure lesson, 64–66
Point of view and reasons activity, 71
Position words lesson, 109–111
Positive environments, 8
Poster activity, 320
Poster sounds activity, 42
Prefix/suffix card game, 59
Primary sources activity, 328
Prime and composite numbers lesson,
    140–142
Prisms, 152–154
Project-based and problem-based
    learning, 20–21
Properties of materials lesson, 197–199
Purposeful and relevant learning, 9–10

Questioning lesson, 51–52

Rap, 20
Rational numbers lesson, 177–179
Read aloud activities, 264, 273, 290
*Reading and Language Arts Worksheets
    Don't Grow Dendrites*, 54, 67
Reading websites, 104
Reciprocal teaching and cooperative
    learning, 21
Recognizing prefixes activity, 58–59
Rectangles lesson, 117–119
Reflection and refraction lesson, 220–222
Relevant learning, 9–10
Research topics lesson, 85–86
Respiration lesson, 217–219
Responsibility lesson, 264–269
Rhyme, 20
Rhyming word book activity, 37
Rhyming words lesson, 36–37
Rhythm, 20
Role play, 16, 21
Role play it activity, 49–50
Roosevelt, Franklin Delano, 319–320
Routines and procedures, classroom, 9
Rylant, C., 67

Sarcasm, 18–19
Science lessons
    birthday egg, 259–261
    cells and cell parts, 229–232
    chemical charges and periodic table,
        223–225
    chemical reactions, 246–247
    coding with glyphs, 203–206
    density, 226–228
    diversity of habitats, 184–187
    DNA model, 243–245
    earth and human activity, 194–196
    engineering design, 215–216
    engineering design-classification,
        240–242
    flowers (sexual reproduction of
        plants), 213–214
    forces of flight, 191–193
    germination and photosynthesis in
        plants, 210–212
    human heart and circulation, 237–239
    interpret fossils-archaeology, 207–209
    ocean ecosystem, 255–258
    plate tectonics, 248–250
    properties of materials, 197–199
    reflection and refraction, 220–222
    respiration, 217–219
    scientific method, 200–202
    solar system, 251–254
    sound vibrations and the ear, 188–190
    states of matter, 233–236
Scientific method lesson, 200–202
*Secretary's Commission on Achieving
    Necessary Skills (SCANS) Report*, 22
Seed cartoons activity, 210
Semantic maps, 18
Serendipity discussion activity, 200
Service project activity, 265
Setting it together activity, 49
Setting mobile activity, 49
Seuss, Dr., 36

7 Habits of Highly Effective People, 25
Shaving cream words activity, 41
Shouting Won't Grow Dendrites: 20
    Techniques to Detour Around the
    Danger Zones, 9
Similes, 19
Singing/body spelling activity, 32
Singing the plot song activity, 64
Slap, clap, snap activity, 38
Snakes and donuts activity, 309–310
Soap bubble experiment activity,
    197–198
Social studies lessons
    American Indian culture, 296–298
    American Revolution, 305–308
    American symbols, 278–279
    branches of the federal government,
        324–326
    citizenship, 270–272
    Civil Rights movement, 321–323
    colonial America, 302–304
    compare and contrast two countries,
        327–330
    Declaration of Independence, 299–301
    economics, 289–290
    European exploration, 331–332
    Franklin Delano Roosevelt, 319–320
    goods and resources, 309–310
    historical figures, 293–295
    key battles and events of the Civil
        War, 315–316
    latitude, longitude, equator, prime
        meridian, 291–292
    Lewis and Clark expedition, 317–318
    maps and globes, 275–277
    Martin Luther King, Jr. Day, 282–288
    military leaders, 311–314
    Paul Revere, 280–281
    personal money management,
        333–336
    places I live, 273–274
    responsibility, 264–269

Societal changes and teaching, 1–2
Socratic seminar, 80–82, 97
Solar system lesson, 251–254
Sound vibrations and the ear lesson,
    188–190
Sousa, D., 3, 18, 22
Splashes of sigh words activity, 33, 35
Square roots, 180–181
Stacked geography activity, 274
States of matter lesson, 233–236
STEAM Programs, 17
Stevens, J., 47
Stibich, M., 22
Story details lesson, 48–50
Story of Ferdinand, The, 51
Storytelling, 15, 21–22
Story writing and illustrating activity,
    33–34
Straight sides shapes activity, 115
Straw shapes activity, 114
Strips of information activity, 311
Strohshneider, D., 190
Student confidence, 12
Subtraction lesson, 112–113

Tangram shapes activity, 123
Tate, M., 53, 64
T-chart activities, 264, 271–272
Teaching
    brain changes and, 2–3
    instructional changes and, 3–4
    societal changes and, 1–2
Technology, 16, 22
Text analysis lesson, 87–88
Text message metaphor activity, 43
Thank You Ma'am, 80
Think, pair, share (TPS) activity,
    297–298
Thomas' Snowsuit, 43–44
3-2-1-Think-Pair-Share activity, 321, 323
Three Little Wolves and the Big Bad Pig,
    The, 74

Tops and Bottoms, 48
Triangles, 136
Tri-fold booklet activity, 324–325
True Story of the Three Little Pigs, The, 74
Two-column note-taking activity, 327
Txt msg activity, 334

Understanding by Design, 26

Venn diagrams, 74, 76, 325
Viewing student work activity, 62
Virtual field trips, 17
Visualization and guided imagery,
    22, 322
Visual predictions activity, 293
Visuals, 22–23, 273
Volume of prisms lesson, 152–154

Walker, A., 92
WebQuest activity, 319–320
What's my opinion? activity, 54
What's the difference? activity, 57
When I Was Young in the Mountains, 67
Wiggins, G., 26
Williams, P., 43, 58
Williams, V., 48
Willis, J., 23
Word analysis skills, 41–42
Word drawing activity, 41
Words
    decoding multisyllabic, 57–59
    high-frequency, 32–35
    rhyming, 36–37
Word splash activity, 307, 332
Word webs, 18
Worksheets Don't Grow Dendrites: 20
    Instructional Strategies that Engage
    the Brain, 13
Work study and apprenticeships, 23
Writing and journals, 23
Writing lesson, 61–63
Writing station activity, 112

A SAGE Publishing Company

Helping educators make the greatest impact

CORWIN HAS ONE MISSION: to enhance education through intentional professional learning.

We build long-term relationships with our authors, educators, clients, and associations who partner with us to develop and continuously improve the best evidence-based practices that establish and support lifelong learning.